Life Before Eighty

Life Before Eighty

Autobiography

Arvid B. Erickson

iUniverse, Inc.
Bloomington

Life Before Eighty
Autobiography

iUniverse books may be ordered through booksellers or by contacting:

iUniverse
1663 Liberty Drive
Bloomington, IN 47403
www.iuniverse.com
1-800-Authors (1-800-288-4677)

Because of the dynamic nature of the Internet, any web addresses or links contained in this book may have changed since publication and may no longer be valid. The views expressed in this work are solely those of the author and do not necessarily reflect the views of the publisher, and the publisher hereby disclaims any responsibility for them.

Any people depicted in stock imagery provided by Thinkstock are models, and such images are being used for illustrative purposes only.

Certain stock imagery © Thinkstock.

ISBN: 978-1-4759-3196-9 (sc)
ISBN: 978-1-4759-3197-6 (e)

Printed in the United States of America

iUniverse rev. date: 7/17/2012

Dedication

Dad, it took me a long time to get your book printed, since I promised you in 1970 – so – this is for you, Dad. Your typical response would be "better late than never".

I chose to print this for the history that might be helpful to those interested in telegraphy, railroading, and logging industries for which there are clubs and interest groups. Since family was an important part of his life I publish "Life Before Eighty" for the descendants of Arvid and Sarah who may become interested in family history and/or in writing.

I include 4 weeks of the newspaper series (with permission) on logging in Central Wisconsin to further document the results of the industry starting in the late 1800's. My thanks to the owner of the Banner Journal and CFO, News Publishing Company Inc.

Leone Erickson Kaylor
Daughter

Foreword

When we were kids in the 1930s, '40s and '50s, with me, Ethel, bringing up the rear of our brood of seven, God's perfect number, our dad Arvid entertained us at dinner over corn on the cob.

Chomp Chomp he would go with his clenched jaw and dentures positioned over one row of the steaming, bursting, golden-yellow homegrown kernels. Methodically and speedily he raced across the line, left to right. Ding Ding he went at the end of the cornrow, performing a carriage return with his head to the left and he began a new row. And onto the next row and the next he raced. We were amused and laughed at his antics.

He was playacting as his own hard-earned and beloved Underwood typewriter, hitting the keys one row at a time with the letters in metal casings that were hinged to fonts to strike the page. Arvid brought this handsome instrument to his first depot job in 1909 and then to the Whitehall Agency in Wisconsin in 1925, as a railroad Depot Agent and Telegrapher. He typed bills of lading, telegrams and all the other transactions that needed to be recorded for the railroad's business in the busiest town on the Green Bay and Western Railroad line.

And in his retirement in 1954 he brought the well-used, sturdy, black typewriter home and set it on his handmade wooden desk in his upstairs bedroom. Throughout his life in free or extra moments at the depot (or handwritten at home) he had been typing hundreds of essays and letters that were filled with his views on philosophy, religion and politics as well as facts of the day. He sent the onionskin paper sheets to newspapers, politicians, relatives and friends and saved a carbon copy for his own files. Now with time on his hands he decided to write a book and to make it a personal record of the common man, touched by world events and about life in his small town. So Dad retrieved the memories, relived the past and typed up his life story.

Ethel Erickson Radmer
February 17, 2011

Acknowledgements

Photographs taken of the author, Arvid B. Erickson in his office, the telegraph key and steam engines have been taken by:
Benjamin W. Erickson, son of Arvid
Award winning amateur photographer
I thank his son Tom, for sharing.

My sister is just as interested as I in seeing our Dad's work get into print while recognizing I needed to follow through on my promise to Dad. Thanks, Ethel, for being there to contribute.

Going through all of this stuff was made much easier due to the helpfulness and encouragement of the professionals at iUniverse. I appreciate all that became involved and for accepting my limitations and assisting me to always move forward at my own pace. As we complete the process, I thank you.

In my drafts I have always used the font American Typewriter because it was the closest to the font my Dad had used in 1960. I am so pleased that it is available for the final printing.

Leone Erickson Kaylor

Contents

Preface to Autobiography of Arvid B. Erickson

Biographies are supposed to be of famous men and women, not a mere individual like myself. But the common man is important too; they are far more numerous.

This one spans a transition period in the history at the world, more important than any other period in times past, especially in the U.S.A. It commences with the 'horse and buggy days' and ends with the commencement of the present 'atomic age'.

Between these two periods, short indeed in the long history of the world, more historical events have taken place throughout the world than in any previous periods of recorded history. But this is not a record of world events, except as they are touched upon in connection with it; that is for historians.

It is a personal record of events taking place with which a common individual came into contact, as well as those with whom he concerned himself and that pushed upon their personal lives during that period.

It may be called a representation of the lives of millions of others who lived and passed on: a portrayal of human incidents and experiences that are typical of the joys and sorrows of life; its successes and failures: tragedies and triumphs as the living and moving drama of human life unfolds which is the common lot of mankind anywhere in the world in any period of time.

Signed A. B. Erickson
Whitehall, Wis.
1-30-60
Revised 1-20-65

--Chapter 1--

A little boy was laying on his back on a warm summer day watching an eagle circling higher and higher into the clear blue skies until it became only a speck barely visible and finally disappearing into the beyond.

As the boy continued to gaze into the vastness of space, he pondered the mysteries of the universe and the worlds within it and wondered what lay beyond his vision and confines of space. Was space unlimited? Did it have a beginning and will it have an ending? Were there other worlds like ours inhabited by people? If so, what were they like? So many questions entered his still undeveloped mind that he was overwhelmed by it all.

One conjecture staggered him and his imagination: Suppose there were no worlds at all; no earth; no planets, no seas, no stars that twinkled in the far distance; no universe and no space. What would there be then? If there were no space, what would be in place of it, if anything? Can a vacuum, or a void exist where there is no space?

All this was too much for a young mind to grasp, so he got up and turned his attention to the realities of his present little world about him, and there was plenty to engage his time and attention which was more within his grasp and understanding. Although there was much immediately at hand to observe, they were not too difficult for him to figure out and arrive at some conclusions, even though immature.

This boy was myself at a very tender age, a comparatively recent arrival on this planet. The question of where he had come from had not yet entered his mind, except that he felt intuitively that his parents had something to do with his being brought into this existence. The mechanics of the thing did not concern him at the moment. Other more interesting aspects of life drew his interest; there was much to explore nearby that was less difficult to understand.

Animal and bird life was abundant in the nearby woods. The blue jay was a lively bird with its colorful plumage. It would turn its head with a hat on it to one side as it looked at one as though to say, "What are you doing in my territory, you brat." The song of the whippoorwill was easy to imitate; it made its nest in the sand in the open with no protection from its enemies. The robins, harbingers of spring, were the most persistent of the singers, perching itself on a limb and sing its heart out to the world in a continuous stream of melodious musical notes. For a small boy, it was the sweetest music this side of heaven to listen to the many varieties of song birds, each with its own particular way of making music. They were endowed by Mother Nature with built-in musical instruments of their own, and they also know how to play them without the necessity of being taught, although the smartest of all birds in the neighborhood, the hawks and crows were not singers and their single notes were for the purpose of warnings of danger to themselves. They were the scavengers; the thieves of the bird kingdom and the little birds did not hesitate to pounce on them in flight and kept it up till they were gone. Man also considered them as thieves, robbing him of chickens and corn, even those planted as seed. A crow always kept his distance, flying over trees, some of them perching themselves on the topmost branch and acted as sentinels to warn others of approaching danger. The owl was difficult to find and see, although, it could easily be heard at night. Small boys of big cities have missed a lot in life, especially during boyhood, in not having the opportunity to listen to what the boys in our neighborhood called the "Bull-frog Symphony", produced by an army of frogs in the swamps nearby. It could best be heard of a warm summer evening when all of nature was quiet; when the birds had gone to roost for the night and all animals had retired to their respective shelters. It was then that the frogs, both male and female, struck up their symphony of song. There were tenor voices among them; sopranos and bases, altos and contraltos, each contributing their share to the grand music; for it was grand to small boys who had not heard any other kind of music produced by man. It was great music because the frogs sang in unison in their own natural way, and it could be heard as coming from the throats of frogs located far up the swamp at a distance; they all heard each other and kept singing far into the night. Possibly this symphony was for the purpose of a lullaby for the birds and animals in the vicinity by which to go to sleep. Who knows all the wondrous ways of Nature in caring for her kind?

Nature has many ways to produce her music, many more than man has. In addition to the birds and frogs, the insect kingdom with its innumerable species have a way each of their own to produce music. Even mosquitoes on the wing sing a song as they seek their victims to anyone who will stop and listen. And who with keen hearing does not enjoy the buzz of a honey bee as it makes its appointed rounds in gathering the nectar of various flowers; They sing also inside their hives, seemingly happy in their job of making sweet honey for mankind.

For nature lovers, nothing is more enjoyable than sitting in the midst of a forest and listening to the wind blowing through the tree tops and branches, producing a music of the forest; and in the distance when a storm is brewing, lightning flashes and thunder combine to show mere man that Nature can be awesome and terrifying while producing a type of music that scares most people, but is exhilarating to the stout-hearted.

And what of the 'Music of the Spheres' that Goethe mentions in his 'Faust': "The sun intones his ancient song, 'mid rival chant of brother spheres. His prescribed course he speeds along in thunderous way throughout the years". That music is for the Gods, not mere men of earth.

But to descend from the clouds and on with my narrative, which concerns itself with the life of one individual, myself, and those with whom he, came into contact.

My Mother was a noble woman, pious and dedicated to her religion. She was fairly well developed morally and spiritually, but lacking in intellectual attainment due to primitive educational facilities of the time of her childhood and in later years when language difficulties prevented extensive reading, although she had the potentials for It. She was almost too good for the harsh environment she found herself in upon arrival in this country as the wife of a pioneer emigrant with all the primitive, hardships that entailed.

She was born in Sundsvall, Sweden in 1852 and married to Nils O. Erickson July 4th in 1875. Before she left Sweden for America in 1881, two boys and two girls, had been born to her, all of whom she lost from the ravages of diphtheria, an uncontrolled disease of the times. She buried them all in her native land. One was 7 months old; another 8 months; other two over one and two years, all passing on within a period of four years. Can we imagine the sorrow and heartache that these misfortunes caused a sensitive soul? Having to leave them forever in her native land, the country of her birth and young womanhood? She was a beautiful girl when she married at ago 23 with high hopes of a bright future with the handsome man she loved. It is fortunate that future events are hidden from

4

our view, especially during happy youth and emerging adulthood.

With a heavy heart she fearlessly set her face toward a new hope and a better promise leaving her native country, a land of beauty and enchantment for a new and strange land in a distant part of the world, across the vast expanse of the Atlantic, to America where she was told great opportunities waited those who would venture there. Her husband had left Sweden for the U.S.A. the year before in 1880. Duty called her, for she must go where he was; to be at his side to aid and comfort him in their new environment. She had married him for better or worse; that was her promise.

So in 1881 she boarded a steam-ship for Quebec, Canada, all alone.

It probably took several weeks to cross, we do not know. She changed to a smaller vessel at Quebec and steamed up the St. Lawrence through the Great Lakes directly to her destination, Muskegon, Michigan, where she was supposed to meet her husband. She did not know where he was located; his only address was 'general delivery'. When she finally arrived there, no one met her. She was alone in a strange city, in a new country. To us now It would seem to be tragic, but probably was not to her, independent and self reliant as she was brought up to be. She did not know any one there and could not speak the language. She was 27 at the time, a fine looking woman with black hair, blue eyes and a pleasing appearance.

She knew her husband was working in a saw mill. She tried to locate someone who could speak her own mother tongue and finally met an emigrant family from her own country and they were able to direct her to large boarding house near the lake-front. Carrying her own luggage she walked the distance to the old fashioned hotel without assistance from any one. She was young, strong and independent, having been reared in a hard school of discipline and experience in an environment of work and self-denial.

She finally reached a large frame structure, two or three stories high located on the lakefront near a large saw-mill. It was an old type of boarding house that catered to saw mill and dock workers with room and board. She did not feel sure of finding her mate there, but took a room anyway for the night in the top story. It was not an elegant place with very primitive furnishings; no heat in the rooms and no running water with kerosene lamps for light. Some of the men who roomed there were rough and tough and liquor flowed freely among them. But she was not afraid and had faith in her fellowman no matter how uncultured they were at the time. Besides she felt capable of defending herself in emergencies if necessary. Although hers was a gentle nature, she could get tough too when necessary. It was early evening in the summer of 1881 when she was sitting and resting in her room wondering what to do next to find her husband. The weather was warm and pleasant and the workers had finished their day's work, eaten their supper and were lounging in front of their boarding house, some of them with their backs to the wall resting and talking to each other, their legs stretched out on the ground.

She opened, the window to look out more easily. The men she saw were not known to her; they were all strangers. She saw a row of legs of other men on the ground leaning against the building, but their owners were not visible to her from where she sat. She fell to observing the knitted socks on those long legs. Being an expert knitter herself, she readily recognized the different types of knitting work done into those socks. As her eyes ran along the row of feet and legs, there was one pair of long legs and feet whose socks were visible to her and which struck her as being familiar; the type of knitting was exactly like that of her own knitting that she had made into socks and sent to her husband while she was still in Sweden. She had knitted several pair and sent to him while waiting for transportation money from him to go to America.

While she was looking she asked herself, "Is it possible that those socks were knitted by me? "They certainly look like those I knitted", she observed. The more she examined them from where she was, the more familiar they became to her. She was getting excited now, "I'll take a chance," she decided. She leaned far out the window and screamed, "Nils, Nils." There was a flurry of excitement among the men below when they saw a good-looking young woman leaning out the window and attracting their attention. There were some 'wise-cracks' by some; all were interested in her. Women were scarce in that part of the world those days and any young woman was more than welcome among them. They fought over available girls and the best man usually won.

She called his name again. Finally he realized that it was his name that was being called and the voice seemed familiar. He unwound his long legs, (for it really was Nils) got to his feet and stretched to his full six feet two inches. When he looked up at the window he knew at once she was his wife Karen. Both ran toward each other and met somewhere inside the building and a happy moment for both ensued. They were united again and ready to face the future and whatever fate had in store for them. Both were young, healthy and free in a virgin land that required the pioneering spirit to develop. They were ready, willing and eager to do their share of it, one couple of many thousands who flocked to this country from many countries in Europe, some of these to get sway from unfavorable communities, countries, and religious conditions in their homeland; but most of them were pioneers called as though by one power beyond them that they could not explain, to do a job that was necessary. These emigrant pioneers were the 'cream of the crop'; the best from each country and they proceeded to give of their best to the new and undeveloped land. They obeyed the command of the ancient prophets to 'have dominion over the land and to increase and multiply their kind', so that we have and now are largely indebted to these people for opening up the country for their descendants.

My Dad also was born in Sundsvall, Sweden in 1851. His father had died early in his life and left his wife to care for two sons. She was a baker and supported them by going from house to house and baked a year's supply of bread, or hard tack for each family. The bread was made of whole-wheat flour ground by the old method of one stone on top the other. It was baked in the form of wheels with a hole in the center so that a large number was strung on a long pole and hung up, generally in the attic of the house, to dry and for storage. That was the origin of the modern day hard-tack that is far more wholesome than bread, soft bread, made form refined flour.

Dad's only brother turned to the sea in his youth and became a merchant-seaman and sailed the 'seven sea's. During a storm in one of the oceans, his vessel, probably a slow cargo ship powered by the wind on sails, with all aboard went down to the sea's bottom. Dad, being quiet and reserved never told us much of anything about his brother except that he was lost at sea.

My father was a tall, slender, handsome young man with a wealth of wavy black hair when he met and married Karen Olson in Sundsvall, Sweden where they both lived. Although they were born and reared in the same city, they did not meet until about a year before they were married on July 4th, 1875. Both wanted to migrate to America as soon as possible as some of their relatives, those on Mother's side, and some friends had already done. Economic conditions in their home land were not good and they thought it would be better in the U.S.A. In addition to that, religious worship was not at all completely free in the Scandinavian countries. Lutheran was the State church, supported by the State, or government, and membership in that faith was compulsory, as was

8

attendance in the church. Although Dad did not give us much information about his homeland and youth, he did relate an incident that took place in church. He and a group of youth were on their knees; they were supposed to remain quiet and pray. Dad's nose was itching and he had to blow it. When the pastor, or teacher whoever he was, heard it, he went over to Dad and reprimanded him severely and even brought his ruler down on his head as punishment. Dad said that was the 'last straw'; that he determined then and there to disobey the church and also to move away at the first opportunity. From that time on his interest in church and religion waned; that was the start of his rebellion.

There is or was a discrepancy, or disagreement among my brothers and sisters in what we thought was Mother's birth-place. Some of them contended it was Orsa in a province near Stockholm that Mother was born, and that she moved to Sundsvall in later youth. Records in Mother's old Bible, pages of which 1 have in my possession, shows that both Mother and Dad were, born in Sundsvall; Mother in 1852 (no date shown) Dad on Sept. 5th, 1851. That is the record 1 rely on; it was recorded by one of her sons at her direction, as I understand it, so it must be correct.

Another item of uncertainty among us was the origin of Dad's and Mother's forebears. The oldest in our family, Anna May, claims that the distant forebears of both came originally from Russia; that Dad's were of the royalty; that his were members of the royal family at Russia; according to that, there was 'royal blood' in Dad's veins, whatever that may mean. She thinks that the original settlers of northern Sweden and Finland were Russians long before Napoleon sent one of his relatives, to Sweden to found the Swedish royal dynasty, over a hundred years ago. That Finland, bordering Russia, in ancient times was Russian territory and its people in very early times crossed over to northern Sweden and Norway, by the way of Lapland of that day. From there they most likely, according to this theory, moved down the Scandinavian Peninsula and became permanent settlers, although very sparsely. It is from these colonies that both Dad's and Mother's distant forebears were supposed to have originated long ago.

Anna May thinks that some of Mother's brothers were of a quite dark color with black hair and dark blue eyes supports her theory that they spring from the original Russians in Finland who were supposed to be very dark in color during those early times. My Dad also was of a dark color, very noticeable during his youth, his hair just about jet black. His and my uncle's appearance was not at all like the present day people, and earlier, of Sweden and Norway, who were blond in color.

The urge to migrate, the pioneering spirit possessed the rank and file in the European countries before and after our civil war, as it has done in previous ages in all climes. Animals of many kinds have that urge also; it is an instinct built into human as well as animal natures. There was a new land across the broad Atlantic that needed to be taken possession of and made fruitful; a continent that the original Vikings discovered long before Columbus' time; the ancient pioneers of whom the Scandinavians of the present day in America are descendants.

So finally my Dad set sail for that new country and arrived in Baltimore, Maryland in 1880, according to the old Bible records. Their last child died of diphtheria in Sweden soon after he arrived in the U.S.A. that left his wife all alone in the world, except for her relatives. The land bordering the Great Lakes was reported to him to be virgin and the Government was practically giving away parcels of it for nominal prices to induce more recruits for settlement. It was later, after the Civil War, that the Congress passed the Homestead Act that encouraged more settlers to come to the West and Mid-West to settle upon the virgin lands.

Dad never told us the route he took from Baltimore to Muskegon, Michigan for that was his destination and he evidently did not know the best route to take and chose Baltimore as the best that he thought. Later he told his wife to travel by ship all the way from Quebec via the Great Lakes vessels. My impression is that from Baltimore he boarded a river boat and sailed up the Chesapeake Bay and the Susquehanna River through a part of Pennsylvania as far as the river was navigable at that time, probably Danville, Pennsylvania. Or he took a vessel up a branch of that river to Williamsport Pennsylvania. From there probably by stage coach, unless the Railroad had been built through there by that time, I do not know. He also may have walked to Erie, Pennsylvania., where he probably boarded a Great Lakes Vessel for Muskegon. He was a great walker and never hesitated to attempt long walks if necessary.

Some years previous to 1880, probably about 1875, my mother's father, Grandpa Olson to us, migrated to the U.S.A. with a party of his county men and four sons via the St. Lawrence waterway. In the group was a man who was dishonest, a swindler, and he managed by hook and crook to take grand-father's money from him, so that when they reached the Welland Canal, he was compelled to leave the boat and attempt to walk the rest of the way to his destination, which presumably was Muskegon, Mich.

While walking and roughing it, as he had to do, his health gave way and died before reaching there. I understand his sons and the rest continued ahead of him. His wife, who was our Grandmother on Mother's side, managed somehow to earn and save enough money for herself and other three daughters to leave Sweden for the U.S.A. and finally landed in Muskegon.

She never saw her husband again. How he died and where buried, we have no knowledge of; probably by State or city authorities enroute. We were told that he was a gentle soul; good natured and trusting his fellowmen so that it was quite easy for others less scrupulous to take undue advantage of him. Grandmother was of a different breed, independent and resourceful and skeptical of those she dealt with and a good manager. She was strong-willed, a good, independent thinker who was suspicious of any and all traveling preachers who tried to influence her, to no avail. She could not and did not accept any pre-conceived religious dogmas that went contrary to her reason and logic. Instead, she pursued the study of philosophy, notably Emanuel Swedenborg and his books and other philosophers that sustained her in her thinking and ideas of life. Upon the death of her husband, she went into the boarding house business in Muskegon, which was a thriving saw mill town at the time, supported and raised the younger members of her family without assistance from anyone.

One of her sons was Uncle Hans, a prosperous farmer near Neillsville, Wisconsin. Another, a well-to-do resident of Rhinelander, a paper mill worker.

The other two uncles were 'lumber-jacks', who moved from one saw-mill town to another and never remained long enough in one place to take root. Cousin Gus, a son of Uncle Hans, was quite tall and lanky and we used to like him very much, being good natured and easy to get along with. He did all sorts of jobs, a handy man and was quite frugal and saving so that he left a small estate at time of death; he never married. A couple cousins inherited his money and property.

The three children of another uncle, Charles, Gust and Sina we were quite well acquainted with. The two boys were good musicians and had an orchestra of sorts. Both passed on prematurely. Sina married and lived most of her life in Ironwood, Michigan where her husband, Geo. Backstrom had a business of some kind and who died before she did. Sina passed on in 1958; I called on her some time previous to that. She willed all her money and property to the Salvation Army. No children.

Of Mother's sisters, I faintly recall Aunt Mary, who also was a very gentle soul, somewhat like my mother. She died in her youth, soon after her marriage. My best recollection is of my Aunt Anna, whose husband was Mr. Bergstrom (cannot recall first name) also an immigrant from Sweden. The couple had a large brood and lived in our neighborhood so that we got to know most of them quite well. Tillie was one of them, who was the mother of Olga, Mrs. John McGuire who lived in Minneapolis and whom we used to visit. John was a railroader, a mechanic in Milwaukee Road shops. Both passed on some years ago. Tillie Berstrom married a Victor Anderson and they lived almost next door to us so that we were well acquainted with their four daughters and one son while we all grew up. One daughter married George Waughtel of Black River Falls; another Wallace Jones an Omaha RR section foreman. Waughtel is a well to do business man in Black River Falls. Herman lived in Minneapolis, as did Vava and Olga. Another Berstrom girl was Rose who married a George Baker of Minneapolis who had a daughter named Adeline about my age. As a teen-ager I used to visit them in Minneapolis and rode with Mr. Baker in his delivery wagon. It was his job to pick up packages at the large stores and deliver them to customers all over the city in a wagon drawn by two horses. I was quite young at the time, probably about 8 or so. It was long before automobiles and Minneapolis was then a thriving small city. It was the era of 'horse and buggy' days.

Dad and Mother rented a cottage on the shores of Lake Michigan in Muskegon and it was there that Anna May was born Feb 5, 1882, their first child in this country. I do not know why they left there, but they did in 1884 and moved to Marine Mills, Minnesota, another saw mill town. Dad had the habit of following the saw-mills wherever they moved when their timber supply was depleted. Twins Alfred and Alfeda were born in Marine Mills July 15th, 1884. During all this time they longed for a home

13

of their own, as most young couple do, but their mistake was the location they chose. He knew that there were saw mills around Black River Falls, Wisconsin so they decided to move to that territory and settle down. Jobs were plentiful and land was cheap during those pioneer days. Finally Dad went there and bought a forty of virgin land in the Township of Manchester, Jackson County about 6 miles east of Black River Falls. It was land that had been cut over by lumber barons some time previously. Later he purchased two more forties in the adjoining township of Brockway. That was about 1886 or so, not sure of exact year. Value of the land as fit for agriculture had not yet been proven.

During those years and some years previous to it much virgin white pine was still standing in and around Jackson County so that many saw mills were operating converting timber into lumber. Saw mills were located in or near white pine forests cutting and slashing the magnificent stand without thought of conserving or replacing the fine trees that were probably hundreds of years old. Many of the cities in the east and south were built up by the lumber from those mills in Wisconsin throughout most of which white and Norway pine had grown for centuries previous to coming of the lumber barons. To cite one example: the cities of St. Louis, Missouri and East St. Louis, Illinois, originally were built of lumber from the Chippewa Valley in Wisconsin. Thus the virgin timber in Wisconsin and elsewhere served the purpose of advancing the economy of our country during the later periods of the 19th century and in later times. Although wasteful methods were used in the process, conservation soon after came to be the slogan of conservation-minded leaders and government officials whose ideas eventually prevailed.

Before Dad and his growing family moved to Marine Mills, Minnesota, he went to his newly acquired land to cut pine logs that were still standing on his land and started to build a cabin, or log house. How he managed to move the logs to the cabin site I do not know. He hewed the logs by hand himself into the right shape and size and notched the ends to fit snugly into the corners. Although it was a simple matter to build a cottage those days, it was very hard work, doing most of it alone without aid from any one. Anna May, who remembered it, told me that Dad worked hard night and day to do the job, resting and sleeping very little. About the only tools he used was a cross cut saw, ax, adz, hammer and other simple tools. The basement was excavated by hand shovel, a back breaking job. But the most necessary requirement was will power and brawn.

Dad had a talent for building anything. He was a carpenter, a stone mason, plasterer, and could adapt himself to any other job that required to be done. When the house was completed it had five rooms, an upstairs room and a small basement made of native rock. How he lived and where while doing this work I do not know. As evidence of how well he built, the house was still standing in 1959, a period of about 73 years and was good for more years to come.

I do not know for sure, but I think the family had moved to Marine Mills about the time he had commenced to build on his land. The saw mill town was situated on the St. Croix River near Stillwater at that time and the Railroad had already been built, by which method they probably traveled to and from Black River Falls. I think it was sometime in 1885 or 1886 that they moved from Marine Mills to their newly built cottage. The twins' birth, Alfred and Alfreda, was recorded in the Lutheran Church of the town, the babies having been baptized in that faith; Mother and Dad had not yet withdrawn from that church denomination. Anna May also was baptized in that faith in Muskegon. In later years Mother became a Baptist.

I can well imagine how proud my parents were when the log house was ready for occupancy! A mansion to a rich man could not have been more satisfying than this crude log house was to them! They owned the land on which it was built. It was a home no matter how humble it was or how primitive. What more could they wish for? They had satisfied the natural urge to own their own home, which is inherent in all of us.

They had three children when they moved in, Anna May, Alfred and Alfreda. The following year, 1887, another set of twins were born to Mother, Albert and Albion Jan. 2nd, 1887, the first to be born in the log house in the woods. Two years later, March 16th, 1889, Arvid first saw the light of a new world, new to him. May 15th, 1891 Mamie was born. Harry followed in Feb. 10th, 1894: then Martha Dec. 4th, 1896. 13 babies had been born to Mother including 2 sets of twins. Arvid was 7 years old when the last one, Martha, came into the world. I recall her as a little girl, a beautiful child, being jealous of Mother. She tried to keep the rest of us away from her when she was around, a childish fancy. She became our favorite she was so pretty and good natured. Eleven of us lived in that humble home for many years; 9 children besides the parents.

Dad was away much of the time earning money for the up-keep of his large brood. When he was home, we felt that he was a stranger to us kids. His was a reserved disposition; not given to talk very much, nor mixing with his family. But he was a good provider; all his earnings went to his family. During his time at home his principal interest was to try and invent something new. From a practical standpoint, his inventions were unsuccessful, mostly due to his disinterest and lack of business inclination. If he had received an education and training in technology, he surely would have made a great success as an inventor and researcher. His talents in that field were latent, undeveloped for lack of bringing them to the surface.

It was his hobby to make models of different kinds of apparatus in mechanics; the only one he applied for a patent on was a portable cement mixer which would have been successful if he had applied business acumen; it could have been, and it was, the forerunner of the modern powered mixers.

What I remember most distinctly was his attempts to solve the problem of 'perpetual motion'. During that period of time there was considerable discussion among men and in the newspapers that expressed opinions one way or another of the feasibility of solving this problem; whether or not it could be done. He was an avid reader of all he could find, which of course was more limited than at present, especially problems in mechanics. His experiments along those lines were failures because of the principle that nothing can be created from nothing; energy cannot be produced without a power of some kind; an effect cannot be produced without a cause. Natural laws were against that sort of thing. Scientists those days were not as far advanced in theoretical thinking as they are at present.

Anyway we boys had lots of fun watching and taking part in the experiments. Dad had missed his calling. He could have made good use of an education in science and mechanics. With his natural talents developed to the full by training, he would have made a great success as an inventor. He did not have much interest in money for business as such. He wanted only to be left alone; to live in peace and in the silent tenor of his ways. He wished to avoid the turmoil and competition of the world in general and the business world in particular. Who can say he wasn't right?

He loved his humble home; the woods nearby and the animals that made their habitat in them. He never tried to kill any of them; he owned no guns or traps for that purpose. He thought animals wished to live too as he did; that he had no right to take animal life. He thought

17

animals were here for a purpose, not to be molested or destroyed by so called higher civilized man.

My brother Albert was influenced to also get into the act of experimenting with 'perpetual motion' models. He made a small one of weights on a sort of 'Ferris wheel' type of thing, thinking that these weights would turn the wheel automatically. Nothing like that happened when it was completed. Dad made several models, one of which I can recall distinctly. It was made of a large wooden wheel with a surface, or rim of a couple feet that faced a tank full of water, half the wheel outside and other half inside the water. He had us kids carry the water to fill the high wooden box, or tank. When it was full and all in readiness, I remember we all almost held our breath expecting the huge wheel to move from the pressure of the water, but nothing happened. If he was disappointed in the experiment, he never showed it in his manner, or his speech. To him it was only an experiment by which he learned something. Although he did not mention it to us, I think he finally came to the conclusion as a result that no machine can run of its own volition; it had to have power from a source outside itself.

A wagon road was hewed out through the woods along a route of the least resistance by the pioneers who were moving into the territory that terminated in Black River Falls, which also was a saw mill town of the period, a distance from our home of 6 or 7 miles. Quite a few families moved into the neighborhood where Dad had built, some of them relatives, all of whom had no idea of the fertility of the soil for purposes of agriculture. They bought land and settled along this primitive road as much as possible. Most of them built log cabins of the pine trees still left standing; others bought lumber in town and built frame houses.

The road by our house also extended in the other direction as far as Shamrock and on to Sparta through cut over land that followed the most direct route and that offered the least work to accomplish. Pioneers had built their abodes at intervals along this two track road and were trying to convert the wilderness into fields for crops. Some of them were native to the U.S.A., or at least Wisconsin, while many were emigrants from various countries in Europe. For instance, the Shamrock community was settled entirely by Irish emigrants over a hundred years ago and their descendants still live there at the present time. When the road had to cross swamps, which were quite numerous a distance down the road from our home, the road builders cut trees and laid them across it and filled it between the logs with soil hauled with teams from nearby. The resulting road across the swamps were called 'corduroy'. This work was all done by men with necessary hand tools and teams with hand scrapers worked with teams and four wheeled wagons by which dirt was moved. Small bridges were constructed of timber and planks laid on timbers across the stream.

When not working in saw mills or at logging camps, the men cleared the best of their land of trees and stumps and put it to the plow. It was very hard work as no machinery was available at the time for the purpose. Stumps were grubbed out by hand and when a tract had been cleared, neighbors pooled their work and teams and broke the land with a large braking plow powered by two teams of four horses and two men, one to drive the horses and the other to handle the plow. The big plow would not always cut through the small stumps and roots when the man who handled the plow had to tug and sweat to get it going again. The work wore out horses as well as the men.

The sad part of it was that the results were not worth the work, but they did not know that at the time. The first crop was generally fair, but after one or two croppings, the yield became less and less due to the sandy nature of the soil in that part of Jackson County; the land was fit only for pine and Norway trees besides jack pine and other varieties of trees. The settlers had to find that out the hard way. After a few years of disappointing harvests, many of them left the county for other more fertile lands and the larger cities where they found employment in abundance. But not my Dad. He would not leave his home; he was there to stay, and he did till the day of his passing at age 79.

--Chapter 2--

During these early days Dad had managed to build a barn of sorts with logs and put a roof on it of straw for cows and another barn for horses. He also built a chicken house and one or two other smaller buildings. I remember vividly as though it was yesterday the tragic and unfortunate occurrence that took place there that was a hard blow to Dad and Mother. It happened on a Sunday afternoon late in the fall, when what crops had been harvested were stored and marsh hay had been piled in stacks on the ground near the barns. Father was away working; Mother and the older kids had gone to a religious meeting at neighbors up the road a ways. Only my Grandmother was in the house. She was supposed to keep an eye on the two little boys left at home, myself and Albion. Instead she kept her nose in a book on philosophy by Emanuel Swedenborg, her favorite at the time; she had no interest in religion or religious meetings.

I have no way of knowing the exact year, but I think it was about 1893 when I was about four, possibly less and Albion was about two years older than myself. I was the leader. His brain had been damaged somewhat by an attack of some kind of fever a year or two earlier that left him somewhat mentally retarded. He was born with a perfect body, but various diseases were not understood those days and could not be controlled as at present. We were playing outside and full of mischief when it occurred to us to burn leaves and hay for fun. I stole into the kitchen and reached up to a shelf and grabbed a handfull of matches behind Grandmother's back. She was so occupied with her book that she paid no attention to me. With matches we set fire to some brush, or I did, my brother helping. That was a lot of fun we thought and easily put the fire out. From brush we went to a small stack of hay and put that out also, or let it burn itself out. We came to a larger hay stack and thought we could set it on fire and put it out easily enough.

The hay was dry and the small blaze soon spread and we were unable to extinguish it. The whole stack was soon ablaze with fire and smoke that spread to another stack near it and from there to the barn and other buildings. In a very short time all the buildings and stacks of hay were on fire out of control. What a fire we had started, and only for fun! I cannot recall that I was afraid, but I probably was; or possibly only felt guilty. Neighbors saw the smoke and came running. A crowd of people soon collected including those who attended the meeting. They could do nothing but stand and watch the fire and try to save the house from catching fire; what they did I cannot recall, but it did not burn. Every other building burned to the ground including the hay, crops and feed; the live stock, what few there were did not burn; they were outside in the pasture, what little pasture there were at the time.

No fire departments were organized at that time to call on; no bucket brigade was attempted as the fire had too much of a headway. Strangely enough Grandmother did not realize that there was a fire until some one went inside to tell her. I had the impression at the time that she was blamed for the catastrophe for not watching us two boys. We were not punished in any way; not even given a lecture on the evils of matches. I was solely responsible, but I do not think I realized it at the time.

It was a hard blow to Dad who came home soon after and immediately started to rebuild. Such is the spirit of pioneers. He took it stoically and never reprimanded me nor Albion. He was not the kind to lay hands on his kids for doing mischief, or for doing wrong. Both my parents never spanked us, but spoke softly and effectively in reprimand and discipline. She ruled with love; her discipline was carried out by tone of voice or by facial expressions and by example in correct living. Both my parents set a good example to their offspring, which was effective.

Grandmother was a smart woman, but this time a 4 year old boy was smarter. Being independent and a good thinker, she was always ready and well posted to argue on any question, especially on religion and philosophy. Although her education and reading material available were quite limited, she had accumulated a wealth of knowledge for her times. As a result she was able to arrive at the facts and reach sound conclusions in almost any field she was conversant with. She was outspoken and never hesitated to argue with itinerant preachers who happened to come to the neighborhood for additional converts. She was a student of the Swedenborgian philosophy which was quite popular at the time, especially among the Scandinavian Emigrants. She probably had access to other philosophical literature as well, but I recall only that one. I remember that she used to remark that the Bible, which my Mother prized highly, was a very controversial book, in her estimation, that did not settle anything.

My further recollection of her was that of her strong individualism and outspoken manner of expressing her opinions, based on her reading, on current subjects of interest. As she sat in her rocking chair with a clay pipe in her mouth, she expounded to say one who would listen on the mysteries of life; of future existence; why we are here and the destiny of the human race, and so on. She told us kids that she started to smoke a pipe as a young girl of 16; that the custom was common among youth and elders at the time. She most always had a bottle of alcohol in the pocket of her dress that she used as medicine, both internally and external rubbing. She would mix a drink for herself with hot water, sugar and alcohol that, she claimed, assisted the stomach to digest good. Never did she use it to excess; moderation in all things was her slogan. She reached the ripe old age of 89 at time of her passing, which was far above the average at a time when the people died early as compared to the present time. Her heart was of gold even though her exterior was not always polished and refined. Her mind was keen and her tongue was sharp to the last as she spent her last days in a small log cabin across the road from our place; alone among her books and memories waiting patiently for her cycle of life to run its full coarse; with a hope and confidence in the future; eager with expectancy for what that future had in store for her and her fellow-man.

In connection with Grandmother's youth and the customs of the time during which she lived her early life in the land of her birth, in her honesty and outspoken manner she used to tell us and others who would listen, of something that was 'taboo' in our parents' home, as well as in the homes of later descendants of the tribe to which I belonged by accident of birth. That was the practice and custom known at the time as 'bundling.' It was a custom condoned and encouraged by society in the Scandinavian countries, and possibly others, during the 18th and 19th centuries. I gathered this information little by little in scraps from, not only Grandmother, but others from time to time. I did not understand it as I grew up until I reached later maturity. When young people of those early days came together for fun and frolic in the winter time, in order to save fuel during the cold, the boys and girls, as well as adults, paired off and got into bed together to keep warm and also to engage in biological relations that

24

is as old as the human race, and as natural. Sometimes two couples used the same bed, as I understood it, and the parents did not attempt to suppress the custom, but rather encouraged it.

The problem those early days was under-population, not over-population as at present. It was thought desirable to speed up the increase in numbers of persons born into the world under any circumstances for various reasons, some of them economic and also for reasons of increased church membership. As soon as they matured biologically young people were encouraged to help in that direction. Marriage was not a problem as that was easily arranged by the authorities, as I understand it. Under the system, it was not necessary to wait for the marriage ceremony to start the process of reproduction, but when it did start; it was made legal by marriage to protect the offspring and mother under the laws and customs of the land.

If we in this modern 20th century see fit to criticize this custom and those who participated in it during those early times, we are reminded that people those days did not travel as they do now, but everybody in each community remained in it and for that reason it was practically impossible for a prospective father to disappear, as they do now. The system also discouraged marriage to girls who proved by the system to be unproductive, and encouraged those who were, thereby contributing to the increase in population, which was desirable. From the moral standpoint, as we understand that term, it would seem to be more in line with a more enlightened ethical conduct by permitting young people to comply with the laws of nature at maturity, rather than to attempt to suppress them and thereby encourage promiscuity among them with its resultant undesirable effects, as is the custom in this modern day and age. I am citing all this to show how our attitudes on morality have changed through the years; a period of time that had spanned 200 years and more. Some day in the far distant future, the human race will have evolved a code of ethics respecting the difficult and intricate problem of human sex relations on a basis of intelligent understanding of the natural laws that apply thereto; they will have developed through the years ahead of us a system of conduct between the opposite sexes that will be more satisfactory from the standpoint of good ethics acceptable to all segments of society that do not run counter to the natural order; it will be done by sex education and an intelligent and frank discussion of the problem by intelligent people.

To return to the subject of this biography, which is myself, if the reader will excuse constant personal references to it and bear with me, I shall try to make this a historical narrative as closely as I can.

As a small boy I was always getting hurt in one way or another. I seem to have been and still am allergic to accidents, mostly mine. There possibly is a natural law of some kind, hidden and not understood by us, that applies in such cases, something on the order of the law of cause and effect which we do understand more or less. The first instance that I can recall was when I was very young. I was playing on a pile of lumber with other small boys that was being used to build a house on my Uncle Hans' land some distance on the other side of the woods from our home. Being bold and reckless, I climbed to the top of the pile, and in doing so, I struck my bare knee against a sharp protruding board that ripped my knee wide open, tearing the flesh badly. One of the men working on the job picked me up and carried me along a path through the woods to where we lived and from there I was taken by horse and buggy to Black River Falls and Dr. Cole who patched it up with several stitches without benefit of anything in the way of anesthetic. One can imagine the terrible pain and screaming by a small child every time the needle went through raw flesh. Mother and a man held me down while the doctor tried to do his best under such adverse circumstances. It pained him also to see such suffering and he had to work fast and furiously to get it over with. In those days unless a doctor was hardened to seeing pain and suffering in others, his was not a pleasant life and in many cases they died prematurely from the strain. Why anesthetic was not used on me, I cannot say, unless it was too expensive at the time, or most likely had not yet come into common usage because of scarcity. Mother never told me how she endured it. It surely must have been difficult for her, sensitive soul that she was.

At another time some years later I and my brother Albert were sawing dry logs into short sticks, fuel wood for the cook stove by hand; we were using a cross cut saw with one of us at each opposite end. We would roll a log onto raised skids where it was held down firmly by hooks while being sawed. But first the log had to be measured into proper lengths for the stove for which we used a measuring stick of the same length. It was my job to hold the stick while Albert used a sharp axe to mark the log into lengths. Just at the instant the axe was coming down, I slipped a little in the snow and ice and my right hand flew under the axe, snipping off my right little finger at the joint, the stub falling to the ground where it froze stiff.

Again I was rushed to Dr. Cole's office and he removed the remaining part of the joint and sewed the ends of the skin that was left. Again no anesthetic was used. Local anesthetic now in use probably had not been perfected at the time. Sometimes I think that pioneer doctors were so used to working on a patient without it, that they did not care to bother about putting me to sleep before operating. They probably preferred to use the old way as being the quickest to get the job done, which of course is only one man's opinion. Under such circumstances it was almost a catastrophe for a person to suffer serious injuries that required surgery. They needed a good, strong heart to withstand the shock and pain, which fortunately for myself, I had inherited from my parents. Only the strongest and fittest could survive.

After I recovered sufficiently to be around again, I found the severed finger frozen in the snow. I did not know what prompted me to do it, but I placed the finger in a small wooden box and buried it in the frozen ground under a tree across the road. The following summer it occurred to me to dig it up and see how it had fared. It was still intact, such as it was, and I wanted to keep it in the house as a souvenir, but Mother made me bury it again and leave it there. So I parted with it reluctantly as a part of me.

Such a story may sound gruesome to some people, but I was young enough at the time not to look at it in that way. All I knew was that I had lost a part of myself and that I should cherish it as such, a childish fancy. In the recent day youngsters are under strict supervision when doing that kind of dangerous work but not those days; we were left to fend for ourselves without supervision by any one; people have improved to that extent at least.

Another instance of lack of supervision was when my sister Martha had one of her fingers cut off with a hatchet she was using in chopping up meat into small pieces for cooking. She was old enough to assist with work in the house at the time. While handling the hatchet somehow her left hand got under it as it came down on one of her middle fingers severing it at the middle joint, the severed part hung to the rest by a small section of skin. Mother hurriedly bound up the hand and rushed her to Dr. Cole in Black River Falls. Dr. Cole was getting old by that time and set in his ways and Mother had quite an argument with him about what to do with the partly severed finger. She ordered him in no uncertain terms to put the severed finger back on the stub and fix it so it would heal back again. The old doctor refused. It was sometimes necessary for pioneers of the time to get tough. She could so when circumstances demanded it and she insisted. The old doctor screamed at her, "You presume to tell me how to do my job? That finger will never grow back on again. Keep away from me while I do the best I can for her." He started to operate when Mother stopped him. It was her turn to get rough with him and she proceeded to give him a piece of her mind. "You do as I say or I'll take the girl to a younger doctor in town who is just starting out (Dr. Eugene Krohn) and I shall tell him what kind of a doctor I think you are." "No, no, don't do that," he was still angry and said, "I will not be responsible for what will happens if I do it your way." Mother ordered him to "Put that finger back on. Never mind the consequences, nature will heal it. I myself will be responsible."

So in his anger he placed it back into position and bandaged it without stitching and without a splint to hold it in place. The final result was that both parts of it healed together properly but not straight. He had carelessly, possible because of anger in being forced, placed them together crooked. It healed alright anyway, but left the finger somewhat crooked, but normal in every other way.

Now, we question the propriety of any one telling a doctor how to do his work, but it should be understood that conditions were different then from the present time. For one thing doctors were far from being fully informed and experienced as they are now. For another, men and women as pioneers were independent and intensely individualistic. As a result tempers flared and clashes often resulted, sometimes fist fights. It was the spirit that made America what it is now, for which their descendants should be thankful to them for the pioneering hardships they had to suffer as they conquered the wilderness and made it fruitful.

Ours was a humble back-woods home, but a home nevertheless and we loved it as such. Woods bordered it on all sides except for a small clearing around the log buildings and the primitive road in front. As small boys we feared to venture very far into the woods because we were told 'wild cats', vicious creatures would pounce on us from the trees if we did. This proved to be a story invented by our elders to keep us from getting lost in the woods, as there really were no such animals. Others abounded, but no 'wild cats'. As we grew older, we explored our primitive surroundings more and more without getting lost. We used the tallest trees as landmarks; we knew where they were located and kept our bearings by them. Sometimes we climbed a tall tree to get a 'bird's-eye' view of the wooded country-side.

Claus Paulson's, neighbors living two or three miles through the woods in front of our home, had some tall trees near their house, tall poplars, that could be seen for miles around. We made a footpath through the woods directly to their place, as well as to other points to which we made trips frequently. We also had a path to a dam on Perry Creek that Henry Gebhardt had built for his cranberry marsh. To get to that we had to cross some swamps, which sometimes were full of water; that did not bother us; we merely took our shoes off to keep them dry.

There were several mounds and hills in the surrounding county-side that were land-marks and that could be seen when we climbed tall trees to get our bearings when necessary. The largest and best known was Castle Mound that stood majestically towering over the surrounding territory. It was a beautiful mound as we observed it, topped by huge rock formations, its sides covered by stately pine trees, its length tapering from the high front to its rear gradually sloping toward the wooded terrain below it. From where we lived, it showed its face to us, the head of it of huge rock formations reaching up into the skies like a sentinel keeping watch over the countryside. Its sides tapered gradually for climbers to venture to the top. The old mound was the first to greet us in the morning as the sun lit up the eastern horizon and it was the last to bid us goodnight as it sank in the shadows of the slowly receding sunlight. We never tired of looking at the mound, easily observable as it was from any direction.

To me it was a symbol of strength and solidarity, unchanging and unmoved in a changing world of human events. To a boy's mind, God placed it there to teach us patience, fortitude and calmness in a world of turmoil and conflict. It beckoned us to come and visit it; to ascend its heights from where we may survey the vast wooded areas around it.

From its heights other smaller mounds raised their bulk from the flat country, all of it covered with woods except for a few clearings here and there. Gebhardt's cranberry marshes could be seen nearby; Cline's hill on which us boys spent many happy hours playing and cooking our meal over a small fire, always on the lookout for the sound of trains that passed frequently below us. A farm known those days as Castle's farm was easily visible from Castle's Mound. A portion of Black River Falls was observed beyond the western end of the mound, nestled along the shores of Black River. In the other direction, far in the distance could be seen two long ribbons of steel extending from the distant horizon and on past the mound to Black River Falls upon which freight and passenger trains moved belching steam and smoke. In another direction were the Oak Ridge hills, over some of which we picked blue berries as small boys. Before the mound became Castle Mound Park, we used to build a fire in the sand leading to a small cave at its head where we cooked coffee for our lunch.

Many were the times that I and my brothers lay in the hay mow on summer nights trying to sleep when we would hear a faint, distant steam whistle announcing the approach of a train on the 'Omaha' main line, part of which paralleled Castle Mound on its way to Black River Falls, about three miles from where we lived. As the train came closer, we could tell by the sound of the wheel clicks whether it was a freight or passenger train. When it reached a point opposite us across the woods and swamps, we sometimes could see between the cracks of the hey mow the speeding lights of the coaches; as it passed Cline's hill, the sounds were temporarily cut off; on the other side the sounds resumed their familiar steady grind and clatter. But when the train passed the head of Castle Mound, and rounded a slight curve toward Black River Falls station, we lost the sound of it. To my immature mind, that train was a symbol of the outside world, a connecting link from my little world to that of a vaster and mysterious one of which I knew nothing.

One Sunday I followed two of my older brothers to the railroad track. I was only a 'shaver' and I had to take two steps to their one. Down the road a ways a 'corduroy' crossed a swamp, a road made of logs laid crosswise with soil filling between the logs rendering it high and dry from swamp water and mud. Beyond that was a small clearing and thence through a tract of woods until we reached Gebhardt's dam that spanned Perry Creek. It was lots of fun for us kids to cross the earthen dam that made a small lake that extended almost to the railroad main line.

There was small wild life in abundance at the dam and in the water. Bullfrogs leaped into the water at our approach; turtles croaked and hid behind roots and shrubs. Snakes were plentiful and we had to keep a sharp eye out for them, bare-footed as we were; but none of them were poisonous that we knew of. Different species of birds were quite numerous; we had not learned the names of some of them, although sometimes we placed our own names on them. The whippoorwill was an elusive bird, seldom seen but easily heard from a distance as it sang its favorite song at night. It nested in the open sandy soil. The owl likewise was heard only at night and hardly ever seen in daylight. The lake contained some fish of sorts, but we never had patience enough to remain rooted to a spot to catch them; we preferred being on the move, there being so much to see and explore.

The railroad main line was a short distance from the dam. That intrigued us as much as anything else, especially myself. This particular Sunday was the first time that I had seen the railroad. I kept myself near the fence fearful of any trains that may come. It was not long before we saw black smoke up the track a ways and soon a huge black monster spouting smoke and steam bore down on us. To me it seemed to be coming where I stood, terrified at its approach. I scampered quickly under the fence wires to be safe on the other side. I thought sure the monster was going to run over me, but happily it didn't. Instead it followed the two rails as it rushed by with a tremendous roar leaving behind a cloud of dust, smoke, steam and cinders. It was only after the engine had passed me that I noted the train of box cars and other types of cars that it was hauling and at its end a caboose with men waving at us from its windows and the rear. What an experience that was for me! But it was fascinating and intrigues me greatly. Young as I was at the time, it left a deep impression on me that has not left me after a lifetime of railroading. After that first trip I was drawn like a magnet to the railroad and many were the happy hours spent either alone or with a group of boys wandering up and down the 'Omaha' main line; throwing stones at glass insulators; placing our ears to the rail for the sound of a train rounding a curve in the distance; listening to the music of the numerous wires strung on telegraph poles along the track as the wind played its chords and symphonies on them. What were those wires for? Why so many of them? Those were only a few of the questions that entered my childish mind.

There was a small railroad bridge across Perry Creek opposite Cline's house that was situated along the track. Adolph Cline, about my age, was a friend of mine and a playmate. He and I and other boys of the surrounding country-side used to stand under the bridge as trains roared by over our heads. Passenger trains especially were a delight as they sped by, full of people. One time my brother Albert was sure he saw a 'preacher' standing at the head of a coach preaching to the passengers, a childish fancy. We would walk for miles up and down the tracks without tiring. One day some time later, as a group of us boys were playing on the track, we saw up the track some one walking toward us. As the figure approached we could see it was a young girl carrying a suit case walking between the rails toward Black River. She seemed determined and as she saw us, she speeded up her pace and walked by us rapidly and never glanced at us. She probably was fearful of what we boys would do to her, but we just stood still and watched her without saying a word to her. We were not the kind to molest girls, or even to speak to strange ones. In later years I have often wondered who the girl was; why she was walking, probably from Millston to Black River Falls because she had no money for railroad fare; probably starting out in the world the first time seeking her place in it, her future obscured from her, fortunately; how did she fare in that world and what finally was her destiny? How interesting it would be now in the evening of my life to be able to visit with her and ascertain how she made out on her journey through this world of woe. I can only hope the world was kind to her.

There was a block telegraph office set up on one side of the track opposite a forest of thick woods near a location called 'Shepps' where a saw mill of pioneer days had been in operation. It was only a shack containing an office chair, the old type, an old fashioned pot belly coal stove and a table along the front windows facing the track on which were several sets of clicking telegraph instruments, and opposite it outside was a high signal most with two arms on top of it that was operated manually from the

34

inside by two levers. We used to walk past it but did not have the nerve to go in and investigate until later. When I was a very young boy I screwed up enough courage to visit him.

Mother put up a lunch for me consisting of pancakes left over from breakfast; that was all. I set out alone across the swamps and woods and up the track where I walked into the telegraph office without invitation. I planned to spend all day with him whether he liked it or not. It was the clicking telegraph instruments that fascinated me. A young man was on duty through the day whom I adored, Mr. Claus W. Wahlquist, whose name I learned later. He was my hero, my ideal. I thought he was wonderful as he manipulated the telegraph keys and listened to the sounders with his ability to read and interpret the different clicks consisting of dots and dashes into understandable language and making a running record on a sheet before him of trains moving into and out of his block. I learned later that it was a manual telegraphy block system they were using on this railroad.

Those early railroad days trains were short and numerous due to the small engines then in use that could haul only a certain amount of tonnage per train. Therefore it was necessary to space them apart by means of block offices placed at comparatively short intervals along the track in addition to the regular offices in the towns and cities. The normal position of the arms on the signal mast was at 'stop', or red which would be horizontal. When a train was due to arrive at the block office west of him, that office would call the block office on the telegraph block wire, which was a wire used exclusively for that purpose, and ask him to 'Block all trains west for extra 35 east.' The operator would then make sure that his signal for west trains was at stop. Then he would say on the block wire, 'I block all trains west for extra 35 east', and sign his initials and office call. Shepps office call was 'SV'. The operator at block office west of him would then place his east signal to 'clear' for the east-bound train, which would be the arm down half ways from the horizontal. When the train passed his office, he would report the train by at such a time to the operator at that particular block office, in addition to reporting the train to the dispatcher 'DS' by the call, or symbol, 'OS' meaning 'on sheet'; on the dispatcher's train sheet. Then the operator at SV office would call the next block office east of him, Millston ON, and tell him to 'Block all trains west for extra 35 east' and he would say he will do so, whereupon SV would clear the block by placing his signal clear for the east bound train, while at same time his west bound signal would remain at stop. When the train had passed Shepps SV office, he would report to the men west of him that it had cleared the block at such a time, when he would then be able to prepare to block for another following train going east. This system worked in both directions for trains running in opposite directions. When two trains were close enough to meet, the train dispatcher, which in this case was at Eau Claire whose call was 'G', would send orders addressed to both trains at offices wide enough apart to permit delivery in ample time by the receiving telegraph operator. This would permit them to block, or clear the block between them for those two trains to meet. One train would take a siding at the meeting point while the superior train would pass without going in on a siding. It is understood, of course, that this system functions only on a single track railroad.

It takes longer to explain the system in detail than it does to actually operate it, for this manual telegraph block system of those days permitted fast movement of trains, one after another rapidly on a single track, because the telegraph was a comparatively very rapid means of communication. It was the fastest of all means up to that time. In later years of course, it was superceded by still faster means. More of that later. Railroads needed far more telegraphers during that period than at any time since to operate their block systems; therefore as a result they were constantly in demand. Telegraph schools (ham factories) sprang up in different cities to train recruits for that purpose to meet the demand.

Mr. Wahlquist treated me kindly on that first day that I visited him, the first time I had been in the telegraph office. My proudest moment was when he requested me to watch and listen to a certain sounder (the block wire) so that he could go outside into the woods and 'do the necessary'. I spent the whole day visiting him and listening to those mysterious sounds from the telegraph sounders; for they really were mysterious to the uninitiated. What was in use then and later was not the original invention of Mr. Morse. The original mechanism consisted of an electric gadget that perforated holes in a roll of narrow paper by electric impulses transmitted from an operator at a distant location. The holes in the paper were of different sizes and square with spaces. These holes represented the Morse code, which Mr. Morse invented, consisting of a combination of dots, dashes and spaces, for each letter. The receiving operator was required to translate these perforations and write them down as words and sentences on a separate sheet of paper. The system was crude and cumbersome, but it did the job, although slowly and laboriously. In the course of time the operators of the gadget learned to distinguish the sound of each dot, dash and space, for they gave off a sound of some kind that one could train himself to read by sound rather than by sight of the perforations. A smart operator soon was able to write down the message by sound, which was more rapid than the original method. The different sounds consisted of the length of the dashes, their number in combination with the dots and spaces for each letter. It was not long before it became customary for all operators of the gadgets, whether in newspaper offices, or in railroad offices of that early period after its invention in 1843, to copy all messages by ear, so that eventually the original gadget was changed to the brass (later aluminum) sounders that were in use at the time I visited Mr. Wahlquist, which I think was the year 1894, or thereabouts. Telegraphers of that period and later, and probably earlier, were called 'brass sounders' from the brass of which the sounders were made. The key by which sending was done, as I understand it, always had remained the same as Mr. Morse had originally invented it.

Mr. Wahlquist was required to remain on duty 12 hours per day, 7 days a week, no meal time off, no paid vacation period, no fringe benefits with a small salary of about forty dollars per month. He slept and ate at the settler's house nearby. But it was interesting work nevertheless, even though long and confining. He was able to converse and gossip with his fingers by calling fellow telegraphers along the line and to listen to the messages and orders and conversations take place over the different wires that ran through his office. I thought it was fascinating, as he explained it all to me, while I listened intently. Although he made a half hearted attempt to discourage me from learning telegraphy, in accordance with the telegrapher union that was trying to organize them, their policy then being to make telegraphers a scarce commodity in order to raise their wages. I became more determined to some day learn it and become a telegrapher; that was my ambition and goal in life. Before I left he told me I was too young to learn telegraphy; that I must attend school more; I must wait a few years; possibly I would change my mind by then. But he did give me the Morse code he had written on a piece of paper. Now I wish I had kept it! I never did change my mind. No matter how long it would require, I would some day be a full fledged telegrapher; that was my firm decision no matter what obstacles were placed in my way. That from a kid of five! Little did I realize then how I would have to fight my way toward that goal, and it was many years before I finally accomplished it.

School did not have much interest for me, although I had no difficulty learning, probably because of the lax educational facilities of the time. Parents were not interested in education, just so we could read and write after a fashion; they themselves were poorly educated, although they were sufficiently intelligent.

Referring to C.W. Wahlquiest again, the next time I saw him was in the Black River Falls depot where he was working second trick. That was quite some years later and I was quite a bit older, although young and ignorant of the ways of the world. He was a fine looking young man, and I recall how easy it was for him to copy train orders, messages and Western Union telegrams with a beautiful telegrapher's hand, typewriters (mills) not yet having come into general use at the time. I recall also how he made a lot of noise when stoking the three pot-bellied stoves he had to keep going.

There were three telegraphers in the Black River Falls office at that time besides the Agent and an assistant. M.J.Harpold was on first trick; C.W. Wahlquist on second; J.J. Gaffney on third, who when I spoke to him, also tried to dissuade me from entering the ranks of the telegraphers because that was the policy of the Order of Railroad Telegraphers, which I always thought was a short sighted policy. W.F.(Bandy) Maddocks was the Agent who also was a telegrapher. Eventually they abandoned that policy. For myself, I never could practice it after I entered their ranks; although the O.R.T. ordered me to do so, I defied them and did all I could to assist young ambitious fellows to get started in the railroad business, knowing how difficult it was for me to get going. I am pardonably proud of my efforts to teach those who came to me and I tried to make good, efficient workers out of those who were well and able. I am also glad that some times I had occasions to, but never did get impatient with young 'hams' on the wire who were slow in receiving and sending Morse. I always slacked up for them and never became angry with them, as some cranky telegraphers did. I am stating these things as matters of fact, not to brag about it.

A year or two after I retired in 1954, I learned that Mr. Wahlquist was still alive and living in New Richmond, Wisconsin on his retirement pension. I wrote him and reminded him of my visiting him in the block office in the woods that day so long ago. I had the pleasure of a period of correspondence with him and reminiscing of the 'good old days'. He was a good letter writer with that old fine telegrapher's hand that was different with a distinction of its own. He finally became too old and feeble to write much and his wife had to answer Christmas greeting card I sent him. He finally passed on to his reward some years later, having run his full course and accomplished his mission in life. I think he was 15 or 20 years older than myself. He must have been far past 80 when he died.

> "Backward turn backward, O
> time in thy flight!
> Make me a boy again, just for
> tonight."

--Chapter 3--

On our frequent trips to the railroad track, Cline's track, Cline's house and other points of interest to us, we would often encounter Mr. Henry Gebhardt at his dam, always with a shovel in his hands repairing it, digging ditches and maintaining his property. He worked alone and mostly by hand in backbreaking work digging and moving soil. A plentiful supply of water was a necessity in his business of growing cranberries, hence the dam from which an ample supply was diverted through a ditch in his cranberry bogs.

One summer day a heavy downpour of rain was too much for his earthen dam. The excess water made a hole in it and soon most of the dam washed down the creek. It was a heart-breaker for Mr. Gebhardt, but he never faltered and set to work at once with a team and scraper to rebuild it. He was a friendly man and always stopped working when he saw us coming to visit and chat. He did not live out his normal life-span which, I think, was due to hard work. He had accumulated a small fortune in his business.

Another good neighbor was William Crome, nicknamed 'Swamp William' because he lived near a swamp. He was an all around handy man, a mechanic, hunter, butcher; he could do anything,. He built a steam engine one time out of an old boiler and scrap iron, as one example of his mechanical ability. Every fall when we had a fat hog to butcher for our winter's supply of meat we called on Billy Crome to do the job. He would come walking up the sandy road with his home made sharp knife and other tools for that purpose. He made an all day's job of it for which Mother paid him 50 cents, plus a noon meal, with which he was fully satisfied. It was our job to assist him with the butchering. We caught the hog for him and held it down on its back while he applied his sharp knife to its throat. I could not bear to see that, so I turned by head and closed my eyes while the wicked knife did its cruel work. My sympathies were with the hog as he staggered around and finally collapsed from loss of blood, after which we went to work on him; first dipping him in a barrel of hot water previously prepared for removing the hair; then stringing him up on a scaffold and removing his insides and cleaning him thoroughly and finally cutting him up into sections for easy handling. Mr. Crome did his job with pains-taking care. He was a very good workman when he put his mind to it. His was a sunny optimistic disposition who always saw the bright side of situations.

He had migrated from Germany as a young man while emigration was in full swing, eventually arriving in Jackson County, probably attracted to that section of the country because of the numerous saw-mills operating at that time, as my Dad and other relatives were. Quite a large group of people, mostly emigrants, were living in that territory during that period. He met a cousin of mine, daughter of my mother's sister or brother, if I recall it correctly, and married her in Black River Falls. They raised quite a large family, but I lost track of them after their folks passed away while I was busy on the railroad.

Our neighbor was Mr. Ostlund, Pete, I believe it was. His wife was an invalid and they had purchased a forty next to ours and built a house on an elevation a little ways back from the road. He was physically a big man, as I recall him, strong as an ox. We did not associate much with him as he did not have any children with whom we could play.

It was Victor Anderson and his wife Tillie with their four girls and one son with whom we were in close contact. They lived up the road a ways, also in a log cabin. Tillie was a daughter of my mother's sister Aunt Anna Bergstrom; that made their offspring our second cousins, and we kids played with them quite a bit. Victor always drove a small horse, or pony hitched to a two wheeled cart with one seat past our place on his way to 'town' for their supply of groceries and the mail. RFD mail service had not yet been inaugurated. Sometimes Mother stopped him and asked him to buy our groceries, also. Coming back his cart was loaded down with supplies for two families. Life was very simple; no elaborate means of transportation was necessary, but only to get there and back, either by foot or horse and buggy, sometimes two horses to a buggy, at no great distance. Roads twisted and turned every which way that followed a path of least resistance. No highway accident that killed people, only a run away horse or two now and then that was not serious. As we boys grew older, we thought it was a great pleasure to ride in a buggy, strapped behind two dapple-greys on our way to town, or to a girl friend's house, or a gathering of some sort, which were quite numerous. We would take turns using the team and buggy to call on girls; my older brother was going steady with Elsie Hix at Shamrock; the next oldest at times had two girls in the buggy with him, Jessie and Lottie Smith, while I called on Florence Linnell now and then in Black River Falls; competition for use of transportation was keen between us during those 'horse and buggy days'.

As a 'shaver' I was rather shy in the presence of the four Anderson girls as we grew up together. I preferred boys to play with. I often wondered as a youngster why girls were different from us boys and why they wore dresses.

43

No one told me and I had to figure it all myself as I grew older. Nature seemed to assist me in understanding the mystery, finally, as natural instincts surged within me. As we grew older and less shy, we found the girls gay and full of fun and easy to visit with, very sociable. We spent many happy evenings together.

On a summer evening the three of us brothers and the older of the Anderson girls would walk the sandy road together, over a 'short cut' where the thick woods bordered closely the road; where the tree tops would form a canopy over us and the road, shutting out some of the sunlight; the fresh, clean fragrance of trees clothed in the green leaves of summer; the wild flowers growing alongside of the road, each variety with an aroma of its own. It probably was the merry month of June, when all of Nature was in tune, we sauntered slowly and finally arrived at a home with a family of young people like ourselves, Peter A. Potter.

Potters lived in a large rambling, frame house set among tall oak trees on the side of an elevation that sloped gently toward the road over which we came. At that time we thought it was a 'mansion' as compared to our own log cabins. It was a family of sons and daughters, the boys some older than ourselves, the youngest girl was Hattie Potter who was home and entertained us with records played with an Edison, long horned phonograph just recently placed on the market. A crank was turned that furnished power to operate the waxed rolls and music would come out through the horn. How wonderful that was, the first we had seen and heard! We heard square dance music, square dances being very popular those days. Even a song by Caruso with his golden voice, as well as a lecture by William Jennings Bryan on the Chautauqua circuit, also very popular during that period. Another was a speech by a famous political speaker of the day, his name eluding me at this late date. I recall he spoke on economics and ended up with 'the price of eggs' repeated several times, probably to emphasize his point. Eggs were only 'a dime a dozen' and he thought that was terrible. Politicians were concerned about such matters those days as they are now. Frank Potter, one of the Potter boys, was a 'fiddler', who played at country square dances together with Ellis Harmon who played the 'dulcimer' an old fashioned stringed instrument that was the fore=runner of the modern electric instrument with strings played with a pick and cross piece, producing pretty much the same kind of music.

The Wiggins family was one of four boys and one girl living about half a mile from the Omaha main line with whom we visited and played. Every Sunday we would walk to Fritz Kluth's home about three miles from where we lived, where Willie Kluth, a boy about my age, joined us together with other boys in the neighborhood when we would tramp the country roads and sometimes through woods looking for fun and sometimes mischief. The railroad track with the Wiggins boys was one of our objectives, and when we were all together we made almost an army, sometimes calling ourselves 'Cox's Army'. Roaming the country-side brought us close to Mother Nature, of which we never tired. People could not travel far those days except short distances by foot or horse and buggy and therefore remained in one location, unless some of us decided to move by train to other places.

One may wonder why we were not in Sunday School on Sunday mornings. There were none in our community. Mother would have sent us if there had been being a religious person. She was a 'practical Christian', who practiced Christian ethics in her daily life, but she never interfered with our freedom except to hold us in line as civil and honest individuals. Dad likewise did not dictate to us nor interfere with our freedom. He had no interest in church creeds or dogma, preferring to live his life without church affiliations. He professed no beliefs, nor creeds, nor did he attempt to interfere with others in their religious worship. He lived an honorable life; hated no one; no misdeeds committed, nor did he cheat in transactions; owed no money nor obligations to any one; paid his way as he went along. He never mentioned God or religion to us at any time; nevertheless, I would call him a practical Christian. The results of such a life surely has its favorable effects in a future existence. Is a person like him punished in the future state because he did not accept the orthodox belief? According to the great law of cause and effect, 'as ye sow, so shall ye reap', he would now be reaping his rewards for the good life he lived regardless of any beliefs or non-beliefs that he adhered to while in physical existence.

I think it was in 1894 that I first attended the Oak Ridge school, which was located about 4 or 5 miles from our home. My first teacher was Carris Dunlovey, who later became Mrs. Oliver P. Kelly in Shamrock. Some years ago while driving through Shamrock I saw Mr. & Mrs. Kelly in the garden of their home and I stopped and renewed my acquaintance with her. She would not have known me unless I reminded her that she taught me in the Oak Ridge school in 1894 about 60 years previously. She and her husband passed on some years later.

It was an old fashioned school, of course, and I was enrolled in 'chart class' where we were taught letters and numbers and a few simple words and to write them. A one room school with grades up to 8 necessarily had to have a simple program of teaching for the one teacher. Nevertheless, we learned the fundamentals such as reading, writing and arithmetic, which was at that time called the three R's. Teacher used a wooden ruler, or a long hickory stick for pointing to the slate board on the wall as well as for maintaining discipline. Some of the kids were 'wild' and defied her at times when she would bear down on them with her ruler. I recall one girl got angry at the teacher and when she came near the girl to reprimand her, she got a good hold of teacher's hair and pulled it with

46

all her strength. It was a battle 'royal' between them, but the teacher finally got the upper hand by the use of her stick. During recess when teacher was out, a boy named Joe King drew on the black-board pictures of a mare and a stallion in a position of sexual intercourse. When the teacher and kids came in, there were those pictures on the board in front of them to plainly see. As I recall it, she merely erased them without a word. It really was a work of art; Joe was a natural born artist and could draw anything.

During recess we boys would roam the thick woods near the school, the woods extending a long ways along the road on both sides of it and far in the rear. In fact, the building was set in the woods along side of the road. No matter how far we were from the school, we could always hear the hand bell teacher used in calling us back. Fist fights were common between some of the rougher boys. Many were the times boys came into the school room with evidence of a fight on their face such as black eyes, bruised skin and sometimes injured hands. Teacher could do nothing about that; it was accepted as 'occupational hazards.' I myself never became embroiled in fist fights, probably because I was adept at diplomacy.

If any of us graduated from that school, we did not receive a diploma. That probably was considered an unnecessary luxury during those days. In the winter time, when the temperature was freezing, we arrived in school frozen badly so that we had to stand around the huge stove in the center of the room until thawed out. It was a long, iron stove that burned long sticks of wood, sometimes green wood. If the snow was too deep, we remained home. Nothing was thought of missing school several days at a time. Education was not important, just so we could read and write and figure. Any 'graduate' of that school had to educate himself after he went out into the world, if he wished to make anything of himself.

We had one advantage those school days that present day kids do not have and that was walking home after school with school mates and having fun with them along the way; stopping here and there to explore the wonders of Nature and the small animals that inhabited the woods along the road; making paths for a 'short cut' through forests of white oak, poplars, birch, jack pine and at intervals a handsome white pine that had been spared by the woodsman, tall, straight with spreading branches that remained green throughout the year. And in season, filling up on blue berries and other fruit and berries.

The school house was used for gatherings and meetings of different kinds, including use as a voting precinct for the district. I cannot recall any political meetings, but I do remember distinctly while a small boy a family came into the community one winter and conducted religious meetings in the school building; they called themselves the 'Christian Crusaders'.

It was cold and wintry one evening some of us from our home walked, or trudged through the snow to the meeting. When near it, a sleigh load of people drove by with a team hitched to a light vehicle on four runners; they were the preacher and his family on their way to 'meetin' from a neighbor where they were staying. The room filled up with people from the neighborhood, bundled in winter clothes of all sorts. The speaker was the common type of a traveling evangelist who made his living for himself and family in that way. I suppose he was dedicated also to his mission in life, that of 'saving souls' from the torment of hell fire and brimstone, which was common practice those days. I cannot recall that part of it, young as I was, but I do remember a song they sang titled "Whiter Than Snow", and the preacher would stop the singing and explain the words as follows: "You know, snow is not exactly white; there are specks of dirt in it. But we will be absolutely white with no specks in it after we are saved." That, to my immature mind, sounded quite rational, which I could understand. But I cannot recall that I took any interest in the contents of his sermon, whatever it was. I also recall that we walked home with an old German emigrant, Fritz Kluth, who lived not far from the school. He wore a beard, but shaved his mustache. He was a likeable old gentleman, sociable and easy to talk to and always optimistic. His son was my age and we were pals quite a bit as we grew up and as young blades, Willie Kluth. We most always walked home together from school to as far as his home.

A few words about religion: Traveling preachers, Baptist, used to come to our house and conduct religious services in our home and elsewhere. Some of them sang solos accompanied with a guitar they brought along, which I enjoyed. When he started on his long sermon, I squirmed and twisted in my hard seat during the two hour talk. When he gave signs of quitting, I rejoiced inwardly, and at the close of the last song, I was the first to bolt out of there and out into the open God's country. Those sermons had no effect on me whatsoever except to build up a rebellion within me that could not be squelched, even as I grew more mature. I recall one portion of it, if not the rest, wherein he predicted dire consequences of eternal torment in a lake of fire that lasts forever and ever without hope of release for those who dared to disbelieve; who would not accept scriptures as he and his group interpreted it literally. To my mind that was a terrible thing to say as coming from God Himself who was supposed to be pure, merciful, full of love and of Divine Justice.

Mother accepted it all without question with the result that she was unhappy; always concerned about her own soul and those of her children. She cried quite a bit over this prospect, worrying about them as they faced a cruel world, or so she mistakenly thought. I recall one of these 'hell-fire and brimstone' preachers admonishing Mother about us boys using our musical talents, or what little we did have, for worldly purposes; he warned her that was the road to 'hell', to play our instruments at parties only to amuse and entertain, not for 'God's glory', etc. They scared the poor woman almost to death, soft-hearted and tender minded that she was. Mother was not at all like her own mother, who was tough minded, realistic and had a healthy skepticism for beliefs, theories and ideas that would not stand up under scrutiny and did not jibe with reason, logic and laws of nature.

As the years rolled on, I came to respect Grandmother's view more and more; to be skeptical of anything at all, religious, political, economical, philosophical that did not respond to good judgment and scientific thinking.

In later years, after we returned from Hazelhurst, Fritz Kluth and his good wife acted as hostess to the young people of the community' always glad to have them in their home. We spent many happy Sundays there with other boys and girls, but girls remained aloof from us, in most cases. Often Mr. Kluth would invite us all to a 'shindig', or 'hoe-down' in their house of a Saturday night and he furnished the music with his accordion. When Albert and I would arrive, Fritz was already seated in one corner of the largest room playing for all he was worth; the floor had been cleared of furniture, bare of rugs, if there were any, chairs placed along the walls for the girls to sit, while we boys stood around. Most of the dances were 'square' dances consisting of four couples to a set. Gilbert Paulson, a young blade of about my brother's age, did the 'calling', and when he was not there, others did it.

In between the square dances, the waltz and the two step were common and popular at the time. As for myself, I recall I wanted to dance with a Miss Gonis, whose first name I have forgotten; I was very shy with girls and had some difficulty getting up enough courage to ask her but finally did. She was just as shy as I was, but we soon got into the swing of it. Those were happy care-free days. Between dances, Stella Kluth, about Martha's age, would dance solos to her Dad's music. We attended many other country dances those days after our return from Hazelhurst, but more of that later.

The family was still together, living in the log cottage up to the time I was about 12, or less. As a youngster I had a certain fascination for thunder storms. I recall one day a terrific rain and thunder storm was raging and I could not resist the urge to run outside into the midst of it. I stood there while the rain pelted me and braced myself against the strong wind just for the fun of it. While doing so, the near tornado tore the straw roof from the horse barn, and how I enjoyed it! I imagined I was a part of the storm as it swirled about me, bent on destruction. To me the natural elements always have had a certain appeal that is difficult to describe. It probably was because they are a part of the world that mere man cannot control; or, had I inherited an affinity for Thor, the Norse god of mythology from distant forebears? The god of thunder and lightening? Who knows?

It was the year 1901 that Father decided to move his family to Hazelhurst, in northern Wisconsin where a large saw mill and box factory were operating to full capacity, employing hundreds of men with fairly good wages for the time. Mother did not object when the head of the house decided on the move; she was a dutiful and obedient wife. Dad was the boss in our house-hold, although he could not always get his boys and girls to obey him, being head-strong themselves.

What I recall of the trip was that a neighbor had been hired with a team and wagon with a high box loaded with bags and baggage and all us kids except Anna May, who had gone to Minneapolis and was working for the Gedney Pickle Co. She was the oldest, age 19 at the time, or possibly younger a year or less. The neighbor, whoever he was, hauled us to Millston, that point being closer to our destination than was Black River Falls, thereby saving on rail fares for the group. Little did I realize on that trip that I would some day become a part of the railroad we traveled on that carried us from Millston to Valley Junction, where we transferred to the Milwaukee Railroad for Babcock, thence to Hazelhurst on the Wisconsin Valley Division of that railroad.

The branch line from Valley Junction to Babcock has long since been discontinued. It was early morning, I recall, when we arrived at Babcock and that I was very sleepy. The trains were of the usual wooden type of coaches, lit by kerosene lamps. The brakeman carried a short ladder with which he reached up to the lamps to light and extinguish them. At the end of each coach was a coal stove that the crew kept fired in cold weather. The steam engine was the old type, comparatively small, that huffed and puffed to get started at each station. It was summer because the trees in the woods that surrounded Babcock were green with summer's foliage, and as we waited for another train to carry us to Hazelhurst, the early morning sun, a huge ball of red on the far distant horizon, was seen to rise slowly, its beams of light following the two ribbons of steel rail that passed the station where we were. The great forest, dark and gloomy when we arrived, awoke from its night of slumber as the rising sun caressed the tree tops and soon flooded it with light and warmth, bringing out the color scheme with which nature had endowed it.

Many years later I drove to Babcock one summer day to have the first look at it since that early morning so long ago and to bring back to my memory the beautiful scene as I observed it then; the forest was still there, not the same trees, but the forest crowding the railroad right of way as it did then; probably the same depot, but the Agent inside was of the younger generation who evinced interest when I told him of that trip and our transferring at his station that morning 60 years ago.

A man's life sometimes may be full of disappointment and despair, but in his serener moments he will acknowledge that, in spite of the suffering entailed, his emotional life slowly opens a new sense in him. He catches now and then glimpses of an undying youth in all things, and the world that seems dreary and ageing will reappear under certain emotional stress as he knew it before life became a tragedy. These glimpses at times are transitory, but they can last as long as the love emotion colors his being. There comes a time for him 'when all the world is young, lad, and all the trees are green and every goose a swan, lad, and every lass a queen.'

Our final arrival at Hazelhurst with 8 kids, two parents and a platform truck full of baggage was unheralded; no welcoming committee with a brass band were on hand; no friends or relatives met us. Mother probably was reminded of the day about 21 years earlier when she herself arrived in this country alone and unheralded to make her way in a new and strange land. But this time she was not alone; she had her husband with her and some very lively offspring. Many thoughtful persons marvel at the way Nature functions through her laws in the reproduction of the species in all kingdoms, especially in the human kingdom. In 21 years Nature had produced 9 offspring by using her body as an incubator, a process of creation that baffles the best of the medical scientists. What force, what creative intelligences and who or what are the directing entities that brings together the necessary materials; creates the many different organs of the proper elements and in the correct shapes and proportions; places them in the right positions in the body for the essential co-ordination and co-operation between them to make a completed, healthy, physical body?

I am not sure of this, but I think Dad, upon arrival, went to a family named Wickstrom's living a short distance from the depot and asked them to house his brood while he got himself a job. They were of the same nationality as our parents with whom they could speak their native tongue. Afterwards, they were friends of our family; it is possible Dad had known them previously.

So Dad sought out Mr. Rummly, the boss of the huge lumber drying yard of the Yawkey Lumber Co. He hired Dad on the spot with no questions asked. Men were in demand, especially a good looking, sturdy, healthy and tall man that he was who seemed very capable of the hard days work, at $1.75 per day, for a 12 hour day, Sundays off for rest. His title: Lumber piler.

The general superintendent of the Yawkey Lumber Co. was Mr. Timmlin. I used to know their given names, but have forgotten them in the flight of time. He assigned us to a house owned by the Company on a ridge with a road in front of it, overlooking a slope and higher land on other side where the school house was located. In the rear of it, the land sloped down to Lake Catherine a short distance away, a beautiful lake that connected with many other lakes through an artificial canal. C.C. Yawkey owned the town, lock stock and barrel, body and soul. He was the owner of all the residences; the company store; the saloon; the town hall; the church; the mill; box factory; lumber yard; thousands of acres of virgin timber in several counties; all the green and dry lumber; the box materials. He coined and used his own money in the town of a metal that appeared to be a form of aluminum, of a light bronze color. Although he paid his men in United States currency, at end of each month in an envelope (no deductions) they had to sign for an amount wanted between pay days in his own coin, dollars, quarters, halves, dimes and nickels and use them for purchases in his general store. These coins were good only in his town.

In a sense he was dictator to his own people. They were compelled to buy in his store and saloon. No one else could engage in business in his town. We attended his church, although it was non-denominational; we went to his town hall for all sorts of activities and the drinking men had to patronize his saloon. For practical purposes, we were his slaves in a sense, but he was a fairly considerate boss. He was not cruel, just a good business man who furnished

54

employment at good wages to hundreds of men. I recall him as short and stocky with black, wavy hair as he strode up the long steps to his office connected with the store and general office, from his mansion type residence on the lake shore in front of the store.

Nevertheless, Hazelhurst was good for us, a change for the better. For the first time I had the opportunity to attend a much better school more regularly than before, as did my brothers and sisters. Everything was different. Teachers took an interest in us, which was not the case in the Oak Ridge school. I for one learned more in far less time in that school than ever before. A man teacher was the best of all of them. He had migrated from Germany; I wish I could recall his name. He drilled us with his driving force, and he had plenty of it. I loved that man, and I have wished many times since then that I could have met him again and told him how much I enjoyed his teaching. His method was direct and to the point. We were called upon to repeat what we had learned the previous day, and if we had forgotten, he drilled us again and again. He has long since passed on to his reward.

The school building itself was of a unique type that we do not see any more. It consisted of three long frame buildings, one story, each separate from the others except that all of them came together at one end forming a sort of lobby that connected with all the others. The first long building paralleled the street in front; another long one was built at right angles and a third in between these outer two, all of them connected up at the angles, or corner of the angle. Each was heated separately with large wood stoves that used slab wood for fuel. The first three grades used the one paralleling the street; the building in between for next three grades and the last that pointed away from street, for seventh and eighth grades. One teacher for each building. I recall best the seventh and eighth grade one where the man teachers taught; women teachers taught in the other two.

During those happy school days, all the pupils were taught the fine art of penmanship. There was no dodging this important and necessary job of learning to write legibly and distinctly. We spent several hours a week practicing with the old fashioned pen and ink with the ink well full of ink always on one corner of our desk. Under our teacher's instructions, we learning how to swing the whole arm and wrist in writing, not only the fingers as at present; the fingers were held in co-operation with the arm and wrist. The wrist had to be level so that a coin could be placed on it and remain there while swinging the arm, thus assuring a beautiful and legible style of penmanship; each letter clear and distinct. This is a lost art in our present day schools, but I believe it will return again, as legible writing is fundamental for an all around educated person. In later years that system of writing stood out in good stead, especially those who learned telegraphy where a good legible hand was necessary in copying train orders, messages and Western Union telegrams, before the advent of the typewriter.

All of us, except the youngest attended school and when we did not attend school, had jobs of one kind or another. None of us were ever taken out of school to do certain jobs. Dad piled green lumber that came direct from the saw mill and hauled on two wheeled carriages by a horse and a sort of two wheeled axle on which one end of the load of lumber would be held down by chains and the driver on top of the load. Each load, depending on size of the lumber, was hauled to and parked at the pile for that particular size of lumber. Dad and his working partner wore leather aprons on which the lumber scraped more or less. He, also, used a sort of tri-pod made of two by four on end of which was a metal spike upon which the boards were balanced and handed up to the piler. He used a roller attachment on the pile to facilitate easy handling of the heavy boards.

There were high plank platforms around the mill on the same level as the saws and machinery that cut the logs into different sized lumber and underneath were all sorts of wheels, pulleys and steam machinery that made the whole thing run. The lumber, when finished, came out on a long moving endless chain run by steam. There were men at intervals on each side who pulled it off the chain and placed on one of the carriages, each of the same kind and size of lumber. A system of plank platforms was extended on the same level throughout the whole huge yard, long lines of platforms paralleling each opposite rows of piles in both directions. These platforms were used for hauling the lumber around the yard with a man and a horse and his two wheeled axle arrangement. Several of them were kept busy hauling. The system of platforms also extended to the box factory at other end of the yard. On the same level dry lumber was hauled for making wooden boxes of various kinds and sizes. On a Sunday when the yard was idle, those of us boys who were fortunate enough to own a bicycle, greatly enjoyed riding over the platforms throughout the huge yards.

When we first arrived, the big saw mill intrigued me and I had to explore it to satisfy my curiosity; I had never seen one like that before. It was situated on the shores of Lake Catherine, a portion of which was partitioned off with a boom from the rest of the lake adjacent to a railroad track that paralleled the lake shore. Flat cars loaded with logs were spotted and dumped into the lake boom down an incline. There was always a raft of logs in the water awaiting the time when each log was guided with a spear in the hands of a man who started the logs up the chute with an endless chain and on into the mill. Another man was there and, using a cant hook, rolled the logs down another short incline. They were placed on the carriage with two men on it that operated the levers. The mechanism caught the logs and held down while the carriage was shuttled back and forth, the huge circular saw sawing the log into boards, planks and timbers, whatever would produce the best material out of the log, also depending on the requirements for a certain size of boards at a given time.

How I enjoyed sitting on a short log stump at the head of the chute and watching the logs come up, rolled over, pushed into the carriage by a huge, steel arm operated by steam. Then they were made secure by the two men with hooks on the carriage, and the log cut up into long boards. How that saw would hum and sing a tune of its own, whining shrilly, and lowering the whine in accord with the speed of the carriage. I never tired of it.

Of all the men in the mill, the man who operated the huge arm and movement of the carriage was the most important man in the mill. He always had two levers in his hand, one just above him and one or two at his feet by which he controlled and operated and co-ordinated the whole operation. He stood in a small compartment facing the circular saw and the carriage track; when a log was to be turned for sawing on the other side of it, he signaled the two men on it to release their hooks by means of levers, then brought the big steel arm up by which the log was turned on the carriage with hooks on the arm, then secured again and run through the whining saw. This operation was repeated for each four sides of the log, the carriage moving rapidly back and forth by the man at the control levers, all of it operated by steam power. He would also signal the men the size of the board he wanted by using his fingers, one for an inch, two for two inches, etc. when they would hitch the log forward that much with their control levers, and the carriage with the log would run it through the saw again and again.

I was not satisfied with just seeing the saw and carriage and the logs being sawed up, but I had to pass slowly through the whole mill and watch every operation; *how the slabs were disposed of by running it over moving rollers to a huge, circular silo where a continuous fire was on full blast burning the waste materials; *how some of it was cut into lengths for fuel wood; *how the different kinds of boards were guided over other sets of rollers; *how ends sawed on platforms with small saws, and finally *how lumber placed on moving chains with stops for each board, at the end of which a man stood ready to estimate the board feet *how each board and plank and timber that passed him he noted on a pegged board behind him, *how after which the lumber was taken off the moving chains and placed on two wheeled carriages standing ready for each kind and variety by a man at his station. The man who stood inspecting and estimating each piece that passed him had to be a good man at arithmetic; he knew at a glance the size of each one and added up the board feet in his head, and when a certain figure was reached, noted it with a peg on his board. The whole operation was fast and efficient and each man at his station was busy all the time. It was a 12 hour per day and 12 hour night operation with two shifts of workmen. The highest paid man in the mill was the 'sawyer' , the man who rushed the logs through the huge saw, five dollars per day, every day and night except Sunday when the mill was idle and repairs made when necessary.

The men were permitted one hour at noon to go home and eat, when the mill stopped whining; the steam whistle blew exactly at 12 noon; 6 PM and 7 AM for meals. The whole town and its population were governed by the mill whistle; even school hours adjusted to it. The noise of the mill and the box factory was heard all over the town and outside it, but to me personally it was sweet music as the circular saw raised its voice high or lowered it to conform to the log that was passing through it, it reminded me, and every one else, that all was well at the old saw mill; that each log had reached the end of its journey after a long life time of growing in the forest as a tree in accord with the natural laws that governed it. What tree is more stately than a tall, magnificent white pine that has withstood the ravages of time for a hundred years and more? Was it its destiny from the very beginning that it should some day arrive in a saw mill and be cut up into boards for the use of man? Or is it foreordained that it would remain in the forest and die a natural death after a long life span of living? In either case, it would seem, that it had fulfilled its destiny in life by growing into a huge, tall tree and in time die in the way of nature, and at the same time propagate offspring and in the end be cut down by a woodsman axe; either way it accomplished its mission in life. "Words are used by fools like me, but only God can make a tree."

My oldest brother did not start school, but went to work in the timber yard, scaling and loading sawed timber that had dried onto flat cars for shipment by railroad to various points. He was 17 or less at the time. I and the rest of them started school, but that was not continuous and steady. The second year Mother thought Albert, being a big boy, should go to work and Dad did not object. So one day she contacted Mr. O'Melia who was boss of the outlying logging camps and asked him to hire him as 'cookee' in a camp. He demurred, saying he was too young, being about 14. But Mother said, "He is a good boy; please give him a job." He replied, "Alright, I will try him out, but you as his parent must be responsible for him, not the company." "That is fine with us; we agree": or words to that effect.

So he was sent to a camp where a Frenchman was the chef and worked all winter with him, getting up at 4:30 every morning and worked until late at night assisting the cook to feed a small army of hungry, hard working men. I recall that I drove out to his camp one day with a passenger in the dead of winter and deep snow; I was working for the cookee owner as driver of livery rigs. I remained all night; filled myself up with doughnuts from a barrel full of them and left for home in the early morning. When the camp broke up in late spring, he

60

was issued a check for quite a large sum of money he had earned all winter. When he presented it to a bank cashier at Minocqua, he was reluctant to hand so much cash to a youngster, especially at the time when so many lumber-jacks were in town getting drunk from their earnings. He told him that he would hide the money in his clothes and hurry to Hazelhurst and give it to his parents, which he did and walked all the way home without incident.

I myself was in demand all over town as a handy boy who could do almost anything. After school and Saturdays, I piled slab-wood for the neighbors in long piles for drying and use as fuel. A huge van drawn by a team of horses would dump the green slabs where wanted and I went to work on the big pile. It had been cut into stove-lengths at the mill, a by-product of it, but most of the slabs were burned as waste in the continuously burning fire in a huge silo near the mill, flames and smoke from which were visible night and day, a reminder presumably by some superstitious people of the fires and burning brimstone of the imaginary hell that lasts forever and ever.

The owner of the livery stable in town, Axel Anderson, who also was a clerk at the company store, hired me many times to make trips with passenger at 50 cents per trip, to different places. Sometimes I would drive a light wagon and team, the wagon containing three or four seats that could carry about 12 people to capacity. My passengers were mostly young men, some of them drunk, that I had instructions to drive to a place that was known as the 'half-way house', located half ways between Hazelhurst and Minocqua. It was a large house near a lake and was occupied by several women. The men piled out, entered the house and remained there all night, until I would return the next day to haul them back. The girls did not show themselves to me, probably because of my youth. They did a thriving business with the men. On the way the men drank brandy from plain bottles, which they passed to me, but Mother had warned me not to learn to drink liquor and of course I obeyed.

I recall a trip I made on winter's day in deep snow to a logging camp in the thick woods some distance from Hazelhurst with one passenger in a cutter and one horse. The route was over a primitive two track logging road that wound through the woods, almost invisible from the deep snow. My passenger was a cook and both of us were bundled up in heavy clothing in the cutter against the bitter cold. When we came to a small bridge over a frozen stream, for some reason the horse veered to one side and the front end of the cutter caught on a small tree and broke the fills and the horse almost getting away from me if I had not had a firm grip on the lines.

We managed to tie up the broken fills with straps and continued to the camp which we reached just before dark. After unhitching and putting the horse in the camp barn taking its harness off, hanging it up and feeding and watering my horse, I went into the cook shack for supper, after which I stayed with the men in the bunk house until they retired for the night. The cook kindly arranged a bunk for me to sleep in that night, and the next morning fed and watered my horse, after which I hitched him up to my cutter and headed for home without further incidents. I made numerous other trips after that to Woodruff, Minocqua, outlying camps, etc., in summer using a buggy and light wagon; in winter with a cutter and light sleigh. Many times Mr. Anderson came to the school to get me to make a trip without any objections from the teacher. I recall once he rapped on the window opposite where I was sitting and motioned me to come out to make a trip and I would walk out of school without the necessity of asking my teacher. One of those days I answered an ad in a city paper about selling something. They shipped me a large box containing all sorts of household luxuries such as cosmetics, soaps, patent medicines and what-not. I set to work at once upon receipt and called on the neighbors in town and before long I had sold contents of the whole box; the ladies were all eager to buy from me, whatever it was. I cannot recall exactly, but I must have received several boxes of goods from this concern, whoever it was, because later on I received two prizes from them for selling so much, one was a gold watch, the old fashioned case that had to be opened to tell the time; the other prize was a set of dishes which I gave to Mother. I kept the watch for a time but later lost it.

Albert's twin brother Albion was sickly after we arrived there. We asked Dr. Ninneman, whose horse I was taking care of at his residence near the lake and who was the company doctor, to come and try to do something for him. All he did was to puncture a boil, or something he had under the arm, which did no good. He passed on some time later and was buried in the cemetery near a small lake with thick woods around it, and a road in front. Albert later, when he had reached full maturity, had a marker placed over it and left instructions that he himself shall be buried along-side his twin brother. He was 14 years 6 months when we buried him, the first burial in our family.

Harry was too young to work and attended school, as did Mamie and Martha. Alfreda, who was 17 or 18 at the time, went to Rhinelander to work. But I recall that she lived with us in the frame house on the ridge for sometime, cannot say how long, because I remember that some of the young blades in town used to come to our house and tried their best to get acquainted with her as she was a very good looking girl at the time. She was quite independent in her way and they had no success with her. Even some married men were attracted to her; one I was working with in the box factory used to call me 'brother-in-law', whatever he meant by that, probably because he wished he had her for a wife because of her good looks. Sometime later she went to Rhinelander were she met and married Sumner J. Hamilton. My oldest sister, Anna May had gone to Minneapolis and eventually married Ed Litchliter, manager of the pickle factory of the Gedney Pickle Company.

We had pleasant and prosperous times in Hazelhurst. We were all earning money except the youngest and Mother who managed the household. Those days a dollar was practically a fortune, at least to us. We liked school and participated in most of its activities; such as they were at the time. C.C. Yawkey had built a church where any denomination could hold services; evidently he understood the need of religious services for his people no matter what their background had been. He was a good manager and businessman although strict in his application of good business principles. He also had built a saloon that catered to the drinking element in the community. There were no attempts at dictating morality, or the code of ethics to the inhabitants; they had complete freedom to think, speak and act within the laws of the state and nation.

The first Sunday school we kids ever attended was in this church. Although I cannot recall the pastor, I do remember Mr. Charlie Steele who was a devout member and worker in both Sunday school and church services. He had a basso voice that could be heard over all others. He also had beautiful, black haired, blue-eyed daughter about my age that the boys liked because of her good looks and cheery disposition, Martha Steele. He also had a son younger than Martha. Mr. Steele took his whole family to church regularly.

Although there was a rough element in town, the majority were decent folks, many of whom carried on church services and functions in connection with it. Mother was an avid participant; she encouraged her brood to go to church, but could do nothing with Dad; he remained home on Sundays and rested and read his papers and other literature. Mother had a beautiful singing voice and made good use of her talents in that direction

64

in church as well as in the town hall where all sorts of social activities took place. I recall especially a duet she sang with a Mr. Dokke, also a good singer, and I enjoyed greatly listening to their fine harmonizing voices. The town hall was the focal point for traveling shows; political meetings; dances; sociables; local talent entertainments; voting precinct and official town meetings. I attended every one I could; I had to know what was going on.

Dad had made a row boat in his spare time which we used rowing all over beautiful Lake Catherine and stopping here and there to catch bass and other species of fish with which the lake abounded naturally. We rowed through the canal and took the boat down an incline onto Lake Tomahawk, which was lower than Lake Catherine, and rowed over that lake until we were exhausted. A chain of lakes connected those two with several others, over which we kids tried to row, but was too hard work. That was before the advent of the more speedy powered boats that required only steering by hand.

During his spare time, Dad experimented with a set of oars he invented that did not require raising up from the water, so that a rower would be able to row in the same direction in which he was looking. It consisted of a set of fins made of lumber that swished back and forth in the same way as a fish uses fins in swimming; they remained in the water at all times while the operator pushed and pulled on his oars that were connected with the apparatus with steel rod arrangement. We tried it out several times and found them to be heavy and cumbersome, and so Dad abandoned the idea, which was sound and required only further experimenting and refining to make it practical. It was only another instance of his lack of initiative in making good use of an idea, which could have proved successful in time.

The people of the town mostly were congenial, of Scandinavian, Bohemian, Polish and French descent, so that it was a melting pot of many nationalities. One day Mr. Yawkey called a mass meeting in the town hall, notifying them when they received their pay of the time and date. It was the year that Robert M. LaFollette Sr. first ran for office, that of Governor. It was called for the purpose of discussing the political issues of the day and Mr. Yawkey was one of the speakers, in fact the principle speaker. In his talk he urged the people to vote for Mr. Peck who was LaFollette's opponent for the office of Governor of Wisconsin at the time. In his speech he predicted many consequences to every one if LaFollette were elected. He extolled the fine principles and virtues of Mr. Peck who was of the conservative turn of mind. Mr. LaFollette was of the more liberal persuasion. I cannot recall that either one appeared in our town during the campaign, probably thinking we as a community was too small and its inhabitants of not much consequence.

The principle issue of that campaign was 'freight rebates' that Mr. LaFollette had raised against his opponent. Before the mass meeting, Mr. Yawkey had arranged with the Milwaukee Railroad depot agent, Mr. Manthy, to bring some of his records to the meeting. Under instructions from Mr. Yawkey, he attempted to prove by the books he brought that rebates were not paid to the Yawkey Lumber Company by the railroad for freight charges they had paid. They were the railroad's best customer and of course the railroad and their agent had to do what they could to protect their good patron.

Of course the station records would not show that rebates, or refunds, had been paid; those records would be in the railroad's general headquarters offices, not at the station. Those records would not be available to anyone, but presumably Mr. Yawkey thought he could persuade his people by the station records that he had not received any 'kick-backs'. Old Bob LaFollette Sr. was the popular figure in the political press of the time and on election day he swept the state and buried his opponent in an avalanche of ballots, including the small town of

Hazelhurst whose inhabitants showed their independent thinking and voting and would not be dictated to on how to vote.

C. C. Yawkey as well and R. M. LaFolloette Sr. have long since disappeared from earthly scenes and we hope they are now on friendly terms, wherever they may be located and enjoying each other's companionship. One achieved fame as a political leader and reformer; the other accumulated a fortune of many millions of dollars. Which of the two were better off? I learned later that Mr. Yawkey had lived to the advanced age of 90.

On Sunday afternoons in the summer time, baseball games were played on the ball diamond on an elevation opposite the railroad track near the depot. Pete Swedenborg was always the umpire; he was also a clerk in the company store. He was the stubborn type of individual and outspoken; woe to the ones who disputed his decisions on the diamond! He was able, and would on occasion, run disputers off the field, for daring to argue with him. He had the build and strength for it. About three PM the ball game stopped and all of us trooped to the depot, including the agent Mr. Menthy who was one of the players. A passenger train's arrival at the depot was a very important event in a small town such a Hazelhurst those days. The train and the telegraph were the only means of contact with the outside world. The railroad supplied all our needs; brought our mail, the papers, express and freight and it carried us as passengers to wherever we wished to travel and bring us back safely without casualties.

The depot agent and telegrapher (he was the railroad's contact with the public, an all around man) unlocked his office and many of us crowded in and surrounded him as he sat at his telegraph table on which were numerous telegraph instruments clicking away merrily. He never objected to us crowding into his office; he was one of us, accommodating and sociable. He listened and found out where the train was at the time and about what time it would arrive which he always announced to us. When we heard the train's whistle, we all filed out onto the plank platform and watched while the engine blew its whistle and rang its bell. Passengers boarded the train while others got off and during this operation, the news-butcher, who was the first to get off with an arm full of Sunday papers from the big cities, did a 'land-office' business with eager customers. It was the 'funny paper' that we were mainly interested in; the 'Katzenjammer Kids;' and; 'Her name was Maud'; and other popular cartoons of the day. Before we went into the waiting room to read the 'funnies; we watched and listened to the small steam locomotive huff and puff, the engineer giving her all the steam he had when the huge wheels would turn rapidly a few times, slipping on the rails, slack up and again turning rapidly until finally the wheels took hold of the rails and slowly got the train moving, gradually picking up speed. All this time the fireman was busy shoveling in soft coal into the firebox to keep up steam for the long haul, the little engine blowing off steam and belching black smoke that trailed in a long stream above and over the coaches.

Had I lost interest in the railroad and telegraphy by this time? My no! I was more interested than ever, as I grew older. The Yawkey Company owned two steam engines of their own with which they hauled logs and freight cars from Tomahawk Junction and connections. I kept a close watch on them at every opportunity, when I wasn't working. Old '99 was an old fashioned steam locomotive that hauled a train of a combination baggage and passenger coach from Hazelhurst to Tomahawk and return daily except Sunday. Besides logs it hauled cars of necessary materials needed and also cars of lumber out-bound less frequently; the Milwaukee Road had a monopoly of lumber and box hooks shipped out.

This particular road over which old '99 operated was owned by the lumber company and competed some with the

Milwaukee Road, but not seriously. I asked the conductor (who happened to be a large, fat man and who roomed at the company boarding house) one day if I could ride his engine '99. Being a good natured man (most fat men are good natured) he consented and instructed his engineer to let me ride. What an experience that was for me who was barely 14 years young! The engine chugged and lurched pulling a coach, caboose and a couple other cars over a road-bed that was far from perfect. The passing scenery was nothing but woods; the only point of interest was the small village of Tomahawk approximately 26 miles from Hazelhurst. I cannot recall what was done there; probably only to turn the engine, pick up some cars, mostly logs, a passenger or two and also express and mail. I rode the engine all the time, not daring to leave it until I reached Hazelhurst again.

They also owned a unique type of engine that did not have the ordinary large driver wheels; in place of them, it had pistons connected with small wheels that turned in opposite direction of the wheels on rails, through which power was transmitted. I believe that type is listed as 4-0-4-4 R 1100. I have a picture of one exactly like it. It was used for hauling logs from outlying camps on flat cars to the pond in front of the mill. Briefly, in the cold winters logging roads were made by gouging out two ruts into which water was poured that froze solid, making a smooth icy path for runners of a huge, wide sleigh carrying logs over which a team hauled it to a rail-head a distance from the logging site. During the winter, when logging operations were at maximum, logs were piled high by this method along-side the company's own railroad. From these piles of logs the big mill was supplied the year around with a constant supply of fresh logs. There were several of these rail heads in the woods to which the company had built a roadbed for rails and over which this little steam engine made frequent trips summer and winter that could haul only a limited number of loads,

69

probably half a dozen or so, because of lack of power. The ancient locomotive was small, but O MY! The Milwaukee Railroad, also, built branches where necessary into the woods for the same purpose; they also piled logs on sidings of their main line where flat cars were loaded with logs and hauled to the mill. It was an all-around, grand-scale efficient operation in the production of lumber; and the railroad had a monopoly of this lucrative traffic. Trucks had not yet been invented.

During school vacation in the summer I asked Charlie Stokes, foreman of the box factory, for a job, but he said I must have a permit from my parents to do so because of my youth; I was under 14. My parents agreed readily and furnished the permit; I was to receive the huge sum of 50 cents per day for a 12 hour day. I was assigned to a machine where boards were sawed and fitted into proper sizes by an experienced man who ran it, and it was my job to remove the completed sides, bottoms, ends of a wooden box from the platform and place on a bench where another older man tied them up into bundles with binder twine. He received $1.75 per day; his work did not require experience or skill any more than mine did, but his pay was much more than mine for same amount and time of work. Child labor!

At the end of the first 12 hour day, my body ached from the work, having to repeat the same operation over again and again. My folks wanted me to work and earn money, but not at that rate and those hours. Mother told me to ask for a raise after I had worked a while. So I, in the course of time, screwed up enough courage one day to ask Mr. Stokes for a raise in pay. He replied that he did not have the authority to do that, and referred me to Mr. Timlin, the general superintendent of the company. When I went to him with my problem, he stated that he could not raise any one's wages without authority from the head-boss himself, C.C. Yawkey. To call on Mr. Yawkey to me was like entering a lion's den, which I did not have the courage to do at that time, although I think now after these many years that he very likely would have granted my request and raised my pay. He was only human, like the rest of us. But most of us had a great deal of respect for him, being the sole owner of the whole outfit as he was and immensely rich. He did not mix with his people; the only time we had glimpses of him was when he walked to and from his private office to his mansion on the lake shore, hardly ever stopping to talk to any one that I could observe. Also, when he stood in front of his audience in the town hall when he wanted to persuade his people to vote the way he wanted them to do. He was a fairly good looking business man, short bodied with wavy black hair; his speech likewise short and crisp and to the point. My father would tower over him in physical stature in comparison; and far more handsome. So my attempt at bargaining with my employer was a complete failure; probably was also for all others who attempted it. No union those days for collective bargaining. But we were happy nevertheless. We lived good and enjoyed life.

I recall Mr. Stokes' habit of chewing plug tobacco and spitting out the juice in front of him no matter where he was, or so it seemed to me. I do not wish to be unfair to any one of my elders and bosses at this late period of my life; they were all human and subject to errors and human frailties as we all are more or less. I did not hate them and do not now; merely recording. As the weeks went on I got to know the men working there and liked them all. I noted some of them trying to cheat, or beat the whistle a few minutes at the noon hour by going to the toilet and thereby get a head start on the rest to go home for dinner. I got into the act also and did it several times, but once too many. Charlie Stokes was watching me this time; waited for me as I belted out at the whistle, caught up with me and gave me a bawling out for it. I cannot remember the exact words he used, but he got the message across to me. I merely kept on walking, and he had to walk along side

71

of me while he did so. I have long since forgiven him, but not forgotten; he had a job to do. After that, I remained glued to my machine until the whistle. He very likely did the same thing to others who were trying to cheat a few minutes on time, company time.

In connection with school at Hazelhurst, I wish to tell about a young man, a Bohemian emigrant who had lost his left arm while hunting one day, and after he had recuperated found himself unable to do the work he had done before the accident. He decided he needed an education in order to make a living in the world with only one arm. So with the help of relatives and others, he entered our school, but was compelled to start in first grade. He was a big man physically, and it seemed ludicrous to us kids to see such a big fellow sitting in the room with the small fry. He was about 20.

First he had to learn to speak English, not having been in the U.S. sufficiently long to have learned it at the time of the accident. He applied himself diligently in the first grade and advanced so rapidly that soon he was passed on to the next higher grade. All the time he learned more and more on how to speak our language better and better. He passed rapidly from grade to grade during the first part of the term so that in the second half and later he had graduated to our eight grade. I remembered him as a big, happy, good natured man who was always looking for fun and having fun with his fellow students. He was strong and even with one arm missing; he could get the better of any boy who cared to grapple with him. His penmanship was perfect; he was by far the best penman in school, his letters and words were the best I have ever seen. He also excelled in all other subjects of study in our grade; he was even better than Albert O'Melia who was supposed to be the smartest boy in school, although he could not handle the language as fluently as Albert. I wish I could remember his name, probably a strange one due to his Bohemian background, but he graduated with flying colors with the rest of his class. I have always understood that he moved to Rhinelander so as to be able to attend high school there; I have since lost track of him. Just think of the feat of entering grade school at first, and graduating from the eighth, all during one school term. He probably did the same in high school. He was not only strong physically; he was strong mentally, as well as emotionally. It requires courage of a high order to do what he did.

Albert O'Melia's family were Irish; his Dad was a superintendent of the logging camps for the company and as such earned more money than the rest of us. Albert was always well dressed in school and always attended. Whereas the other boys came to school dressed in almost any kind of clothing, he always wore a dress suit with pants that ended at his knees and long stockings. He wore a gold watch chain across his breast with a gold watch in his vest pocket and a tie with his shirt. One would think that other boys would sneer at him and ridicule him for his Dude clothes, but he was not the type that invited that sort of thing, for he really was an aristocrat that commanded respect. We respected him for his smartness and his ability to pass his exams easily and to solve any problem presented to him. We heard later that he went through high school in Rhinelander in three years. From there he was sent to the University of Wisconsin and graduated in three years as a lawyer. Later he became district attorney of Oneida County. His only son also took up the law as a profession.

Albert had a younger sister named Margaret O'Melia who was cast in a different mold from her brother. She was a quiet lovable girl, red haired, friendly and easy to talk with. I used to skate with her on a small lake near town, Lake Catherine not always being safe in warmer weather in the winter time. But all of us kids did skate on lake Catherine when the ice was frozen thick. We built a bon-fire on the shore of a moon lit night around which we would warm ourselves between sessions on the ice. It was in the company store in the evening after supper that the young people would gather, the store always being open till late every night. The boys especially would gather there just to visit each other, not to do any mischief; we never thought of mischief. The best place to sit was on the counter where bolts of cloth were measured off for the ladies, but there was room for only a few. The lake shore facing the store, the mill and the town was all clear of pine trees those days, so that we had a clear view of the great expanse of the lake. There also was ample room there to play ball if and when we wished. We made our own play-ground and managed our own games without the aid of a supervisor, as at present.

I suppose each of us can say that there were certain periods in our lives in past years that we really can call happy and care-free. In most cases it probably would be during days of youth when everything was new and strange with no monotony as in later years. It is refreshing and good for one's disposition and sense of justice to live in retrospect and in memory of these by-gone days. Such retrospect periodically creates in us a sense of balance between those good years and the more difficult ones of later times.

As a person nears the end of the trail after a life time of living, and as events of past years pass before one's consciousness in panoramic sequences, one needs to keep fresh in memory the good times, the happy moments and the pleasant fellowships in order to counter-balance those that were not so pleasant and that may upset the balance when dwelt upon too long. Life is a balance sheet; we need credits to offset the debits. The more credits, the better. Individuals are somewhat like corporations in respect to the profit motive. We came into physical existence for the purpose of accumulating as many credits as possible under the circumstances in which we find ourselves, so that at the end of the life-span allotted to us, we may extract the quintessence of service performed for our fellowman and take them with us as dividends to whatever is the next phase of our continued existence.

"So merit winneth the happier age,
Which by demerit halteth short of end;
Yet must the Law of Love reign King of all
Before the kalpas end.

Such is the Law which moves to
righteousness,
Which none at last can turn aside or stay;
The heart of it is Love, the end of it
Is peace and consummation sweet. Obey!"

--Chapter 4--

But happy times must eventually end. We had lived in Hazelhurst four years when father decided to return to his beloved homestead in the woods. Mother did not object; her attitude was that the husband is the head of the household, the bread winner and as such must be obeyed whether the move was desirable or not. From the vantage point of 'hind-sight' and experiences in later years for all of the family, the move was the wrong one; we should have moved to Rhinelander instead where conditions would have been far better in every respect.

When an individual, or the head of a family, reaches a point in life where two pathways point in different directions, one or the other is chosen. A number of individuals are affected for better or for worse by that one decision. One path leads to disruptions, disappointments, unfavorable environments, and retardation of the evolutionary process of progress and advancement in all fields of human endeavors for those concerned; the other leads to happiness, good fortune, favorable environments and a speed-up of the process of advancement and progress for the same individuals. Such can be the consequences for better or worse by a single decision of one individual.

I myself did not go back with the folks because I had moved to Rhinelander the year previous and was working as a clerk and delivery boy in a grocery store. Albert remained on his job as cookee; Freda was in Rhinelander and Anna May in Minneapolis. The oldest brother accompanied the rest of the family to Oak Ridge. Later Albert moved back there. I decided I was going to pursue my own course in life as I wished it. I was just as head-strong as Dad was.

Dad's principle reason for moving back to Black River Falls, he said, was that the prospects for the timber supply in that area would be depleted in another year or two when employment for the men would cease. But that was not a good reason for not moving to Rhinelander where employment prospects were practically unlimited. Was it 'fate' that compelled him to do what Dad did? Plato said it, "there's a Destiny that shapes our ends, rough hew them how we will." I am not too sure about that. True, a parent can shape the destiny of his offspring by his actions, but a member of the family is free to shape his own destiny, especially if he is possessed of a strong will. I think now that what Plato referred to was the inexorable laws of nature to which we are all subject such as birth and death; laws of reproduction; those governing the body and its organs; gravity; cyclic laws; evolution and many others. Three are all fixed for us, but outside those fixed laws, we are free to create our own destiny, our own environments, which is possible for a man of strong will to do. A strong will is an asset for anyone, provided an educated intelligence functions with it. If we did not have the freedom of intelligent choice, man's progress would halt. If an arbitrary system were imposed on us, and if choices were made for us by authorities outside ourselves, such as a Supreme Being, then indeed a fixed destiny would hedge us about; we would then become automatons, mere machines, unable to advance. Stagnation would ensue as far as each of us is concerned; evolution would cease to operate. Fortunately a better system is in effect for us. So I for one set out to carve my own destiny, my own career; to do what I wanted as a free individual as far as that was possible under the fixed laws that governed.

There was an old Swedish peddler who operated a grocery store in Rhinelander and who liked to travel among his country-men in the small towns surrounding it. He always carried a supply of groceries and dry goods in amounts sufficient to fill a small conveyance he had with him; in the winter a bob sled with uprights in rear to push it over the snow, and in summer a contraption with four wheels under it. He always came by the train via Tomahawk to Hazelhurst and would vend his wares from house to house. Later, I often wondered why Yawkey did not stop him from competing with him in the sale of goods, but he probably thought better of it as of no consequence to his own grocery business.

Mother used to enjoy his visits; they were both from the same homeland and I believe raised in the same community. She always bought something from him; a good customer. On one trip, I recall, he paid particular attention to me; I was about 15 or 16 at the time. He asked me if I cared to come to Rhinelander and work for him in his store. It is possible he made the offer out of consideration of Mother and her friendship. Of course she and I were in favor of it and I agreed at once. When it came to jobs, Mother, and Dad also, were 'on the job' plugging for us.

And so it came to pass that I boarded the Milwaukee railroad local passenger train one day for Hesford Junction where I changed trains for Rhinelander. From then on, I was on my own and have been ever since. In a way I was glad to get away from the parental influence, although my parents hardly ever interfered with my activities; I was free in most respects. I had freedom to go to dances; shows; parties. I was free to search for empty whiskey and beer bottles around town and sell them to the saloon bartender, 5 cents for beer and 10 cents each for plain glass whiskey and brandy bottles. My folks did not interfere when the men in the Yawkey office sent me on errands to buy liquor for them at the saloon; they did not wish to be seen in the saloon with the common man. I always paid my own way when admission fees required to activities; always had money of my own that I had earned myself. Not once that I can recall have I ever asked my folks for money. By the way, whiskey and brandy and alcohol were shipped on to the saloon in large barrels at that time and the bartender had to fill the plain bottles himself for sale to customers. Beer came in large wooden kegs.

Although I was young, I was not afraid to face the world and what it had in store for me as I traveled from home that first time. When I arrived at Rhinelander, Adam Johnson the peddler and grocery store owner, and his good wife took me into their own house to room and board while in his employ. They had a house full of kids themselves and treated me as one of their own.

My job was to hitch a horse to a delivery wagon in the mornings and call on customers to take orders from them for groceries and to deliver the orders in the afternoon. I enjoyed the work; it was something new and different. The owner was gone most of the time and a manager was in charge in addition to myself. One day I was suspected by the manager of being the cause of a shortage in cash in the till. He called me on the 'carpet' and asked me to explain. It was only a few silver dollars he figured he was short. I cannot recall how I explained it, if any, but I know I had not taken it. The manager-clerk was not a congenial man, and it seemed to me he was suspicious of most everybody. The owner, Old Adam, interceded in my behalf and kept me on the job. He and his wife were kindly souls; they were blessed or burdened with a large brood. In later years, after they had grown up and their parents had passed on, they became sturdy and reliable citizens of the community. The old peddler and his wife had done a good job of rearing and educating their offspring, descendants of sturdy, Scandinavian stock. There was a hall upstairs above the store and on Saturday nights dances were held there and I used to go up there and watch the room full of dancers and to listen to the orchestra. That also was something new for me, as the only music I had heard previously were traveling show people with a few stringed instruments in the Hazelhurst hall. One time a member of one troupe liked the town so well that he and his wife decided to live there; he made his living by giving lessons on the guitar and mandolin, one of his pupils being my oldest brother who took lessons on the mandolin. Later on when we became older, Albert and I also acquired some sort of skill on those instruments. But this orchestra above the store was entirely different; it was music from many instruments and I thought it was 'heavenly' as they played popular dance music of the day.

I cannot recall why or when I left the grocery store job, but I find myself next working in a refrigerator factory where the old fashioned, wooden ones were manufactured that required ice for cooling. I was assigned to a machine that planed the sides of hardwood boards that went into the manufacture of the ice refrigerators. It was my job to run the boards over a whirling, roller type planer with sharp knives that planed them smooth, and when I had completed one hand truck full, it was wheeled to a gluer who glued the boards into the proper sizes. I remember that I worked so fast that the trucks filled up too fast for the gluer and he told me to 'slack up' that he could not keep up with me, as he was supposed to do. One day I happened to hold my hand too close to the whirling knives as I planed a board and one of my fingers was zipped on the end, just enough to tear a little skin off it and that necessitated a call on the doctor. After that I did not feel inclined to continue on that particular job. Work was plentiful in the city for any one who wanted to work.

My next job was with an ice company harvesting ice from a lake and stored in an ice house for use in summer;

a man by the name of Kepler owned the business. One day while out on the lake it was bitterly cold with a strong, cold wind blowing. I did not realize it at first, but when I got to the house where I was boarding, my uncle's, I found that my face had frozen; it thawed in the warm room and my aunt Josie assisted me to restore it to normal. That job lasted only a few weeks when the large frame building was filled with cakes of ice.

Some time before that my sister Freda had married Sumner Hamilton and he asked me to live with them and go to high school. She was to have her first baby, Harry, and I was to help out as much as I could. One of the first things I did for them was to build an out-door toilet in a wood-shed on the lot where they lived, house and lot being owned by Sumner's mother. I carried water; brought in wood; split the large chunks of wood; sawed up slab wood and did errands for the family. I did not like high school and I and a boy by the name of Clark played 'hooky' and amused ourselves by loafing around the Soo Line railroad switch yards.

Sumner was a city fireman. While I was with them, a fire broke out in the lumberyard on the north side of the city next to a residential district. Previous to that he used to let me ride with him on trips to small fires and on practice runs. He was driver of a team that hauled a hose wagon. It was interesting to watch the horses being hitched to the wagon in the fire house. When the doors in front of the horses were flung open, a whip behind them automatically alerted them for quick action when they would run to their appointed places under the harness and with one snap it came down on the horses, the collars fastened and a buckle snapped and away they went galloping for all they were worth up the street. Sumner was on the seat with the lines in his hand before the harness came down, while the other firemen all jumped on as it moved out of the building, one of them sounding the gong. It was a sight to behold to see those horses galloping, followed by another team hauling a fire engine that was used to get up steam for increasing pressure of the water at a fire. Previous to a run, kindling and fuel were all ready to ignite the moment a call came in, fire in the engine was already burning and smoking when it got started.

This particular fire, after it got started in a dry and flammable lumberyard, spread rapidly by a stiff wind; leaped across a street bordering the lumberyard and on to the houses. It burned a wide swath, practically the whole of the north side of the city and jumped the Soo Line railroad tracks to the houses on the other side.

Sumner was on his fire wagon all day and all night. He fed his horses from a nose-bag whenever he could and watered them from fire hydrants. Fire companies from surrounding towns rushed their equipment over the railroad on special trains, but all they could do was to try and keep the fire contained and from spreading further destruction. It was Rhinelander's most disastrous fire before or since.

During those days I spent some of my spare time in the Soo Line railroad yards and round house watching locomotives and trains and in the telegraph office that was located in the freight house listening to the music of the telegraph. In the evenings sometimes I visited the second trick telegrapher who was quite friendly and watched him send and receive train orders and telegrams, and how I envied him his ability to do so! I also roamed the Chicago & North Western railroad freight yards and freight and telegraph office, almost making a pest of myself. But they understood my interest in the railroad business and were quite courteous with me, although they did nothing to get me started in the railroad world which I still longed to do.

During this period of time, think in the winter, Uncle Gust hired me to do a job that I am quite sure present day youth would not think of doing. He had a huge pile of pine slab trimmings from the paper mill, or a saw mill in the city that required sawing up into stove lengths. His whole back yard was full of the stuff and I agreed to saw it all with a buck saw by hand. So I went to work on it with a saw and a 'horse' and kept at it for weeks. When I finally finished, he said I had done a terrific job and paid me. During the time I did this job, I stayed with them, board and room free.

I had not seen my folks for a long time, a couple years or more, and I was starting to get lonesome for them and the rest of the family. I was not particularly eager to go back to Oak Ridge, but thought it would be nice to see them again. I was not doing very well in school; I thought it held me down too much; I wanted freedom to do what I longed to do, learn telegraphy. I wasn't getting anywhere in that direction. Furthermore, Freda did not want me around any more after her son Harry was born; that I was not doing enough to pay for room and board; took too much to feed me, etc.

I had always had a warm personal regard for Sumner, her husband. He was good to me; always pleasant and good natured, but Freda was just the opposite. So I decided to quit the city; to shake its dust from my feet. On my way to the depot to board a train for Black River Falls, I was walking carrying my worldly goods in a suit case, when I met Sumner on his way home. He felt bad that I was leaving; hated to see me go. He accompanied me to the depot to see me off. In later years I visited him a few times and always found him cheerful, good natured and optimistic. He passed on at age 60. Life had not been good to him; its struggles, temptations, disappointments and frustrations were more than he could take; weak willed that he was at times. He died of a stroke.

Before I leave the Rhinelander scene, I'd like to reminisce a little further and tell a couple incidents of ancient history. One was that I saw the very first feature moving picture that had been made in 1903, just a few years previously. I was attracted to it by a 'barker' standing on the side-walk in front of a store building selling all within hearing of his voice of 'The Great Train Robbery', only ten cents. Of course I paid my dime and went inside to see what it was all about. The projector was set up in front near the door and the patrons all stood around it with a white cloth for a screen a little ways up front. How I enjoyed looking at that picture, probably because it involved a railroad and a telegraph operator. It required only a few minutes to run it through, after which the owner, manager and barker went outside again to attract more customers. I paid my dime several times to go in and see it again and again. The picture was rather primitive and 'flickered' quite a bit, but we did not know of anything better, so we could not complain.

The Salvation Army every night used to march down the main street from their upstairs headquarters and stop at a corner down town, playing their band instruments as they marched. There was one song they sang quite often that I remember to this day; "And oh what a weeping and wailing, as the lost ones were told of their fate; they cried to the rocks and the mountains, they prayed but their prayers were too late."

To this day I have never been able to reconcile the contents of this song to a God of Divine Justice. I thought then and still of the same opinion that God must be a cruel tyrant to permit His people to suffer such a terrible punishment merely for not believing as they were told by these Salvation Army people and others of like persuasion. Merely a belief one way or another! According to that understanding, a mere belief nullifies laws and systems of Nature that are fundamental and inexorable!

I was happy to see the family again. It was the spring of 1907; I was 18 and had not yet realized my ambition. I thought strongly that I must try to do something about it now that I was with the folks again. I did some farm work for them. While I was plowing in a field not far from the

84

railroad line and while I heard trains passing, I studied the Morse code that I had in my pocket; it probably was the one C.W. Wahlquist had given me many years before as a small boy. Every time the team wanted to rest at the end of a furrow, I pulled it out and tried my best to memorize it better and better. Farm work did not appeal to me, although I did some farm jobs for neighbors that summer and following year. All they paid was a dollar a day, always in silver dollars; why silver, I do not know, unless it was due to Bryan's campaign for silver (16 to 1) that I heard my elders debate while I was very young.

During the summer of 1907 and the following year, I mixed with the young people of the neighborhood, boys and girls, which I had not done much of in Rhinelander, except for a few boy friends. Girls were not on my mind too much until I got home. Brother Albert had matured into a handsome young man and he also was attracted to them. He had learned to play the guitar and I the mandolin which we played together as a duet at parties and to amuse ourselves and others who would listen. The girls were smitten with him more than with myself. Olga Anderson, a neighbor girl about his age, also was smitten, especially when he would strum his guitar and sing a love song to her of a moon-lit summer evening! I do not blame the girl, being at the sentimental age. Eventually she married John McGuire of Minneapolis and both have since passed on. They were a happy couple, industrious and frugal and good managers. They raised a family of 2 boys and 2 girls, just what she wanted and had planned for. I have always thought that they were an ideal married couple who managed their affairs in such a good way as to produce for themselves a happy and fruitful life.

During that period of time I met the first girl that I had ever 'kept company' with, Mattie Ketchum. The Ketchum's were a family of four girls and a boy and lived in the same community, Oak Ridge 3 or 4 miles from our family home. This community, or neighborhood was called Oak Ridge because of the many oak trees and ridges, especially one ridge that divided it into two. The Ketchum's only son, Harry, I understood in later life to have joined the U.S. Army and eventually was promoted to the rank of General, or possibly Major General. In later years I lost all contact with them; I tried to renew contact with them, or at least find out how they had all fared, but I failed in my attempt.

Mattie was a small girl and lively. I enjoyed her company and friendship while it lasted, which was not long. We thought nothing of walking miles together over sandy roads that curved through thick wooded forests. We talked, while strolling, of inconsequential matters, as is the custom of inexperienced youth in any time. We had not 'gas machines' to take us to saloons, not even a horse and buggy. My older brothers had a practical monopoly on the use of the two dapple greys and new buggy the family had at the time.

What eventually became of the girl and how she fared in later life is something I have often wondered about. If there is such an ethereal immutable law as fate that carries with it an inveterate decree in respect to our lot in life, that is something most of us know nothing about, unless we care to study a philosophy that explains it as Karma. Be that as it may, she and I at that time stood at a fork in the road of life; one pointed the path for her to take, while the other drew me over a different pathway.

There was another family that we were well acquainted with, one of two girls and several boys, the Albion Mattson family who lived next to Perry Creek on the first road to Black River Falls about half way from our home. The oldest girl, Nettie, I remember as sickly; she died of consumption, as tuberculosis was known at that time. There were several sons in the family and the one I knew best was August Mattson who was a little older than myself and who later became an undertaker in Black River Falls. Another went into the jewelry business in a distant city;

all were good business men. The youngest in the family, a girl named Inga about my own age, was a sociable and friendly girl. Every time we walked past their house, which was a nice frame cottage, she most always stopped us to visit. On a summer day when it was hot and dusty on the dirt road, and as I reached their home on my way to or from town, I would become thirsty and I most always stopped for a drink of fresh cool water that I pumped directly from the ground on their premises. Inga and her mother always bade me in to sit down and visit.

One Sunday summer afternoon I was walking toward Black River Falls on the old pioneer dirt road and when opposite their house, Inga came out and invited me inside where she introduced me to Florence Linnell, a good friend of hers from Black River Falls who was visiting her. Florence was a brunette; dark haired with large dark eyes, probably dark grey, if I recall correctly. She really was a beautiful girl. Her face and figure were the type that appeals to the opposite sex; probably 16 or 17 years of age. She was quiet and reserved; not much of a talker. She fascinated me from the beginning. As they say, I was 'smitten' with her; yet she seemed to be distant and beyond me. She was difficult to get acquainted with, probably because I was not the aggressive type when it came to females. But I had a good time anyway the few hours I was there most of the time playing flinch with the two girls. I met her a few times after that; took her to a country dance in a horse and buggy once. I tried to see her more often but without success, so I wrote her but she hardly ever answered. Later I learned she had a boy friend, which of course made me feel blue and downhearted. She finally married him later, and I went my way that differed from hers.

It was very difficult for a young man in my circumstances to get started on the railroad, especially when I did not know any one who would take me on as a student in a telegraph office. No one would try to assist me except Mother, not even an encouraging word. She wanted me to get started in the railroad world, probably because that was my wish and ambition. While I was home and working at odd jobs around the country, I did the next best thing I could think of: I ordered a student's telegraph set, sounder and key and blue vitriol for battery, plus the necessary zinc and copper fittings from a Sears Roebuck catalogue. When I received them, I set them up on a small table in a bedroom off the living room. I spent many happy hours practicing sending the Morse code on the set. I soon became proficient in sending, but my receiving was deficient. I tried to get one of my older brothers to learn the code and send to me, but they had no interest whatever in my efforts. In later years my oldest brother admitted he was sorry he did not go along with me at the time and learn it together. There is no doubt that he would have been better off in every way if he had done so and entered railroad work. My other older brother was too impatient to concentrate on the Morse code; everything had to go in a hurry for him; he had other ideas.

One day during this period I ran across an ad in a magazine of some kind probably a farm paper, advertising a sort of tape recorder gadget that had a roll of paper with indentations on it that represented dots and dashes of the Morse code and that would operate a telegraph sounder when run through a metal roller connected with the sounder; this would send a message, or several messages in the Morse code that could be read from the sounder. When I received it and set it up, I had one of my sisters, sometimes a brother turn the crank for me so I could decipher it and write it on paper. It wasn't long before I learned to copy all of it; after repeated turning the crank and running the paper through, I knew it by heart, and that was as far as I could go. I decided then that I simply must go to a telegraph school if I wanted to get anywhere with my ambition.

I wrote several telegraph schools that had advertised in papers and magazines for information. Telegraphers being in such demand; several schools sprang up around the country during that period of time. How I read and re-read those catalogues! There was one in particular in a city in Florida that took my fancy. I longed to go there and enroll, but it was so far away and I had no money; I had spent the money I had earned, not yet having learned the value of it, which I did later. I finally decided to go to Eau Claire and enter the Northwestern Telegraph School, the nearest one to me. They promised in their literature to place me on a job on a railroad at graduation; that sounded great to me! But the money question still faced me.

Mother and I talked it over and we decided to go see the banker in Black River Falls about borrowing one hundred dollars, which we figured would be sufficient to get me through school. All he required he said, was a note signed by myself and my Dad, which was done and the loan was arranged. Dad's credit was good anywhere in town without question; A No.1 credit.

So with one hundred bucks neatly folded in a leather folder in my pocket, I started out from Black River Falls in the latter part, or middle part of March 1909, probably on my birthday March 16th. I am not sure of date. At that time all passenger trains stopped at the old depot now used by McGillvery Lumber Co. and trains crossed the river just above the dam; abutments for the trestle still remains in the river as relics of the old original railroad that had been built some years previously.

Speaking of McGillvery, I want to deviate a little from my story and to a related 4th of July celebration in Black River Falls that I am reminded of and is interesting from the stand-point of ancient history of that period. The parade was passing through the streets which I was watching from the sidewalks, which were largely made of wooden planks, when a team drawing a flat topped wagon on which a speaker was holding forth as it moved along the street, gesturing with his arms as he spoke. If I am not mistaken, it was the original Mr. McGillvery who I believe was a congressman at the time. A 4th of July celebration those days was not complete without a speaker of the day. As the team, wagon and speaker moved slowly, I with some other kids ran along-side it and listened to and watched the speaker raise and lower his voice as he put his message across to his listeners. At the time I must have been about 7 to 8 years of age, am not sure. Why the speaker did not remain in one place while giving his speech, I cannot say. Probably he was on his way to a location for that purpose and kept talking while being moved from place to place. That is only my guess, as I am not sure. I also recall that at meal time that day, we went into a long room that contained one or two long tables that were filled with all kinds of food, men and women and kids sitting eating all they could for 25 cents per meal.

To get back to my story, I boarded the local passenger train at Black River Falls after buying a ticket to Eau Claire and the next that I remember was that of the large depot there and the crowds of people on the platform, more than I had ever seen in one place before. Upon arrival I went directly to the telegraph school which was located upstairs in a store building on Barstow Street. Mr. L.P. Loken was the owner and teacher at the Northwestern Telegraph School, having previously been employed on the Omaha railroad as a telegrapher on the western division, as I recall. He was a kindly man, interested in his pupils who would do all he could for them to get started. He took me into his house as a roomer after I had paid him in cash for part of the tuition and room, the balance I deposited in a bank. One hundred dollars was almost a fortune during that time. I was on my way at last! My boyhood dreams were about to be realized! I was enrolled in a school and to take a course that I really liked the first time in my life. Mr. Loken assigned me to a table at other end of the room, and as I walked into that room full of young fellows, all strange boys to me. They looked at me as though to 'size' me up and I felt somewhat frightened, but it soon passed as Mr. Loken tested me on the wire. He found that I was a good sender for a beginner, but needed to practice receiving.

Tables were lined up in rows down the length of the room, each of them wired to one circuit with sounders and keys fastened on top the table and 2 to 4 boys sitting at each table; the room was full of students. L.F. Loken sat at the head table and kept sending perfect Morse to us for hours at a time. How sweet those sounds were to me! "The sweetest music in this world to me, is the musical click of the telegraph key."

In a smaller room to one end batteries were set up for power, the old fashioned blue vitriol type. There was an extra circuit set up for the slower receivers and I was on that for a while until I became more proficient where we could break in on the sender and talk back and forth. We called ourselves 'hams' and the school a 'ham factory.' One day a train dispatcher Mr. Loken knew came in. He sat, or stood at one of the tables and manipulated the key talking to Mr. Loken on the wire, and fast. I thought that was wonderful. I found that learning to receive required concentrated attention for long periods and also a lot of patience. Mr. Loken certainly had a lot of that. He was the perfect teacher, I thought and we all loved that man. During certain periods we were required to master the typewriter, or 'mill' as we called it, but that was haphazard; we were not taught the scientific way of the touch system, merely 'hunt and peck', or 'pick & peck'. It was not too long before I was able to copy with the best of them.

School is most always a happy time for youngsters as well as young people and this school certainly was for me. My fellow 'hams' were good mixers, congenial and 'happy-go-lucky'- sort of guys. I enjoyed their companionship and made many friends. During June we attended ball games on Saturdays at the ball park, think it was Carson Park. Mr. Loken and I attended that Congregational Church on Sundays; the same building still stands.

For some reason I left Loken's and roomed at a rooming house farther up Barstow street across the river and had meals at a restaurant. I and another student slept in the same room and the some bed. He turned out to be a sleep walker. As soon as he was sound asleep, he would get up and stand in the room with his eyes closed and sometimes snoring while standing. Several times he walked to the window, opened it and stood in front of it as though to jump through it and to the ground below, we were on the second floor. He never did that, but walked down the stairs a few times but soon came back without disturbing any one else in the house and back to bed again. To me this was very strange indeed, not having seen it before. How does one explain this phenomenon? What causes it? I'll leave that to the scientists.

Again, all good things must come to an end. My hundred bucks lasted three months for tuition, room, food and incidentals. I told Mr. Loken my money had run out and he took me at once to the Omaha railroad passenger station, the upstairs of which was used as division headquarters, including the train dispatcher's office. The chief train dispatcher was Mr. J.B. Elliott. He was a large man, tall and heavy set with quite a prominent 'corporation.'

When we came, he happened to be standing on the platform in front of the stairs leading to his office. Mr. Loken knew him well and addressed him, "I have a ham here who wants to go to work for you." That was all that was said. All he did was to ask my name, then went upstairs and back in a few minutes and handed me a pass to St. Paul. That was my first free pass on a railroad, and I have received many of them since then. Mr. Elliott told me to contact Mr. C. E. Davison, Chief Operator in 'A' office in the general office building, on the first floor and he would assign me to a job. That was all; no questions; no exams; no physical; no forms to fill out; nothing. That was July 1st 1909.

I arrived in St. Paul in the evening; slept in a hotel that night and the next morning I contacted Mr. Davison, "Old Davy", as he was familiarly called by most every one. I always called him Mr. Davison; he was my senior, old enough to be my father, and I respected him very highly. He did not ask me any questions either, nor any kind of an examination; not even for eye sight, nor hearing ability. Only said I can go to work at once in the telegraph office, of which he was the head; his desk was at on the end of it. I was to work as a messenger boy and introduced me to the other messenger who delivered telegrams, reports, etc. to offices in the building, and I was to deliver to offices outside the building, across the street, to freight house, and to the Western Union office up the street. His name was George GeBauer. That was July 2nd 1909. That was the actual start of my railroad career, such as it has been.

George GeBauer Picked up the telegrams and reports from each telegrapher; sorted them as to individuals addressed in piles every half hour, after which we delivered them. The first one in the morning was the '7 AM' report from each of the four division offices, Eau Claire; Spooner; St. James and Omaha, Nebraska. Telegraphers came on duty at 7 AM; off one hour for noon meal and through at 6 PM, Sundays off. The 8 hour day had not yet been thought of. Several copies were made of the 7 AM report using this tissue paper, the same kind as train order paper. All the officials received a copy; J.T. Clark, President; A.W. Trenholm, General Manager; F.R. Pechin, General Superintendent; G.L. Ossman, Car Service Agent; H.M. Pearce, Traffic Manager; A.M. Fenton, General Freight Agent; G.H. MacRae, Certified Public Accountant; M.R.

Drochau, Freight Claim Agent; Geo. Boyce, Supervisor Telegrapher & Signals; E.E. Wood, General Baggage Agent. These men received most of the telegrams also as well as those sent. Several others received and sent telegrams in the constant stream throughout the day. Walker Wiesel was the oldest telegrapher in the office. Next oldest was George Schaller; A.T. Bone; G.F. Stucke; Ray Slaker. Boomer telegraphers would work there a while, then go. They kept on the move from one telegraph office to another and from one railroad to another. After I left several other telegraphers were hired, some for additions and others for replacements: H.L. Kveel; J.B. Head; E.A. Faudel; G.J. Adams. This latter came from Black River Falls, as I did. The two messengers were paid $25.00 per month, payable once a month, I am not sure, but I don't think the telegraphers were paid more than sixty or seventy five dollars per month during that period. One man was on duty all night, and he generally was Ray Slaker. To save the work of sending a large file of telegrams to Chicago, office call SJ, he would place them in a large 'train telegram envelope'; put on his straw hat and walk to the union depot a couple blocks away and hand it to the train baggage man on the night passenger train for Chicago to be delivered in the morning to offices in Chicago. Ray Slaker, I recall, was a very handsome young man; he wore the most fashionable clothes with the sound, stiff brimmed straw hat in style for young men at the time. He was a son of the division superintendent at Eau Claire.

Tom Bagan worked the SJ Chicago wire, the heaviest in the office. He would sit at his table with his sounder next to his ear by means of a 'resonator' and copy one telegram after another just as fast as the operator in SJ could send him on the double key board 'mill' without breaking in on him. After 'clearing' SJ of his file. Tom would send him a pile that had accumulated in front of him, sending with his right hand and with his left noting time, office call and receiving operator's personal sign simultaneously. All the telegraphers those days sent with their 'fist', the vibroplex or 'bug' had not yet been invented. Tom hardly ever looked up from his work; he kept 'glued' to the wire and his mill, except to spit tobacco juice into a spittoon kept beside him. He did not have time, nor the inclination, to converse with the other telegraphers in the office. George Schaller, on the other hand, was a talkative, sociable sort of man. His wire work did not call for so much concentrated effort as the SJ wire; he worked the local division wires; he also clicked off the time signals over all the divisions hooked up into one wire, commencing 1058 AM, the last signal, or click at exactly 11 AM as he received it from Washington DC. It was the duty of all Agent-Telegraphers over the entire railroad to be on hand at that particular hour to get the correct time and check their clocks and watches, at the same time receive '23' messages, if any from their division offices. Woe to the agent who did not respond, or OK the message sent to all agents, and to acknowledge the time by giving his office call! He was reprimanded on the wire later when he did not appear to answer his call from the dispatcher; and for all other agents to hear it, which was not at all pleasant for him. Mr. Schaller was able to receive a message on his mill and converse with any one in front of him, both at the same time. That requires skill.

We messengers had a desk, or table of our own on which a sounder hooked up to the dispatcher's wire from Eau Claire. There was no key, just the sounder, so that we could not break in on the fast wire, which was too fast for us students; but we were required to listen to it in our spare time and try to learn to copy that fast stuff. Sometimes we kept the sounder screwed up too loud for Mr. Wiesel, whose desk was nearby, and it irritated him; he always came over and adjusted it to lower sound. I don't believe Mr. Wiesel was able to continue the grind in that office very long after I left later that year of 1909. He was quite old and nervous at that time. It was too much to expect a man to sit at a desk and send and receive messages continuously 11 to 12 hours every day with only Sundays off. None of them lived to a ripe old age, except possibly A.B. Bone, who spent 58 years of his life in the one office telegraphing. The trouble was they had no opportunity to get up and walk around, or to exercise, even moderate exercise. A man had to have a very strong, healthy constitution to be able to withstand such abuse to his body.

On that job I must have been fairly well thought of as a reliable and honest worker; probably that was the reason I was entrusted one day with a large envelope that contained something valuable by George Boyce's chief clerk to be delivered to the cashier at the freight office nearby. I was instructed to deliver it at once, which I agreed to do. I placed the envelope in my coat pocket, and promptly forgot all about it until later in the day I discovered I still had it in my pocket. I was scared stiff; I dropped everything and hurried over with it at once. Fortunately, no one concerned knew I had 'slipped' up on the job, at least nobody said anything to me. That, of course, taught me a lesson.

C.B. Davison was the chief operator and boss of the office. He hired all the telegraphers for the entire railroad. Sometimes he had as many as 10 applicants at one time. He placed them all in a circle in front of him as he sat at his desk and lectured them on the rules of the railroad in respect to a telegrapher's duties. He never failed to tell them about the operator who was the cause of a wreck and engine smash up because he had disregarded the rules. He kept stressing the importance of the most important rule in the book: "In case of doubt, adopt the safe course." The only examinations the men took were for color, eye-sight and hearing which Mr. Davison himself administered. Each man in turn was placed at a desk with a sounder in front of him and required to receive a perfect copy of a train order without breaking in on the sender, who was Mr. Davison himself, using a small circuit with the necessary telegraph instruments, keys and sounders. His Morse was not too good and he purposely speeded up his sending to test an applicant's ability to telegraph, especially to receive and copy legibly. A man had to make a perfect copy without breaking before he could pass and if he failed, Mr. Davison kept sending to him until he did have a perfect one. Telegraphers were in great demand and for that reason qualifications were none too strict.

Mr. Davison was a kindly man and I never heard him utter a harsh word to anyone. I loved the old gentleman. He had some minor eccentricities such as always carrying an umbrella no matter what the weather. When I came to the office on Sunday mornings, he was always there sitting at his desk reading the Sunday papers almost out loud to himself. He was always well dressed, wearing high stiff collars and shoes well shined. I never learned what his personal life was.

There was a district fire department house located next door to the old Omaha railroad general office building with the telegraph office on the ground floor and its windows facing the fire house. In the summer the windows were kept open for ventilation and the firemen would come to the windows on their side, stick their heads into the office and ask the telegraphers for news of important events of the day. The telegraph was the principle means of communication those days, either railroad or Western Union. The telephone had not yet come into general use. That summer of 1909 Billy Pepke and another prize fighter, think it was Joe Gans, or Battling Nelson, fought one day for the light weight championship and the firemen sat on the window sills receiving reports from one of the telegraphers of the progress of the fight by rounds. These reports were 'hot off the wire' and did not cost the firemen a cent; and they received the news at the same time as the city newspapers did on their press wires. News of other important events of the day also were provided the firemen by the telegraphers as an accommodation to them. There were no wars, or even rumors of them during that period; all was quiet and peaceful. There was no unemployment and men were more numerous than women those days. There was no competition between men and women in any field except that of the men competing for the favors, interest and friendship and love of the available females, young and old. All an unattached female had to do was to show herself to the man and they would flock around her competing for the chance to escort her to a dance, to church or to any social activity of the time. Girls became wives and it was their job to run the home and make it happy for her man and offspring. That was all that was required of her. There was no thought of girls entering the business or professional world except as clerks and secretaries, assistants to the man; it was a man's world.

I cannot recall seeing one girl working in the building in any of the offices to which we messengers delivered telegrams; or in any of the offices in other buildings nearby. Certainly there were no female telegraphers; such an occupation for women was not thought of, or heard of. That was a man's job. It was not until many years later that women were permitted to learn telegraphy and work in Western Union telegraph offices, but the railroad managements made it a rule not hire them, except in a few rare instances, when necessity required it. Can we imagine what the course of the business and economic world would have taken if Kaiser Wilhelm had not seen fit to start World War 1 five years later? Would science have progressed as far as it has since that time? Certainly the male population would have remained on an equal basis, or nearly so with the female population as Nature intended it should in numbers. Man is wont to disrupt Nature's equilibrium at certain times by rash acts after which much time is required to restore it to its normal condition again.

Mr. Davison was hard pressed for more telegraphers all the time, so he decided I should take the final exam and send me out, although I was not fully ready, or prepared. He did not test my eyes or ears; just kept sending train orders to me until I had a perfect copy without breaking. He had to have one that contained no errors for his and my records. He wrote out a pass for me to Bingham Lake, Minnesota and instructed me to go there and work third trick the next night, October 12th 1909. I arrived there late at night in a howling wind storm that was sweeping across the prairies, a fitting welcome to a 'ham' operator.

After contacting the Agent J.K. Smith, I went on duty at 10 PM October 13th my first telegraph job. Everything was new to me. I knew absolutely nothing about station accounting; the management was slack in that respect, figuring it was up to the individual to teach himself. All I learned in 'A' office was to telegraph. On my first job, I was required to write up the freight received book. When I asked the second trick operator to show me how to do it, he became angry at me and would not teach me. His name was Hyde, which also appropriately applied to his skin, and as thick. It was there that I discovered how mean and discourteous some railroad men could be and I was commencing to get an idea of how cruel the old world could be to a young man starting out in life. I finally learned how to post freight way bills in the freight received book, but had to do it myself by 'hit & miss'. I was compelled to learn all my work the hard way; no one would 'stoop' to teach me. That was considered beneath the dignity of some hard boiled men.

The dispatcher's office, DI, was at St. James. I was not asked to copy a train order the first night. I had no difficulty in reporting trains to the dispatcher by the call 'OS', meaning 'on sheet', his train sheet I got into the system of the manual block by telegraph without much of any difficulty. The operator at Butterfield, east of me, was a gentleman and gave me every assistance. When I could not read the dispatcher, he repeated what the dispatcher said to me more slowly on the side block wire what he was trying to tell me, a ham that I was. I'll never forget this man for his consideration of me at that time. There were real gentlemen in railroad service, just as there were cranks.

It was in the morning that my difficulties really started. A branch line ran off the main line from Bingham Lake to Currie, Minnesota. With six stations and I was required to copy the telegraph car report from each agent on the branch every morning and send them to St. James side wire man before the first trick operator, A. Backer, came on duty. When they called me, I simply could not copy that stuff. I knew nothing of the form that was used. Those fellows raised 'Cain' with me when they found I was a 'ham' and a poor one. There was one crank especially named Warner at Stordon who made it miserable for me. He was unreasonable. He would not recall that he himself was a 'ham' a beginner at one time who needed consideration. When he raved at me, I could read him alright, but when he sent 'cars', I could not read it, much less copy it. That first morning the first trick man had to take the 'cars' for me and send them to St. James. He was a gentleman and understood my predicament; he understood how it was to start out without proper training and did all he could to assist me. All the time I was there, not once did he say a cross word to me. When I left, he told me that I had done very well for a beginner and that he hated to see me leave. He had a fine family of a boy and a girl and a good looking wife. From my experience at that station, I determined that I would never be impatient and rude with a beginner. I only hope I have carried that resolution out satisfactorily.

On my second night on the job I copied my first '19' train order, and strange to say, I did it without breaking in on the dispatcher. For one thing, he sent very good

Morse that was quite easy to read; for another he sent slowly, realizing he was working with a beginner. I have often wished that I had kept a copy of that order, a carbon copy, as a memento. But at that time I could not look into the future very far. I was young and lacked experience and wisdom. In a week or two I was able to copy the 'cars' in the mornings and had it all cleaned up before Mr. Bacher came on duty. I eventually got into the swing and routine of things and after having to take several bawlings out by Hyde and Agent J.E. Smith, who also was on the cranky order. The local train-men on way freights and the branch were not much better.

There were three telegraphers working at that office, each one on duty 10 hours that overlapped each other's schedule; when not telegraphing they did book work and other necessary duties. Lighting was by kerosene lamps which we had to keep cleaned and filled. Some of us also did janitor work in the depot; also kept the light in the train order signal mast filled and lighting; and of course we sold tickets for local passenger trains. My salary was $52.50 per month, payable once a month, no deductions. The agent J.E. Smith did not seem to do much of anything except to supervise and run the cash book and balance sheet. I do not know what his salary was. After becoming acquainted with my work and the people, I really liked the place. All those with whom I came into contact were congenial.

During that period, and long afterwards, a telegrapher was looked upon as a very important person (VIP). Wherever I went I was respected because of my connection with the railroad, which was an important institution in the lives of the people during those times. It was the life blood of their economy, as was the telegraph their means of fast communication with the outside world in addition to the mails that were hauled by the railroad. The telephone had not yet come into general use, nor had electric lighting. The railroad had made possible the settling of this vast prairie with its fertile soil by emigrants from foreign countries. Native homesteaders and their descendants were grateful to the railroad for that and for the service they performed for them in transporting their grains to markets.

At that time grain growers in the surrounding prairies used horses in hauling their grain in wagons with high boxes to huge elevators in town from where it was shipped by rail to markets. Sometimes the volume of grain shipments were so great that many cars congested the yards while waiting for trains to haul them; the oldest cars on hand were moved first. This congestion was due to inadequate steam power that the railroad had at the time. People came to town to trade and for various activities, always in buggies. The 4th of July celebration was the greatest event of the year in all those small communities of the West. They remained in one community mostly.

I roomed and boarded at the home of Mr. & Mrs. Warner, an elderly couple. Mrs. Warner put up a midnight lunch for me. Their old fashioned brick house still stands, as I saw it recently. I recall that Mr. Warner made frequent trips to Mountain Lake, a nearby town, for a wagon load of cases of beer for the local saloons and that I went with him on one trip; we had to make our way over prairie lands that had no roads at that time. Another telegrapher besides myself roomed at Warner's. Mr. Warner was an ardent member of the Odd Fellows Lodge at Windom, the county seat of that county next town West of Gingham Lake. He wanted me to join and said that he would recommend me to the Lodge officials, but that I had to wait until I had reached voting age, 21. I agreed, but not very whole-heartedly; I was not a 'joiner'. So it came to pass on March 16th, 1910, I, Mr. Warner and a couple section laborers took the hand car out of its house along-side the track and pumped our way to Windom, using 'elbow grease' for motive power. At the lodge, I was accepted largely because of my connection with the railroad, especially as a telegrapher. I was initiated in the first degree that evening and later took one or two more degrees. We got back in time for me to get to work at 10 PM. I never cared much for lodge work; it did not appeal to me, so I stopped paying my dues and was dropped from their rolls. But the lodge still has records of my joining, as I found out when I wrote them some time ago.

Those days it was practically impossible for a railroad telegrapher to avoid meeting girls, especially an unattached one, as I was. One winter Sunday morning, after the service at the Methodist church, the only one in town, I was standing outside with others when a young girl came up to me and spoke to me (Cannot recall what she said). She wore a long dress and with a waist up to her neck and a huge hat on her head, the style at the time. Her face was round with large blue eyes; fair complexion and rosy cheeks. She was not tall or slim. One would classify her as a blond. She was quite pleasant and easy to get acquainted with and talk to. She was jolly and good-natured. We got together in no time and walked on the board side-walk to her home up the same street a short distance from the church. In front of her home was a gate, the house surrounded by a picket fence. She was the only child of a German couple who had migrated from Germany during pioneer days; her name, Marie Ewert. We were together many times after that meeting and became good friends. I recall a program of some kind held in the church some time later when she sang a popular ditty of the day: "With rings on my fingers, bells on my toes, elephants to ride upon, my little Irish rose," etc. She had a fine contralto voice.

I had forgotten about Florence Linnell in Black River Falls in the rush of business and work of the world of which I had become a part. She was far from my mind and she had sent me only a card or two since I left her. Just then I was taken up with this German girl who was always on hand and willing and glad to see me.

I must now relate an incident that was not to my credit, if I am going to honestly charge myself with both debits and credits in my life's balance sheet. I committed an error that could have been disastrous. Old Davy in 'A' office had drilled us time and again with the slogan, "in case of doubt, adopt the safe course." It was the most important rule in the book.

One stormy night a blizzard was raging across the Minnesota prairies when I had occasion to be in a position of doubt concerning a freight train, and I failed to put that rule into effect. That one failure has been uppermost in my mind all the years since and a constant reminder to always be on the alert in respect to train movements and train orders. The night passenger train from Minneapolis to Omaha No. 9, that I would hold, or block all east bound trains for it placing that signal to stop. At the same time Windom, MN, west of me called on the block wire and told me to block all trains west for a freight eastbound, which I did by placing west signal to stop. Both my signals, east and west, were at stop, or red. Soon BU, Butterfield reported No. 9 west bound past there, entering the block. Windom also reported the freight past at about the same time, entering the block west of me. It was 14 miles from Butterfield to my station, and 5 miles from Windom, so that under normal conditions the freight train would easily have cleared the block at my station by taking the siding in ample time for No. 9 passenger train west. But the storm, as I soon learned, had delayed the freight and caused it to stall on the main line between the two stations. The crew was compelled to uncouple half the train in order to move one engine, with the power they had, and leave the rear half of it on the main line while the engine proceeded to Bingham Lake with the head end of train to place in on siding there. This siding was around a slight curve, as I recall, from my office. I kept looking for the freight's headlight through the window into that snow storm and terrific wind that was howling. I was getting anxious to clear the block for the passenger train. Finally I saw the light at the siding. I did not want to stop No. 9 if I could help it. As I stared through the storm I thought I saw a high ball signal with a lantern light, but I was not absolutely sure. Under the rule I was supposed to keep my signal to stop and issue a red clearance to the engineers and conductor for the train to stop and proceed with caution until they were sure of a clear block ahead of them to the next station. Instead of doing that, I did a terrible thing; I cleared my signal west bound for No. 9! The train was coming down the track and rolled to a stop at my station and a lone passenger got off. At that moment the head light of the balance of the freight train came into view around the curve and entered the siding; it had doubled in. I saw then what a mistake I had made. To clear myself, I hurriedly put my board, or red signal to stop and issued red clearance cards for the crew on the passenger train and went out on the platform with it to hand to the engineers and conductor. When I went to the head engine, the engineer was on the platform and he was very angry and bawled me out severely. He screamed, "Do you realize what you have done? That if I had not stopped, to let off a passenger, we would have kept going and run head on into that freight train? Why wasn't your signal at stop? Why was it clear when a train was in the block ahead of us?" He kept raving at me until the conductor took a hand and assured him that he would report the incident to headquarters office. I did not realize at the time what that meant, which would have been instant dismissal and the end of my railroad career. The engineer was satisfied to leave the matter in the hands of his conductor, after which the train proceeded slowly down the track and made sure the freight, all of it, was in the clear, when the passenger train proceeded. But before they left, the conductor took me aside and said in an under-tone that he would not report the incident; that I should not worry about it, but that I should take this to heart and be a good lesson to me and to be very careful in the future in such cases.

All this happened in just a few minutes in a blinding storm, but the effect of it remained with me the rest of my life. The sleeping passengers on the train had no way of knowing about the drama that had been enacted outside on the station platform; that a lone passenger having to get off there had saved them from a horrible wreck and possible death and injuries to many of them! What a tragedy that would have been! And I would have been to blame for it under the rules then in effect. True to his word, the conductor did not report it. That saved me and my career and it also taught me a lesson; it made me a better railroad worker after that. It showed that many railroad men were gentlemen those days, even soft-hearted when they had a reputation of being stern and severe. Therefore I have always been indebted to his kindness and consideration. I have often wondered if he realized how much good he did that night by not reporting me. Certainly no good would have been accomplished by reporting it; I would not then have been in a better position to perform my duties more efficiently and the railroad would have lost the services of a man who had learned a bitter lesson and better able to abide by the rules. Experience even to the point of possible disaster assists one to rectify deficiencies and become better qualified as a result. I only wish I could have had the opportunity to express my appreciation and thanks to him before he left earthly scenes. But our destinies in life took different paths. In later years I met quite a few railroad men like him, but there were plenty of the other kind.

Marie Ewer continued to be a good friend of mine while I was there. We took many walks together up and down the board walks; along the railroad track and to the lake outside of town a short distance where the railroad operated a pump enclosed in a building along-side the lake to pump water for their locomotives. She was a pleasant, good natured girl and I was quite fond of her as she was of me. When the time finally came for me to leave there for other stations, and new experiences, she hated to see me go. She was a good soul and when I was at Rushmore as relief agent, she came there to see me. She tried to keep track of me by letter and I did likewise, but I made so many changes after that that we lost track of each other. The last time I saw her was when I went with her on the train from Rushmore to her home in Bingham Lake on a Saturday night. When I had to return to my work, she saw me off at the depot Sunday night, sad but smiling. She had treated me royally, but I am not so sure about myself. Fond memories of inexperienced youth!

"No ranging down this lower track,
    The path we come by, thorn and flower,
Is shadowed by the growing hour,
    Lest life should fail in looking back.

Act first, this earth, a stage so gloomed with woe,
    One all but sickens at the shifting scenes.
And yet be patient, Our Playwright may show
    In some fifth act what this wild drama means."

Tennyson---

--Chapter 5--

During that period, telegraph jobs were not bulletined; in other words vacancies were filled with available men by the management; they were not advertised for men to bid on them so that the oldest in seniority would secure the position permanently, as was later put into effect. It was for that reason that the management kept me at Bingham Lake from October 18th, 1909 until June 20th, 1910 when they wanted me to do some relief work.

They sent me to Avoca, Minnesota first to relieve the agent-telegrapher there for a few days. That was the first position I had as agent-telegrapher and it was there that I made out my first application to the American Express Company for employment to handle express business on a 10% commission basis. I have a copy of that application and it is dated June 23rd, 1910. I was there about a week not long enough to get the books out of balance. July 1st I was sent to Rushmore, Minn. and remained there until about Aug. 15th, 1910. It was there that I first attempted to make out monthly reports and the balance sheet. Something that I had not been trained to do, nor any experience with up to that time. When the accounting department did not receive reports from that station at the end of July, after that had wired me to get them out, they sent a traveling auditor out there to see what was the trouble. When he arrived and saw how young and inexperienced I was, he did not say a word against me, but rather remarked about the operating department's foolish practice of sending young students to these difficult assignments without training them in the intricacies of station accounting. That was the way he reported it to his superior officers. I did not receive any complaints whatsoever from them. Most of the blame went to the Chief train dispatcher who ordered his men to where he wanted them without inquiring as to their ability in handling station accounts.

During those early days railroad accounting was far more elaborate than at present. A daily balance sheet had to be made out and sent to the general accounting office showing every detail of business transactions for each day. Other daily, weekly and monthly reports of many kinds were required by the different departments at both general and division offices. All reports were written in copying ink, or indelible pencil and copies made on thin tissue sheets in large books, one for each kind of report. A moist rag was spread over each sheet and placed in a hand press which was screwed down tight to make a good copy and left long enough to make a good impression. Way bills for freight forwarded were handled in this same way, a very cumbersome and time consuming process. Carbon paper had not yet been invented, and if so, railroads were the last to use them.

During the many years that have elapsed since that period, accounting procedures have been constantly simplified and streamlined, with fewer and fewer reports with less work. For one example, remittances, both cash and checks, had to be placed in an American Express envelope for that purpose, stitched through with a string, the ends of the strings and flaps sealed with heated sealing wax, the wax impressed with a metal stamp with the express company's name on it, entered in a receipt book and receipt taken from the express messenger on the train. At present remittance are simply placed in the U.S Mails. Freight, passenger and express tariffs also were very numerous and extensive and cumbersome requiring two large filing cabinets at the smaller stations, each tariff added to it, cancelled, amended and suspended by the use of supplements of many and various kinds, dates, places, and so on. This tariff system took up much of the agent's time in filing, discarding, replacing other tariffs in the cabinets. And every tariff and supplement had to be filed upon receipt. It was a terrific job.

For a couple days the auditor had me collect freight bills and doing what I could with the reports under his guidance.

He taught me much that I needed to know; gave me pointers and instructions on how to write up the cash book, which was the most important book in the office, and to make out the monthly balance sheet and make it balance properly in addition to the numerous other duties in respect to accounting and remitting proceeds of the collections. With his valuable assistance we finally brought the books and balance sheet up to date and set me on a course of correct procedures in the manifold duties I was required to perform in order to keep the accounts in balance. He was a gentleman in every respect, and a good teacher. I learned much from him. After completing his assignment, he left for his office at St. Paul. After that I had no difficulty to speak of.

I must have left there soon after that, for during the following months I found myself at Org, Minnesota, Sibley, Iowa, Savage, Minnesota, and finally at Vernon Center, Minnesota, in most instances relieving the agent. Org, Minnesota was mostly a telegraph relay office on the main line and at the start of the branch line running to Sioux Falls, South Dakota. All telegrams for stations on this branch and to and from stations on the main line were sent to Org for relaying to the different offices. I enjoyed greatly the work of telegraphing, especially in this relay office where I was alone and undisturbed. I recall that at

Sibley, Iowa, while I was relieving the night operator, the agent, Mr. Cunningham complained to me that the gas light bill had increased abnormally and warned me to be sure and turn the lights out in the waiting room after the local passenger train had left, which of course I did. He was a frugal man and wanted to protect the interests of his company, which of course is a desirable trait to have for any one. I also recall that at Savage I used to look out through the windows and see Dan Patch take practice runs on the private race track located across the main line. Dan Patch, of course, was a very famous race horse of the time owned by M. M. Savage, a Minneapolis businessman, retail mail order firm of the Savage Co. This stallion held the record of 1:55 per mile as a harness racer, the fastest of them all before or since. I was on first trick and in the evenings I mixed with the boys of the community playing pool mostly and some of the young blades kept humming a popular song of the day, "I wonder who is kissing her now, etc."

It was at Vernon Center where I made another of my mistakes, but this time it was personal, not against the company, thank goodness. I went there to relieve the agent Mr. Mann, who had drawn, or was appointed to another better position somewhere. Working with him was an assistant named J.M. Ball, a young man some older than myself, and of course we became pals. The depot at Vernon Center had a high platform of planks surrounding it on all sides except the front. The office was of the very old fashioned type enclosed with slate permitting customers to look into and through the office; no privacy. Mr. Mann transferred the accounts to me, railroad, express and Western Union; that was soon after the first of October 1910.

He had a son, O.S. Mann, working the side wire at St. James. Next AM when I sent 'cars' to him he was very abusive; I was not good enough for him. He was mean to all operators he worked with. In spite of that, he eventually became the chief train dispatcher at St. James. J.E. Kickey was the chief when I was on that western division. I cannot remember how I countered his abuse, but I hope it was sufficient to give him something to think about. I was commencing to learn that the best medicine for those kinds of individuals was to give them a dose of their own medicine, which is all they can understand in most such cases.

I believe I would have remained on the western division if it had not been for J. M. Ball. He started almost at once to speak in glowing terms about Texas, especially Dallas and Ft. Worth. He had a friend with the Western Union, he told me, a telegrapher that he wanted to go and see and wanted me to go along with him. He kept talking so glowingly of the South that I was commencing to be persuaded by his glib talk. Ball was not a telegrapher, but I learned later that he was a boomer of sorts, going from one railroad job to another and from one railroad to another. If I had known that at the time, I probably would not have listened to him. But I did permit myself to be 'taken in' by his speech and manners, and so I wired J.E. Hickey to please relieve me as soon as possible as I wished to resign effective at once. Ball did likewise. Next day I received a letter from him acknowledging receipt of my resignation and he would arrange for my relief as soon as possible. I placed that letter in my coat pocket, never dreaming it would serve me very well when we arrived at a certain small town in Texas.

And so it came to pass that I left the employ of the Omaha Railroad on October 24TH, 1910. We did not wait for our pay checks; they were to be forwarded to us in Dallas, Texas. But later I had the check sent to me at Ft. Worth. I and Ball decided to 'ride the rods' to Ft. Worth just for the experience and fun of it, although we did not actually ride the rods; that was not necessary. Neither was it necessary for us to travel that way at all; we had ample cash to go first class if we wanted to. We, also, were well dressed. My suit was almost new; both of us wore derby hats, the style those days. I sent my suit case with clothes ahead by express. We traveled light, only the clothes we had on, money and some letters, including the one from J.E. Kickey, CTD.

We got on the local passenger to Mankato and from there on the main line. I doubt if I would have had the nerve to 'best my way' on freight and passenger trains if Ball had not led the way, as he seemed to be proficient in that mode of travel. I did not feel I was cheating in any way because I could have had a free pass to travel down and back if I had remained with the company and not resigned; I was entitled to free transportation no matter what method I used. This trip was the first and last that I 'hitch-hiked' by rail; 'bumming it' were the words used at that time to describe that kind of traveling, 'hitch-hiking' not having yet been invented.

It was in late October 1910 in the start of a winter blizzard, or fall storm that we hopped into an empty box car on a freight going south from Mankato. We rode all that evening and night in freezing temperature until we arrived in Omaha, Nebraska where the weather was not so cold. We slept that night in a hotel room in Omaha. From there we made short trips on freight trains between terminals and were gaining experience all the time. When train crews were on the alert for 'bums', which we actually were, we hid behind cars in yards, or a coal shed and made runs for empty box cars as the train moved out of the yards.

As we got farther south, weather became comparatively warm and at night we tried riding on top of box cars for a change. In time we tired of traveling by slow freights, and thought we would try to get on a fast passenger train. As we gained confidence by experience, we thought we could do it easily. I cannot remember what town it was, but late in the evening while the train was loading passengers, mail and express, we were on the other side of the train where it was dark, and as it started to move, we swung onto grab irons of a baggage car and climbed to the top. No one saw us as we reached the top of the baggage car we could find nothing to hang onto. All we could do was to lay flat on the rounded roof, our arms and legs stretched out and head down with our derby hats pushed down over our heads. It was a precarious position to be in and dangerous, but we were young, reckless and foolish, but full of confidence. As the train gathered speed, one can imagine the wind sweeping against us, but we hung on for dear life. We must have rode that way most of the night. After that dangerous ride we had to rest the following day and loafed in the warm sunshine on the outskirts of a small town deep in the heart of the Southland. We had decided by then to try a better and safer method next time.

We looked over the next passenger train that came along and found that a couple of baggage or express cars on the end of the train was not being used by the crew in walking through the train, so next time we climbed into the vestibule of the first one we saw, an opening between two cars and stood, or crouched there. Vestibules were not closed those days as at present. We rode for a long time that way in comparative comfort; all that day until in the evening the train stopped at a station. We stood up hard against the door to keep out of sight as we had learned to do, when we heard foot-steps on the gravel that stopped opposite where we were. We saw an arm extended towards us with a wicked looking revolver pointed in our direction and the man behind it said in his southern drawl, "Reckon you'd better come 'off'en there." We did, and promptly. A water tank stood opposite and beyond a short way the station with the platform full of people, some of them watching us and the drama being enacted before them. The board on and off the depot read, 'Justin, Texas.' It seemed we were just in at Justin, Texas deep in the heart of Texas. What an undignified position to be in!

We were on the Santa Fe Railroad at the time; previous to that, the Rock Island. After the man with the gun had made sure that we were not carrying fire-arms, he lowered his and pocketed it in his holster. We were somewhat dirty, but did not look like bums at all; fairly respectable with good clothes still in good order. He looked us over carefully and told us he thought we did not look like 'bums'. He wanted to know all about us. We said we were railroad men and were traveling this way just for the lark. He asked for identification papers of some kind to prove our statements. That was when the letter I had in my pocket from J.E. Hickey of the Omaha Railroad at St. James, Minnesota came in handy for us. After reading it, he drawled, "Well, I'll tell you what I'll do. Seeing as how you fellers are railroad boys, instead of arresting and locking you up, I'll let you go providing you leave town by walking and not ride another train, unless you pay for your transportation to your destination. The next station on the railroad is Ft. Worth, 25 miles from here. How about that?" We promised readily, not realizing then how much of a walk it would be. We were very short of money: certainly not enough to buy tickets, and so we started to walk after the train had left, in the same direction, glad we could get out of an embarrassing situation so easily. The next few days were the toughest I have ever experienced. There were no towns between Justin and Ft. Worth, Texas, so we had no more chances to ride and were compelled to walk the whole distance. The worst part was lack of money. Fortunately the weather was nice, the nights warm and sleeping under the stars was not difficult. We slept in a church building one night: another on the bank of a creek. We kept walking steadily until hunger forced us to beg for food.

Talk about losing one's dignity! 'Pride goeth before a fall.' Mine had fallen badly. It was an ordeal that sapped our strength, but we made it at last when the light of Ft. Worth appeared ahead of us. We had been walking on the railroad track most of the time, and those lights certainly looked good to us. Ft. Worth, Texas at that time was a small city. We made our way to the apartment of Ball's friend who fed us with a good meal. Food never tasted better. It was a great feeling to get into a bed again. We cleaned up, shaved and pressed our clothes which helped us regain our self-respect again once more.

One cannot appreciate a good bed and food until compelled to do without them for a while. I had to go to work at once as I was just about broke except for the check that had arrived at the apartment of Ball's friend. They tried to get me to sign it over to them saying it would be as a loan, but I became suspicious of both of them. His friend was not working for the Western Union, probably because of illness. He looked pale and sickly and I found out soon enough that he was afflicted with a venereal disease that necessitated treatments there in his apartment. When they failed to get my check, they asked to borrow my suitcase, which I agreed to; it was not of much value anyhow. They never returned it. I left them promptly and was glad to get away from the two slickers. I cashed my check which enabled me to look around for employment.

I went to the dispatcher's office of the C.R.I.&G. Railroad in Ft. Worth first and asked for a job as a telegrapher. The chief (cannot recall his name) put me on a wire to see what I could do. I sent a few messages for him and copied a few. He seemed to be satisfied with my ability and without questions or examinations of any kind, except to get my name, he wrote out a pass for me to go to Graham, Texas to work the day job as telegrapher. Graham was the terminus for the branch from Ft. Worth and only one telegrapher was employed there besides the agent, chief clerk and express agent. It was about in the middle of November 1910. Graham was a cattle and cotton shipping point. Several carloads of long-horn cattle were shipped from there every week, and during the peak season, almost a train load. Baled cotton in carloads were also shipped every day to eastern points, some of it for export overseas. It was a good business town, although primitive in many ways. Streets were dusty; sidewalk of wooden planks or boards. Cowboys were numerous and every store front had hitching posts. The depot was the busiest place in town, being the only outlet for passengers, freight, express as well as long distance communications by wire.

I liked by job very much. My hours were from 8 AM to 6 PM with an hour off for noon meal. I did all the telegraphing for the railroad and Western Union as well as some book work. The pay was quite a bit higher than the same kind of position up north. The agent was quite old whose name I do not recall, but I do remember the clerk's name, R. A. Moore. He did all the billing and had to know tariffs, routing and rates. He was some older then myself and I liked him and palled around with him quite a bit. The express man was an Englishman whose accent was so pronounced that I could hardly understand him. I think he was employed by the express company on a salary basis; the express business was very good, having to use a separate room for the packages. R. A. Moore was also a telegrapher and a local chairman of the Order of Railroad Telegraphers. He was a prince of a young man, but when I beat him at pool, he could not take it; he wished to be unbeatable in everything.

Moore's wife would come to the depot quite often. After getting acquainted with me, she brought along a girl friend of hers, a Miss Graham, daughter of the mayor of the town whose grandfather had founded it years before. She was a dark-haired brunette, rather small in stature, quite attractive and jolly. She made herself agreeable to me with more than necessary attention. We went to a few places together and she invited me to her home, but never

117

had occasion to go there for some reason. She was just a good friend and a jolly companion while I was there.

I spent Christmas that winter in Graham, but I cannot recall how I fared except that the agent handed out cigars to the office force, including me. Western Union business was very good. Our relay office was Dallas 'DA' and my office call was 'GM'. I used to have to call 'DA' for minutes at a time before an operator happened to come near my wire and heard me calling. That was before the Western Union developed an electric gadget that would ring a bell, or flash a light on the many different wires entering a main relay office when the specified combination of dashes was made on the wire by any operator out on the line.

Although I liked it there, I was starting to be lonesome for Wisconsin and Minnesota, my original stomping grounds where my own people lived. Texas was hot and dusty, even in winter. Its people seemed to me to be lazy and slow moving, contrary to the people up north who were always running about. So when an older telegrapher, older in seniority, came to 'bump' me (displace) I was quite pleased when he relieved me in the early part of January 1911. In later years I have often wondered what path my destiny would have taken if I had chosen to remain in Texas. Would I have eventually become interested in oil wells and made myself a millionaire? The grounds on which I tread undoubtedly was rich in petroleum, as it has since proven to be. Oil was unheard of in Texas at that time; at least not on the scale that it became in later years. Man spins his web of life unmindful of the future nor of the consequences of his actions from day to day. As youth, the future is mercifully hidden from us lest it disturb and disrupt the orderly process of living, if we knew it in advance. Pre-knowledge of future events is undesirable for thinking human beings, which probably is the reason that prophesies are unpopular.

Before I headed for my home country, I went to Dallas, Texas to attend an airplane meet that had been widely advertised. I spent a couple days there and enjoyed it very much. The meet was held on the fair grounds, and I sat in the grand-stand watching every type of plane invented up to that time do their stunts; for they really were stunts only that did not seem to have any value; the airplane at that time was only an expensive toy in the heads of people who could afford to play with it. Again, the future of such a machine was unforeseeable, as was the automobile of later times.

Aviators from this country and Europe were there with their huge toys trying to impress the spectators with their possibilities. The famous Frenchman, Bleriot who was the first to fly over the English Channel, was on hand with his monoplane type of airship, while others had the biplane type. Bleriot was the most successful. When he flew up into the air, he did not return and we all wondered what had become of him. The evening newspapers had glaring headlines about his flight and speculated about where he had landed, if at all. The morning papers told us what he had done. After flying around for a while, he landed in an open field nearby as he thought it would be too dark to return to the fair grounds. The next day he came back and made a safe landing at the meet, which made him a hero to all of us. Other aviators crashed on taking off, some into fences. One flew right in front of us in the grand stand. None of them were injured, happily. Since those early pioneering days for the airplane, many hundreds of thousands of people have been killed and injured as a result of it. The same is said of the automobile. If all of us had known in advance at that time the sacrifice of human lives that the airplane and the automobile would bring about as they were developed during the ensuing years, would we have dropped them as dangerous engines of destruction? A hypothetical questions like that cannot be answered.

Some of us think and say that the sacrifice of human lives is necessary if progress is to be made in any and all fields of human endeavor; that it is not such a terrible catastrophe for people to lose their lives because there is no such a thing as loss of anything really; it is only an expression we use that is not true. Nothing really is lost; it merely changes its form of existence. Life is a continuous process that exists on all levels no matter where it is located at any given time. Life renews itself continuously and when an individual dies accidentally or otherwise, he does not 'lose' anything except the temporary use of his body; and even that is not 'lost'; it merely disintegrates into atoms that returns to their constituent elements. The life itself returns again to another body in time and continues the process of evolution; of making progress and advancing man's knowledge and experimenting in all fields to further still more human advancement by continuing where he left off previously.

January 10th, 1911 I bought a ticket to St. Paul. When I entered 'A' offices again, Mr. Davison welcomed me back and asked where I had been. He said he wanted me to go to work for the company again; that he wanted a man in Bennett, Wisconsin at once; so I went there and relieved the Agent-Telegrapher the next day. Bennett was only a small village whose principle occupation was logging and work in a small saw mill that cut the logs into lumber, ties and belts for paper mills and shipped out by rail in car lots.

It was in the middle of winter with much snow and severe cold that kept most of us inside the small hotel where I roomed and ate with a few boarders and two girls school teachers. I spent many evenings talking to the girls, especially Miss Ebba Abrahamson whose favorite topic was philosophy and religion. She called herself an atheist, not believing in a God or a future existence for the individual. I argued the opposite point of view in a friendly manner. She was afflicted with a weak heart and had to be very careful. One evening she had a mild attack; went to bed and called the land-lady to stay with her in her room. She was fearful of dying and could not face it alone. I thought at the time that a belief in a Supreme Being with Divine Justice would stand her in good stead in such circumstance even though a belief does not change the natural laws that apply; it would at least console her and comfort her in such a crisis. She recovered from the attack and we resumed our talks. She was an educated and intelligent woman, gentle and feminine.

One evening to while away the time of a long wintry night, the two girls, myself and two other young men in the community went to the depot and had a private dance in the waiting room under the light of kerosene lamps that hung on the walls. One of the guys brought his fiddle and furnished the music for the four of us who 'tripped the light fantastic' far into the night; and a pleasant time was had by all. That was how I celebrated my 22nd birthday, although I said nothing about it to the rest.

The regular man having resumed his job at Bennett, I was instructed by the dispatcher at Eau Claire to go to Burkhardt, Wisconsin, another small community. The young agent there had resigned and had refused to wait for a relief man for some reason. As a result, in order to get me there quickly, the dispatcher, ordered the helper engine from Hudson to take me there at once, as I was needed there to care for the company's business. The key had been left in the way bill box outside and I took over without benefit of a transfer by the auditor. The principle business at that station was provided by the Burkhardt Milling Co. with carloads of flour and feed shipped out and grains shipped in. In later years the big mills, operated by water power at that time, was taken over by a co-operative concern.

From there I was called to Boardman for a while in relief work. After that to Cable, Wisconsin and thence to Hayward as relief telegrapher where I came in on the tail end of the famous John Dietz case. Hayward was the county seat and the nearest telegraph office from the site of the John Dietz home where he had his gun battle with the power and light company that was trying to oust him from his property in order to build a dam on the Thorn Apple River in the vicinity of his home. He was a hero to most people because of his defiant stand against a corporation. He became well known throughout the United States and some foreign countries. Newspapers sent their reporters to Hayward from the big cities to report on the excitement created by Mr. Dietz and his family, especially his daughter Myra, who stood by her father while they were shooting it out with the deputies. Press traffic became so heavy at the telegraph office in the passenger depot that the Western Union were compelled to send press operators over there to handle it as it was too much for the regular telegraphers who were there. When I arrived the excitement started to peter out.

From Hayward I was sent to Trego, Wisconsin to work third trick in the electrically operated interlocking plant at the juncture of two main lines, one to Duluth-Superior, the other to Bayfield-Ashland. I had not been there very long when an engineer of an extra freight disregarded a small stop signal, ran through an open switch and put the plant out of temporary operation. I had placed the signal against him and opened the derail switch in order to line up for a regular train on the main line. This was the first interlocking plant I had worked at; I was getting all sorts of experience. While the plant was out of operation, trains were routed and signals given by hand. It was repaired and placed back into service in a couple days. The engineer was penalized by a forced layoff of thirty days; I kept on working. Three telegrapher-lever men were on duty there on eight hour shifts. Also an agent. Fred D. Sinclair was on first; his brother Ray D. Sinclair on second and myself on third. There was also a telegrapher there, as I recall, by the name of Quinn who had something to do with the plant; what it was I do not remember. He may have been a maintainer of the plant. Fred Anderson, the agent, was a tall lanky, good natured young man who was in charge of the depot that was situated on the main line to Ashland, the plant in between the two tracks. During the season of blue berry picking, the blue-berry express traffic was so heavy that he had to hire another man to assist.

One of the buyers and shippers of blue berries was swamped with the enormous crop that year (1911) and hired me on part time while off duty from the plant to assist at sorting and crating the berries. The reason for the huge crop was that the brush, small trees and old blue berry vines in the woods surrounding had been burned over, purposely so that the new vines would grow and a good crop insured. That was a principle requirement for a good blue berry crop. In later years, conservation practices stopped it.

I used to enjoy watching the Trego, Wisconsin every morning as daylight replaced the night darkness, coming down the track from Spooner; its steam engine belching smoke, and as it passed the plant, I was always at the window high above the track looking out and waving to the engineer, who would respond with a wave of his hand, and sometimes a toot of his whistle. It was the time of the day when the early morning sun was about to show his red rays over the distant horizon; when life all around us was about to awaken from its night of slumber, human, animal and vegetable life, and commence a new day of work and play. This was the best time of day when all were refreshed and eager for what it would bring forth for each individual. It was a time of day when Nature in all her glory responded to the warm rays of the rising sun; a symbol of the eternal resurrection of all life in response to the constant urge for renewal of life; in response to the law of life that it shall come back again and resume where it left off the previous day, the week, the month, the year or the century before.

Although the woods around there were burned and its growth returned for the purpose of speeding up the growth of blue berries, this same urge of Nature to renew itself overcame the destructive forces of humans to destroy; the seeds of growth could not be destroyed, but only awaited the morning to break forth from their temporary confinement to sprout, blossom and bloom again in new growth, new plants, new trees and fresh vegetation. Thus Nature functions in her renewal, her resurrection of life and form

I was at Trego most of the summer of 1911 and in the fall some time I was sent to Shell Lake to work first trick telegrapher. Three telegraphers and the agent worked in that office. I was on first, Palmer Imslund on second and Cy. Johnson on third. I recall that Palmer used to press his ties in the office press that was used for making tissue copies of letters, way bills and reports. He placed his ties in the press, then screw it down tight and by morning they were mostly pressed. He was a jolly young man, a red head and did some entertaining at gatherings. He was an imitator and could also sound off almost any hand instrument with his mouth, throat and lips. In later years he left the railroad and worked with Eddie Canter as an entertainer, but later on resumed telegraphing for a railroad in Michigan, D. & I. R. in the dispatcher's office as side wire man. He was an expert telegraph operator.

L.B. Marquette was the agent and I recall that one day handed me a slip of paper as he sat at his desk and I at the telegraph table with the following notation on it: 11-11-11-11 AM and remarked "This date has never before been written and never will again." As a matter of fact he was right. It was 11 AM Nov. 11th, 1911. It was on October 6th, 1911, some weeks previous to that date, that I heard Hudson (HN) tell some on the wire that Black River Falls, my home town, had met disaster by flood waters from a washed out dam at Hatfield that swept the main business district, the whole of it, down the Black River. Many of the residences also went down the river.

Shell Lake was a pleasant place to work; the large lake was a short walk from the depot and could be seen from the window. I stayed at a hotel in town and the manager of it was the same man who had managed the boarding house in Hazelhurst some years previously whose name I cannot recall. The depot was a busy place, as all small town depots were those days; I think we had two local passenger trains each way and two way freights, besides regular and freight trains. The railroad business was good and many men were required to run it. I did practically all the Western Union wire work, being on day time and our relay office was St. Paul 'Z' office, the same office to which I used to deliver telegrams while a messenger in 'A' office. Shell Lake office call was 'WS'

I must have left Shell Lake in the spring or early summer of 1912 as I find myself at Hammond, Wisconsin that summer for a short time relieving A.D. Shire, the agent. One Sunday morning one of the girls in the hotel asked me to go to the Methodist church with her. During the song service I did my share of singing. I must have sang 'loud and clear', because Monday morning a lady called on me at the depot and stated she wanted me to sing in the choir; she had been told by the girl about my singing. But I was sorry to inform her that I was leaving Hammond the next day and would be unable to accommodate her.

During this period Woodville first trick was on the bulletin for bidding and I applied for it with the result that I drew it, not expecting to do so. I happened to be the oldest in seniority at the time on that division and was assigned to it.

This was the first job I had drawn on a bulletin.

--Chapter 6--

There were three tricks at Woodville. I was on first; P.R. Anderson on second and W.E. Poerake on third and C.A. Pope the agent. We had the branch line to Weston to handle, which included Elmwood and Spring Valley. Western Union traffic, railroad messages and car reports were relayed at Woodville, (WD). At that time the main line was single track and followed a different route than the double track of later times. Trains were numerous and short as compared to present day trains. We handled many train orders every day. We were on duty 10 hours per day and 7 days per week and no meal hour off. The hours overlapped for the telegraphers who did clerical work and janitor duties on the overlapping hours. Not having time to go to lunch, Mrs. Myrvold brought it to me. She owned and operated the hotel where I roomed and ate near the depot. She was a widow with two daughters. It was a very busy office with many freight and passenger trains on both the main line and the branch with heavy freight, passenger, express and mail traffic.

Stories of serious accidents to individuals are not pleasant, but I should relate this one to show the hazards of railroading for train-men during that period. A freight conductor, a young man named Wilcox on an extra, after he had been in the office for orders, in attempting to board the engine, a heavy fabric curtain covering the entrance to the cab got in his way and he failed to make the grab iron, lost his balance and fell with both legs under one of the drivers of the engine that was moving at the time, cutting off both of them just below the knee. Every one was excited but they managed to carry the poor man into the waiting room, laid him on the floor and rounded up the doctor B.G. Stockman. He could not do much for him except to try to stop the flow of blood and ease the pain, but soon became unconscious. The train dispatcher ordered the limited to stop at Woodville to take him to Eau Claire and finally to the hospital. He was placed on a cot and had to wait over an hour for the train. We heard later that they barely saved him from dying, having lost so much blood. Transfusions were not in use at that time. Several months later I saw him on a train and I could hardly recognize him, he was so pale and frail. He was trying to get used to artificial legs with the help; of crutches. Injuries and deaths were more numerous then and hospital and medical services inadequate for railroad employees than at present.

The manual block system was in use at the time. A wire called the 'block wire' for the exclusive use of telegraphers in blocking trains was equipped with a switch at each station to enable him to cut the wire, or switch from one side of him to the other, thereby to promptly block trains and to clear the block for others following. The signal arms outside were operated by hand with levers inside the office. The same signal arms were also used for delivering train orders and stopping trains. In later years, after the main line had been relocated and double tracked, electric automatic signal systems were installed which eliminated many block telegraph office jobs.

The Chief Train Dispatcher at Eau Claire (C) at the time was F.G. Little, who had taken over from J.B. Elliottt. An old veteran dispatcher named Lamb was on first trick dispatching trains when I first came there. His Morse was terrible, the bane to new telegraphers, to whom he showed no mercy; even the older experienced men had trouble copying him. It was not long before he became too old and was retired and replace by a younger man name H.E. Stubbs. His Morse was perfect and we all enjoyed working with him. Mr. Glennon was the second trick dispatcher, but I cannot recall name of the third man. Rosecranz, (Old Rosy) was the day side wire man. The other two were R.F. North (SM) and later Grimenz. Side wire office call was 'MS'. These men sent and received messages all over the division and copied 'cars' every morning for the car dispatcher. Several other telegraphers came on later.

Up to 1912 the main line of the CSTPM&O Railroad was circuitous with many difficult grades; it had originally been constructed along the lines of least resistance that entailed the least expense in time and money. Since these early railroad times, traffic constantly increased due to expanding industries and agriculture with new towns built along the right-of-way and increasing populations. These factors caused railroad managements to realize that their facilities were becoming more and more inadequate and in time forced them to expand them to meet the constantly increasing demands for their services.

The main line from Chicago north for a considerable distance had been straightened and double tracked some years previously by the C&NW Rail Road. Also, the Black River Falls cut-off had been built by the Omaha eliminating the long curve into the city. It remained for them to complete the job of straightening, relocating and double-tracking the railroad into the Twin Cities. In the summer of 1912 surveying crews set up headquarters in Woodville in a store building and commenced surveying the territory north and south of there, while other parties worked towards the Twin Cities. Woodville became an important center, first for surveyors, then for construction crews. A whole new right-of-way had to be mapped out and the land acquired for that purpose sufficiently wide for double tracks. Practically a new railroad was to be built which would eventually eliminate the old trackage with the old installations together with some depots and additions to others in some locations. This time they were making sure that the main line would be as straight as possible over the available terrain. Huge fills and many cuts became necessary to accomplish this purpose. Bridges and overheads at new and different locations, all built for permanency were necessary, planned and constructed.

I was in the midst of all this activity during the balance of 1912, the whole of 1913 and a part of 1914 handling telegraph communications and wire reports for the different crews; the extra work entailed by work trains and the increased volume of company traffic and construction crew; materials. The surveying crew members with whom I came into personal contact were: W.H. Johnson head engineer, a middle aged man; his son whose name I cannot recall at this late date; Travis Kennedy son of the division superintendent T.W. Kennedy; J.E. Bunker; Geo. Coffin and one or two others whose names have escaped my memory. We were all young fellows, except the head man. We all roomed at Mrs. Myrvold's boarding house, or hotel, the only one in town. Also ate our meals there. A couple of girl school teachers also lived at the hotel. All these young people, including the regular residents in town, were full of life and energy of youth and made it a lively place as long as they were there. They put on several parties and dances. There weren't enough girls to go around for all of them with the result that rivalries sprung up among the boys for the available girls. This was fine for the girls with so many to choose from, and the best man won in most cases. Times were good; everyone prosperous with good paying jobs, good pay for the times. There were no wars to take the men away and everyone seemed happy.

I shall make this portion of my narrative as brief as possible, the unfortunate episodes that occurred while at

Woodville in 1913 and later, as they were most unpleasant for me then and in later times. My health started to fail, my body breaking out in a rash; in time both sides of my neck commenced to swell larger and larger as time went on. I became listless, just about half dead, so much so that I could not participate in any activity except to hold down my job and it was a wonder I was able to do that.

Dr. B. G. Stockman could not, and did not try, to diagnose it accurately; instead he sent me to Dr. A.E. Comstock at St. Paul who was a surgeon. His specialty was surgery which was first coming into use more and more at that time. He did not attempt to diagnose my case either; did not ask me one question in respect to my difficulty. But he did ask what I did for a living and if I was able to pay to the operation. That was the first I knew that I had to be operated on. I was so weak physically and mentally that I could not discuss my case with him, and he did not offer to discuss it. Instead I was led 'like sheep to the slaughter', if that expression can be pardoned, because that is the way I have felt ever since.

He instructed me to go to the hospital; that I would be operated on the following day. It was not an operation as that is understood in this modern day of medical practice, when it is done scientifically and for a good purpose. Surgery then was a 'hit and miss' proposition; he merely experimented on me, and it was a 'miss'. He tore tissues out of both sides and after sewing up the wounds, I was worse than before; he did not cure me. Later a nurse told me that Dr. Comstock had entered my name in hospital records as 'tubercular' glands of the neck. I cannot recall how long I laid in the hospital, but while there, my brother Albert was the only person to call on me; did not even receive as much as a card from my folks or rest of the family. When I left I all but collapsed on the walk outside. It was my strong heart that kept me alive.

I resumed my work at Woodville with my neck bandaged, the wounds draining puss and waste matter.

C.A. Pope the agent with whom I worked in the office was afraid of being contaminated; he was one of those who was constantly protecting himself against imaginary germs and bacteria. Just a few years later he died prematurely of a heart attack. I have outlived him by a good many years. Was that ironic, or was it poetic justice? Dr. Comstock as well as Dr. Stockman also passed on prematurely many years ago, but I myself am more alive than ever. Again, ironic, or poetic justice?

About that time I happened to see a copy of one of Bernarr McFadden's magazines, forgot its name, that specialized in health and natural methods to keep healthy, especially diet. Fasting and physical exercise; he was a famous physical culteralist of the day. It was then that I started to study and learn all I could about body care and proper foods, and I have always, since then, contended that McFadden was an inspiration to me at that time and since, and that by following his instructions I regained my health, although it was a very slow process.

I had to go back to Dr. Comstock's office at St. Paul periodically for him to change dressings; that is all he did; no check up whatsoever. The railroad management gave me a hand full of passes for the purpose. I had to be relieved many times to go to St. Paul, sometimes for longer periods; once I went to my folk's home to try to recuperate. It was a time that tested my courage and patience and my will to continue to live. Once when Dr. Comstock was changing the bandages, he remarked to an assistant Doctor that he had lost a patient on the operating table that morning. I did not have the nerve nor the will to say to him that I wished that would have happened to me.

One day we received instructions from Eau Claire for all operators and agents to be on hand on a certain date for uniform inspection. The Assistant Superintendent, C.W. Tower was the inspector, who was nothing but a tailor's agent to take orders for new uniforms if what we wore did not suit him. He practically forced all of the men to accept his dictation and sign up for new uniforms, payment to be deducted from pay checks. When he came to me, Mr. Tower stopped him; "no new uniform for that man; he has been sick; pass him up". And of course the mean tailor's agent had to respect Mr. Tower's orders. That goes to show that there were officials on the railroad those days that were human, even though there were plenty of the other kind. Mr. Tower was a gentleman, 'and a scholar'.

I managed somehow to remain on the roster with the co-operation of the management regardless of my long periods of being off duty to recuperate. At the end of one of those periods the Chief Train Dispatcher sent me to Altoona, Wisconsin to work third trick for a while. Previous to that I had bought a tent so that I would be able to sleep outside as much as possible thinking that more fresh air, especially at night, would assist me to get well faster. I brought it to Altoona with me and set it up on railroad grounds near the depot and slept in it during part of that winter: no matter how cold it was, I slept in it. But I found that did not help me much. By studying my body and how it functioned and reading all I could find on diet and health, I learned that my difficulty was faulty elimination. I had inherited that tendency from my Mother and uncle. Although Mother did not die directly as a result of it, I think it contributed to the disease she was afflicted with and edema, or dropsy that brought on her final end. My uncle died of an acute obstruction in the intestines which was caused, without a doubt in my mind, by a life time of faulty elimination. He was 78 at death. As soon as I felt sure what caused my difficulty, I started using rubber syringes with hot water into my rectum to make sure of complete elimination and clean rectum. As a result I started to get better, slowly at first, and completely recovered in time. This is not a pleasant subject, but it is necessary to have this knowledge in order to avoid afflictions of various kinds. From my experience

I am convinced that more diseases than we think are caused by faulty and incomplete elimination. Animals have several bowel movements per day and are healthy. Man carries his waste matter with him all day long, every day in the year by thinking falsely that he has a complete elimination once a day: that is absolutely wrong. We need to clean out our rectum two and three times per day, if not naturally, then by means of hot water with a syringes: we need to assist nature , to co-operate with her.

What I have learned about how to keep well was not gleaned from doctors, but by application of my mental faculties to the problem of good health. Not one of those that I contacted told me what to do, or what was the cause of my affliction, although it is their business to know all about such matters. My experience with them has been unpleasant and unsatisfactory, I am sorry to say. What knowledge I have gained regarding it I have had to learn the "hard way." I believe my parents would say the same if they were here to tell us. Possibly I am prejudiced; if so it is due to the age in which I was born and lived the first part of my life when medical science was in its infancy, as compared to present day medical knowledge.

During this period of time my Mother also was sick, but she put on a bold front and did not say much about it. Modern medicine has learned all about her affliction since her time: they now know how to cure and control it. My sister Mamie was caring for her during her illness and final passing. When I saw her last, Mother was confined to bed in her old home, tired of life and its problems and willing, even eager to leave it for good. She did not possess the fighting spirit, but was satisfied to permit Nature to take its course and die a natural death.

And so it came to pass that on November 26th, 1913, she who had given birth to 13 offspring; who had faced the vicissitudes and harshness of pioneer life was released at last from life's restrictions and obstructions, when she became free to take up an abode elsewhere that would be more in keeping with her nature, a place of beauty, of peace and quiet contentment. She has followed the foot steps of countless billions of other human beings who had preceded her in times past, and would continue during eons of time in the future.

It was not a 'calamity' for us to 'lose' her: we thought it was a gain for her. Although we loved her as a Mother, few tears were shed for our seeming loss;. Grief is a selfish emotion denoting loss of something when it really is not a loss. In some ways I envied her. I myself had yet to live my appointed cycle of life on earth with its attendant conflicts, handicaps and restrictions, unaware of what the future had in store for me. But she had finished hers and was now enjoying the fruits of her labors in accordance with the fundamental natural laws applicable; a well earned rest in a place of comparative bliss. Her earthy life span was finished at age 61.

> "Loved ones, though our waking vision
>   Know your forms no more,
> Earth's illusions shall not hold us;
>   Well we know your live enfold us
> Even as before.
>
> Death? 'Tis but a stepping forward,
>   No diverse at all;
> Swifter than of old the meeting,
>   Warmer, heartier the greeting,
> When you hear our call.
>
> And at night when softest slumber
>   Deals these earthly eyes:
> Lo, a new day dawneth brightly
>   To your world we rise........

D.W.M.Burn

--Chapter 7--

Life goes on in spite of sickness and death; it moves relentlessly regardless of disappointments and embarrassments. I returned to Woodville and resumed my work although I was still weak and sick physically, mentally, emotionally and spiritually. I determined to conquer disabilities and handicaps. I remained there during the winter of 1913-1914 and the summer of 1914. The surveyors had completed their work and left, as had the construction crews. I believe the railroad did the construction work with their own crews not by contractors. A new passenger depot had been built high on the embankment and fill at the new double track main line just north of the village. A long covered stairway connected the new depot platform with the one below at where the branch trains stopped and handled passengers, baggage, mail and express for towns on the branch line. An elevator operated by a gasoline engine lowered and hoisted trucks containing mail, baggage and express. Everything was brand new and I moved into the new depot that had two waiting rooms and the office between. I do not know the date I moved in, probably some time in June or July of 1914. I was the first telegrapher ticket agent in that office. I still held down first trick and for that reason I was assigned to the new office; the other two telegraph jobs were abolished, the men going to other stations on different jobs.

Many other telegraph block office jobs were abolished also due to the new electric automatic signal systems installed on the new double tracks. All I did in the new office was to handle the telegraph work for the branch line; sell tickets; check baggage; 'OS' trains to the dispatcher and work with the side wire operator at 'MS' Eau Claire; there was no need for the dispatcher to issue train orders for trains to meet any more. Trains west moved on the right hand track and those east on the left without having to meet opposing trains; in fact it was now a 'right-handed' railroad.

The double track railway was now practically straight and level with gradual curves. Longer freight trains hauled by the new type of 'Mikado' locomotive rolled by with much more tonnage and with fewer stops. As a result a new name was coined: 'drags'. Passenger train schedules were speeded up due to straighter tracks and heavier rails. Elimination of meets also contributed to the increased speed of both freights and passenger trains. Automatic block signals placed at intervals rendered the old fashioned manual block system obsolete. This created new jobs for signal maintainers. At first my hours were from 7 AM to 7 PM, but later reduced to 8 hours per day as a result of the so called new 'Adamson Act'. Verily a new era entered the railroad transportation world.

Although some train and engine crews found themselves without jobs as a result of all those changes which we call 'progress", in time readjustments were made for the men and employment was provided for those willing and able to work. Times were good. The economy expanded on every hand. Labor Unions were becoming stronger. I had joined the Order of Railroad Telegraphers (ORT), one of the oldest and most conservative of labor unions. When I became ill, I had to stop paying dues but in later years I rejoined. Our wages were being hiked little by little as time went on, as well as wages were initiated. I had a good job; I liked it there in the office on the high embankment; I could look down on everyone else. It was there that I bought my first typewriter, an old fashioned 'mill' whose carriage had to be lifted up to see what I was writing. Cannot recall the make, probably a Remington.

General Chairman of the C.R.T. was W.J. Liddance, a veteran. O.D. Tenny, Secretary-Treasurer, M.J. Herpold of Black River Falls local chairman, a good friend of mine in Weston, the end of the branch line, was ambitious to learn to telegraph and had mastered the Morse code sufficiently to send a little on our wire. A.E. Boe, the agent there, assisted him quite a bit. He called me one day and asked if I would send to him on our wire, which I did during periods I was not busy on other wires. We kept it up for some time and soon he was able to copy very well for a youngster and beginner. He was very smart and learned rapidly; his name, A.K. Holmberg. He was my first student and I have assisted many more since then. It was not long before he went to St. Paul and the management hired him at once as a telegrapher on the Western Division and eventually he was called to 'A' office as a full fledged and fast telegraph operator, the office where I had my start as a messenger in 1909. In a few years he entered the Traffic Department and became a traveling freight agent out of Sioux Fall, South Dakota. The last I heard of him he was General Agent at Eau Claire. He called on me at Whitehall one day some time after the Second World War. He has always appreciated my assisting him.

I have a news paper clipping in one of my scrap books dated Sept. 19th, 1941 with a group picture of railroad men on the Omaha as follows: A.K. Holmberg; S.R. Sitney, Roadmaster; J.J. Prentice, Division Superintendent, Spooner; Carl R. Grey, Jr. Executive Vice President Omaha Railroad; S.B. Dickey, Agent Worthington; and E.L. Pardee, General Passenger Agent. Worthington Minnesota, businessmen and Omaha Railroad officials had joined in an informal celebration of the 70th anniversary of the coming of the railroad to Worthington, Minnesota back in 1871.

The agents on the branch to Weston were A.E. Boe, Weston; Mullholand, Elmwood; Spence, Spring Valley. Boe sold life insurance for the Equitable Life Assurance Assoc. during his spare time on the side and sold a policy to me while I was at Woodville, but illness prevented me from keeping up the premiums.

Officers of the Eastern Division at the time were T.W. Kennedy, Superintendent, G.W. Tower, Assistant Superintendent, F.G. Little, CTD, later replaced by J.J. Prentice who later became Superintendent, Spooner. Train dispatchers were H.E. Stubbs; Olennon and a couple others I cannot recall. Side wire telegraphers were R.F. Worth, who in later times became Postmaster at Chippewa Falls and still later became an Attorney. There were others whose names I have forgotten.

During my spare time at Woodville, and later at Hustler, I used to cut in on the fast wire Eau Claire to St. Paul and enjoy listening to R.F. North send messages to 'A' St. Paul. He had a perfect sending hand, far better than any one using a 'bug'. He signed 'SM!. His sending was a steady rhythm, and so perfect that the operator at 'A' never needed to break in on him. Every message was numbered, followed by 'MS SM Eau Claire, date, time, etc.' It was not the contents of the messages that interested me, but the steady and rhythmatic sending of perfect Morse at the same steady pace that flowed over the wire that intrigued me; it was music to one who could read and decipher the dots and dashes and spaces into words and sentences with meaning, much as an expert on music can interpret and understand the musical sounds of a symphony orchestra.

Mr. Rosencrantz worked the day side wire job at MS for many years. He was a fast hard worker and expected others to do the same by copying his fast stuff without breaking. He never slacked up for the 'ham' operator, but kept right on his fast pace until the poor 'ham' was able to write it all down. There were many offices between Minneapolis and Elroy those days that kept old Rosy 'RO' busy all the time. He had a style of sending of his own that was the bane of some of the telegraphers, sending fast and furious. He had the habit of using short, sawed off lead pencils in writing and always wore a skull cap while on duty.

J.J. Prentice who was Chief Train Dispatcher for many years was promoted to Assistant Superintendent of the Eastern Division and later Superintendent of the Northern Division. at Spooner. G.F. Boutlette replaced him as C.T.D. and F.E. Nicols replaced T.W. Kennedy as Division Superintendent. Superintendent who was getting old and finally retired.

Most of the time I was on the Eastern Division, H.E. Stubbs was the day time train dispatcher, and he was a good man. His Morse also was just about perfect. He remained long after I left the Omaha and the last I heard of him he had retired on his pension and a well earned rest.

When a wreck blocks a main line temporarily, the train dispatcher has to wait for it to be cleared up, when his work is diminished and trains grind to a halt. It was after the line had been cleared of the wreck, that it was interesting to listen to Mr. Stubbs go into action on his wire as the commander he was; when orders flowed steadily from his mind through his fingers to operators along the line one after another that appeared bewildering to those listening. Every detail over the entire division about every train that was waiting was stored in his mind and orders and messages and instructions in a steady stream were sent by his strong fingers to operators and trains with precision and dispatch until traffic was moving again and everything under his control.

The traveling and shipping public little realize nor can appreciate the work done by those efficient and faithful men who are behind the scenes in an upstairs office, as they manipulate and move trains as pawns on a master board, the train sheet in front of him, ordering and moving them as the master players they are. The train dispatcher cannot permit anyone to interfere with his orders. Even the president of the railroad cannot over-rule him. His authority in respect to train movements is supreme while on duty. He runs the railroad, the most important men on any railroad. Next to him are the telegraph and telephone operators out on the line who work with him and carry out his orders and instructions.

Our union had some time previously persuaded the management to put into effect the modern system of bulletining vacancies for our craft once a month for each division. Under it the oldest in seniority who applied was assigned to a telegraph job or an agency, provided the applicant qualified. On the July 1914 bulletin the Hustler telegrapher-agent position was up for bids. I felt I should leave Woodville, the town in which I had experienced so much 'grief', so I applied for it, not expecting to get it. But I happened to be the oldest in seniority who applied so was assigned to it at the close of the month. I hoped now that my fortunes would turn for the better.

During the summer of 1914 there had been much talk in the newspapers of the possibility of war in the near future. The papers kept us posted daily and I followed the news closely in the St. Paul Daily News. Kaiser Wilhelm of Germany was rattling his sword and strutting around with a chip on his shoulder. He did all he could to start troubles with whoever wished to defy him or quarrel with him. With his superb army, he thought he was invincible. It was France he was aiming at, his ancient enemy. And so world events shaped themselves up in such a way that on the very day the German armies were invading Belgium. I, a little insignificant me, also marched up the side walks of Woodville towards the depot, carrying all my worldly goods in a suit-case, somewhat despondent and still weak in body from illness, and boarded the local train for Hustler. I was 'shaking the dust' off my feet of the village where I had almost met my 'waterloo'.

The following quotation applies to human beings as well as nations: "Ho! Ye who suffer know. Ye suffer from yourselves. None else compels. Ye are not bound. The heart of being is celestial rest; Stronger than woe is will; That which was good doth pass to better-best."

A strong will is an asset for any one, provided it is used for the individual's own 'better-best,' as well as for the good of mankind. Decisions arrived at by logical thought and supplemented by power of a strong will, assists one to maintain a balance between the many factors that may influence us one way or another; to resist the pitfalls of life; to follow independence of thought in all fields; in short to be individualistic in the classic manner.

Kaiser Wilhelm certainly was not a good thinker; his actions were based on his emotions, not his intellect, if he had an intellect. As I review past events in perspective almost a life time later, I mark that day in August 1914 as a turning point, not only for myself personally, but for the history of the world, when Kaiser Wilhelm took it upon himself to change the course of history. All the wars and revolutions that have since plagued the world, had their origin in the Kaiser's fool-hardy decision to send his armies marching across the nations of Europe. It was in the province of this one man to have prevented the bloody wars that followed since then, with the wholesale slaughter of human beings for no good purpose. It was he who lit the fires of warfare with its repercussions of dictatorships, nations, fascism, communism and their attendant evils of slavery, destruction, starvation and disruptions of established governments.

I know that there are large numbers of intelligent people in the world who believe in and think that there is in existence, invisible to us, a Ruling Hierarchy of the world, who have in their charge the evolution of the earth and its inhabitants, animal and human. It is presumed that the Supreme Being of our solar system whom we call God, or of the Galaxy to which our system belongs, organized this hierarchy and stuffed it with the most advanced of His Agents, or Assistants for the purpose of supervising, directing and assisting the people of earth to make progress; to advance and to evolve in all fields of human endeavor.

Was it the plan of this Ruling Hierarchy of our world to cause to be brought about catastrophes of far reaching dimensions during this period of time in order to teach the leaders and their peoples of earth the folly of warfare and of the dictatorial governments that followed? Were these drastic means necessary to bring into existence, first a League of Nations and later a United Nations organization, and later possibly an International Police Force to maintain law and order?

Looking backwards over our comparatively short period of recorded history, we find that at times revolutions have been necessary to change bad conditions for the better; wars to abolish slavery; wars to establish democracies; revolutions to uproot decaying governments; to stop dictators and many other changes towards betterment in governments, economics, science, education and a host of others. Who knows but that a Napoleon, a Bismarck or a Kaiser were not required to expose the fallacy of militarism: Who can say that a Mussolini or a Hitler was not needed to show us the folly of dictatorial Nazism and fascism? Or a Stalin and a Lenin to try out and expose to us the cruel consequences of dictatorial communism and the devilish theories of Marx? Would science have advanced as rapidly or as far without the impetus and challenge of opposing forms of governments? Would capital and labor, which used to be bitter enemies, have gotten together to cooperate for the common good without this threat from communistic forces?

No progress has ever been made in times past, or at present or in the future without penalties of some kind. The human race must try everything once in order to learn more lessons. Advancement through the evolutionary process in all fields has always been at a cost of one kind or another. Nations, like individuals, are subject to the same law of actions and reaction; of cause and effect, as well as the law of the evolutionary process that makes for progress and advancement.

There is one result, or effect of all this warfare, conflict, turmoil and slaughter of innocents, and that is, as any thoughtful person may observe, the improvement of the spiritual aspect of man. As we see the suffering of people throughout the world, our sympathies are aroused that otherwise would have remained dormant. We are concerned with the sick and injured now more than before. The aged and feeble are cared for better than ever. We give children more love and attention and are solicitous of their welfare and their education and proper bringing up. Boys going off to war are given the best of training to survive the rigors of warfare; their parents hoping and praying they will come back alive. Our injured soldiers are given the best of medical care. We have established all sorts of organizations that have for their sole object the welfare of our fellow-men. We make laws for their social welfare; erect buildings and establish institutions for many kinds for the benefit of the unfortunate; the handicapped; the mentally retarded; the chronically ill. We try to rehabilitate the criminals among us and we do all we can to prevent delinquency among the youth. We try to assist the poverty stricken to help themselves, and so on and on. As a result of all this suffering brought on by warfare, revolutions, and cruel dictators, the people as a whole are more and more conscious of a Supreme Being and are flocking to the churches and other institutions for comfort and solace and asking themselves where and how they themselves have been negligent; how they can better themselves spiritually, morally and in other ways thereby they are consciously, or unconsciously speeding up their progress, their advancement and evolution along those particular lines.

We are stressing education now more than ever before as an effect of the upheavals, the rapid changes in scientific research and discoveries and in technology in all fields; as a result of new governments being established in the so called backward countries requiring new and better leadership. As a result of the unrest that has sprung from the many recent wars and consequent upheavals in all segments of society, the youth of the world are bestirring as never before demanding attention and calling for improved conditions in governments and the economy and social betterments. They are using their recent found freedoms to express themselves on all phases of social reform. As a result of the better education they are now receiving they have become better thinkers and more intelligent than their elders in many cases. All this is to the good, for the world needs new and better thinking to replace the old, some of whose minds are not in concrete and unable to advance.

The objective of the evolutionary process is the well-rounded man; progress towards betterment intellectually, morally, spiritually, emotionally; advancement toward the ultimate perfected individual. In the normal and slow process, evolution required almost unlimited time to accomplish its purpose, for it is a very slow process. Now, since the time of Kaiser Wilhelm, and others before him, the evolutionary process of change has been considerably speeded up in all fields of human endeavor. This speed up would not have taken place had not the Kaiser of Germany, and others following, sparked it. The world wide changes we have seen and are seeing now, which were all necessary, had to be started by something, or some one high in government who had the authority to start it all. The present series of world wide changes was started in 1914 and has continued since, and it will continue for a time into the future when eventually all the peoples of the world will be completely free to follows their own natural best; to develop their own governments and their own economy and to co-operate peaceably with all the rest of the world in peaceful pursuit of their welfare and happiness. That is the way it is supposed to be, for evolution functions best when there is complete freedom for all individuals.

In the light of the over-all plan that the Ruling Hierarchy of our world has for the people of earth, the killing of millions of human beings is only incidental, although that has serious consequences for us all in the sorrow and suffering it causes. As stated, that sorrow and suffering is an important factor in advancement of our virtues, bringing out the best in us, which is all to the good. For, the passing away of an individual whether naturally, accidentally, or in warfare is not as serious as it seems to be on its surface. The individual himself is not losing anything he is only discarding a physical body. His consciousness, ability to think and cognize remains with him; he merely changes his form of existence from this physical to an immaterial form of his continued existence; to a far better, freer one where his ability to think is enhanced many fold.

To return to my narrative. I longed for a home and a family. Strange to relate, it was not primarily the sex urge for which I wanted a wife, but rather for a home. At the time the home instinct with me was the stronger of the two, which probably was due to ill health depleting my energies. I wanted some one to care for me in illness; some one who would wish to share my fortunes and misfortunes; a home-maker; a loving companion.

Some time before my move to Hustler I happened to meet a girl, a waitress at the Campbell Hotel in Merrillan,

Wisconsin. At the time I was on my way either to or from my folk's home when I stopped to change trains at Merrillan. My sister Martha, also, happened to be there at the time and she introduced me to Miss Sarah Larson who hailed from West Garden Valley, where my mother used to journey at times for companionship among some of her country men and women of by gone days, and also to attend religious services in a Baptist Chapel in that community. Sarah welcomed and encouraged me to call when I could. We went to her folk's home later. My mother had known her folks well.

They had been pioneers in that community and had cleared virgin land of timber and built up a productive farm. We were both the same age; both professed the same religion. I learned to like her. She was raised in a farming community as I was. She was not the 'high-hat' type of girl as some others I had known. She had a good reputation and a good manager of financial affairs. In the course of time I asked her if she would take me, such as I was, for better or worse as a life partner. She agreed to that and said she would try to do the best she knew how for me and I for her.

When I set out for Hustler from Woodville that hot day in August 1914, I had a renewed hope, a stronger faith in the future, regardless of my sickness and the war clouds that hung over Europe. I arrived Hustler August 15th, 1914. I stopped at the only hotel in town that was run by Mrs. Otto C. Smith, whose husband was the hotel bar tender and later employed by the railroad as a section laborer. The next day both the railroad and express auditors came and checked me in at the station. A.R. Chase had been agent there for some time before I came, but he had left for another position and the relief man was there at the time; cannot recall his name. John Moore also had been agent there for many years prior to A. R. Chase when he went to another station.

I found Hustler station to be nice and pleasant; a waiting room; a freight room and the office in between. I grew to like it and the little village. Some good people lived there, a mixture of Scandinavian and German extraction. My hours were 7 AM to 7 PM 7 days a week. My duties, in addition to telegraph and station work were to care for the two switch lights; carry the U.S. Mail between depot and post office for the passenger trains; keep the train order signal light burning; the kerosene lamps in office and waiting room, all lights using kerosene, and keeping the waiting and office floors spick and span. I was proud of my station and tried hard to please my employers.

All the freight for Clifton, which was called an 'island town' those days because it had no railroad, came through my station. Several cars of live stock shipped per week as well as potatoes and grain in carloads forwarded as well as a carload of butter a week; lumber, coal, cement and other building materials received besides a large volume of L.C.L. freight and express. Every two or three days we had a platform truck load of live poultry by express for the Chicago market. Business was very good. My waiting room would be full of passengers twice a day waiting for passenger trains for whom I had sold tickets, both local and interchange.

Jim Wilson, a retired farmer, was a regular caller at the depot for train. Sometimes he carried the sealed pouch of first class mail for me, leaving the heavy sacks of parcel post for me to carry. He enjoyed visiting and talking to the waiting passengers seated on the benches. He was a story teller, most of his stories which ended up with 'Its a long road that has no turn in it!' Sometimes while standing in front of the people, he went through a dance routine solo which most always ended up with his dropping down on the floor and going up and down on his rump, to the delight and amusement of his audience. He was a character, friendly and sociable.

I became friendly with James Freeborn who ran a patent medicine and delicatessen store in town. He and I rented a house owned by Mrs. O.J. Steele for the huge sum of $7.00 per month and we batched it for a while in that house. He was about my age, a friendly and neighborly Irishman whose parents had migrated from Ireland during pioneer days. While we were living there, a big wooden box came for me one day by freight from Merrillan. It contained the 'hope chest' of my wife to be. When I opened it and saw all those women's clothes and articles, it gave me a strange feeling; it cast a sort of 'spell' over me. Jimmie understood when we rented the house together that I was to occupy it with my wife soon after our marriage, to which he agreed. I asked for relief for the Thanksgiving period that year. We had set the wedding date for the day following Thanksgiving, November 21st, 1914.

About that time I joined the Baptist chapel in the community, the church to which my mother had belonged. I did that as a free agent because I felt I should belong to an organization of that sort, more for security and consolation than for any other reason. I do not feel the need for a so called 'salvation'; I could not see what I should be 'saved' from; I was not a criminal or a law breaker, and I had been trying to live a good life as much as I could; I did not feel guilty of anything. It was the stabilizing influence of the church and its moral teachings that I thought would be beneficial to me and my family. I did not think that 'salvation' consisted of being 'saved' from an eternal punishment that was said to be the case if we did not accept it literally as they said it. I thought that would be altogether too drastic for a mere belief or a non-belief. Rather salvation would be a gradual and steady process of improvement of one's self; advancement in morals' in ethics; spiritual awareness of a Supreme Being with Divine Justice; progress towards betterment in intellect, good thinking. That is the only 'salvation' worthwhile, because by so doing we save ourselves from the consequences of our own follies.

Everything was all set for the wedding. We asked Rev. A.R. Klien the Methodist minister from Merrillan to officiate. The ceremony took place in the brides' house. The house was full of guests and relatives and friends. Afterwards, a bountiful repast was served in the evening for all present. It was late when the last one had departed. We remained in the house for the night and next day left for Black River Falls by train from Alma Center, some one taking us in a horse and buggy to the depot and for picture taking by A.J. Roisland. That evening we boarded a train from Black River Falls to Chicago, having reserved a Pullman berth. Thus a new phase of life was begun as others had before us, an experience as old as humanity itself, a response to Nature's call to mate.

"Beloved bride and bridegroom may
Your wedding day be bright,
And may the light of silver stars,
Adorn your wedding night.

There will be disappointments and
There will be little tears,
But they will serve to strengthen you,
Throughout the married years."

--Chapter 8--

After our trip to Chicago and a few other points, we arrived at Hustler to start housekeeping in the Steele house which previously had been furnished. As soon as word got around that a newly married couple had arrived in the house, a crowd of people assembled in front of it in the evening after dark and put on a 'shivaree' for us with noise making gadgets and whooped it up until I came out and gave them some money with which to buy cigars and drinks.

I resumed my work at the depot and we soon got down to the business of living a married life. We had many callers; soon we became acquainted with most everybody in town and several in the country-side. We started to go to the Baptist church; our first Christmas was spent in that church with a Christmas program and a tree decorated with all the trimmings including wax candles. The pastor was an Irish emigrant with the map of Ireland stamped on his face and an Irish brogue that was difficult to decipher. His name was McGorty. 'McGorty, be gory.' He had attended a Bible school in Minneapolis that was founded and run by Dr. W.B. Riley, whom he often mentioned in his sermons. It later became known as the Northwestern Schools.

Julius Mueller was the postmaster with the post office in his store. He was a good business man and in time accumulated a small fortune, but he died a little past his prime and could not enjoy it very much. He had two sons, one of who became cashier in the bank of which Julius Mueller was President. W.W. Smith was the cashier at the time. In later years he met his death in the prime of life together with his girl friend at a railroad crossing. W.F. Talg was the lumber dealer and also bought and shipped potatoes as well as retailer of foods. He was a very tall man as compared to his wife who was so much shorter, a typical 'Mutt and Jeff'. Mr. Talg always came into the office and paid freight bills in cash, at times up to seven hundred dollars and more.

In the fall of 1915 we were to have our first baby and Grandma had agreed to come and assist in the great event. She had officiated many times previously at such events in the role of 'mid-wife', a practice that was common among the pioneers of her time. When I look back now after these many years I am inclined to view the event from a humorous stand-point, although it was not humorous to us at the time. My Mother-in-law was of an altogether different type from my mother. She possessed the necessary ingredients for a true pioneer with her discipline, independence and resourcefulness. There was nothing weak about her and she would not tolerate weakness in any one around her.

Fortunately it was on a Sunday and my day off or most of it. Grandma's orders were not to call the Doctor; she would take care of everything. The excitement started in the forenoon. Towards noon labor pains increased and screams became more frequent. I told her, "I'm going to call the doctor". The old mid-wife said, "no. This is not as bad as it sounds." We closed all the windows and doors so as not to alarm the neighbors. She tried to reassure her daughter who was commencing to become alarmed herself. We all forgot about the noon meal. I should have defied her and called the doctor at the beginning, but she was a woman to be reckoned with; besides her daughter felt confident that her mother could handle the job satisfactorily. At 1:30 PM I could not stand it any longer, and regardless of her, I ran to the depot to telephone Dr. Cron at Camp Douglas to come quick. He was slow in coming with his horse and buggy. The old lady was still adamant and insisted the doctor was not needed and kept saying, "Everything is going to be alright." Well, it turned out all right finally after those terrible hours of labor without any anesthetics, nor other assistance that a doctor would have provided. The Big Boy finally arrived at 2:55 PM October 10th, 1915. After that she ordered me to 'go right back and telephone the doctor not to come; we don't need him now; its all over and under control." I refused. That was when she really got angry. There was a glint of steel in her eyes that I could not ignore. I went outside. The doctor had already tied his horse to a hitching post in front of Talg's house, next door neighbor; we had no post in front of ours. I met him carrying his satchel and tried to explain the situation to him. I must have made a poor impression as he kept right on walking and into the house. The old lady did not dare tell him where to get off at, although she was capable of it, and said nothing. Dr. Crone finished the job and pronounced everything Okay, including the Boy, who was of pretty good size for his age. The doctor charged us $9.00, which he said was half his regular charge for such cases.

One may wonder why the old mid-wife was so insistent on keeping the doctor away. The main reason was her frugality. It went against her second nature to spend money foolishly, and this would be foolish because she was there to avoid the unnecessary expense of a doctor. We were at a loss what to name him, not having had any experience with such matters before. His mother said, "You give him his first name and I'll furnish the second, Ward, in honor of a former employer of mine, owner of a laundry for whom I worked in Minneapolis." I raked my head for an appropriate name. I wanted something heady. I myself had been afflicted with a handle that most people had difficulty in pronouncing and remembering. So, I said to myself, what about Ben, or Benjamin. If that name was to honor anyone, it would be a famous name in our history, or it could be in honor of one of the citizens in town, Ben Tremain, who later became a Member of the State Assembly and held that office for many years from our district. He also got to be a good business man and had accumulated a lot of property during his life time. Mom was agreeable to it, so we duly recorded his name in the records Juneau County at Mauston, Wisconsin as having been born and his name shall henceforth be Benjamin Ward Erickson. What a name! What a Boy! He was a strong, healthy youngster with powerful lungs that he could use effectively.

That is a mere outline of how we brought a new human being into physical existence via the same route that countless others had done before him. At the time we had absolutely no conception nor the true meaning of a human being born among us. Even the mechanics of the thing was vague and difficult to understand. We had no control of the process except to get it started. The Mother who is the incubator of the human race, has nothing whatever to say about it, once the process has commenced. The most learned of the medical scientists are unable to ascertain and state exactly what the actual process is; the power or force which governs it; the timely and accurate construction of the myriad atoms and molecules and particles that go into the different parts of the body to be, forming the different organs and limbs and the many other functional organs and systems of the body.

One of these for example is the marvelous construction of the eye with its power to perceive the pre-existing light. How were the intricate parts of the eye brought to such precision and delicate adjustment as to be able to catch light and pass it through the membrane and cornea, on through the aqueous fluid and the contractile aperture of the pupil, on through the crystalline lens and the vitreous humor to reach the retina? This is a long path taken by light through transparent objects, or organs until it finally reaches the optic nerve in the rear of them, which nerve carries the light to the brain and eventually to the consciousness of man.

Another wonderful example is the ear, with its delicate adjustment of the three semi-circular canals inside the ear, each pointing to one of the three dimensions in space. Logical thought and mathematical ability are in proportion to the accuracy of the adjustment of these semi-circular canals. Musical ability is also dependent upon the same factor; but in addition, the musician required extreme delicacy of the 'Fibres of Corti', of which there are about ten thousand in the human ear, each capable of interpreting about twenty five gradations of tone. In the ears of the majority of people they do not respond to more than from three to ten of possible gradations. Among ordinary musical people the greatest degree of efficiency is about fifteen sounds to each fiber. But the master musician requires a greater range to be able to distinguish the different notes and to detect the slightest discord in the most complicated chords.

Now, does all this merely 'happen' to be? Did it all come about as a result of fortuitous aggregations of atoms: In attempting to answer questions of this sort, it is necessary, I think, that we consider how human beings bring about their own factual miracles of creation. They do not just 'happen', nor come into being by themselves. They required first the minds of men to design them. then to manufacture them out of the materials that were produced by Mother Earth. The human mind is the creating factor; the Entity that creates, controls and uses them. If we give serious thought to what the human mind is composed of, we must necessarily conclude that it is a 'Spiritual Entity'. Certainly it is not a physical one.

Accordingly, we must likewise conclude that the mysterious force, or power that science cannot 'put their finger' on that designs and created the human body with its intricate organisms must necessarily be intelligent Entities that are invisible to us and which function from a higher plane, just as our minds think and function from a higher plane that is different and above the physical. These intelligent Creators have in their charge the process of reproduction, the assembling of the many different particles of materials that are necessary for the purpose, creating the many different intricate organs and placing them in their proper locations, all on a schedule of perfect timing. These Creative Entities use the laws of nature that apply, such as that of heredity; of genetics; evolution and others.

The Spanish-American war occurred during the very early years of my life; I was too young to remember much about it, but I do recall that at school whenever a coward showed up by refusing to protect himself in a fist fight, he was called a 'Spaniard', which at the time meant 'coward'. In 1914 when the First World War commenced, that was my first experience in reading and hearing about a war. I thought it was a terrible thing; that so called Christian nations and their people could kill each other wholesale as they did. President Wilson had been elected in 1912, and if I recall correctly, I had voted for him in Woodville. When the war started, he urged all Americans to be neutral by issuing large posters and newspaper ads and articles asking us to be calm and not to take sides in the conflict. He was determined to keep this country out of the war, and he succeeded up to a certain point.

In the 1916 national election, Woodrow Wilson ran for re-election on his record as having kept us out of the war. Charles Evans Hughes opposed him on the Republican ticket, and on election night, on the basis of returns that evening, Hughes seemed to be the sure winner. But next morning when more complete returns

155

were received from California, Wilson was the winner. Hughes was an 'isolationist' and appealed to the voters on that basis, but that did not seem to be sufficient for the voters in the western part of the United States. It was not long after Wilson was inaugurated that trouble started for us. Germany was getting bolder in her attacks; a German submarine sank one of our passenger boats, claiming it carried contraband for her enemies contrary to international law. American public opinion became inflamed, including members of congress. A few of them remained cool, such as Sen. R.M. Lafollette of Wisconsin and a 'hand-full' of others. But the majority of congress members were not disposed to remain cool; they wanted to throw neutrality out the window, and soon declared war on Germany. It remained for President Wilson to sign the war declaration, or not to do it. It was in his power to plunge the U.S. into war, or not to do so. He chose to sign. History changed its course as a result of that signing as far as we were concerned, and also probably the whole of Europe. That was the end of our traditional isolationism as it was inaugurated by President Washington. We have been engaged in European conflicts ever since.

Destiny can be seen at times to take a hand in Human events and to shape our course, rough hew them how we will. Men, being short-sighted, can see no farther than his present generation, but actions and their peoples are only pawns in the hands of Destiny, moving and manipulating them as a great chess player does. "It is all a chequer-board of nights and days, Where Destiny with man for pieces play; Hither and thither moves and mates and plays, And one by one back in the closet days."

I was drafted for war service together with hundreds of other young men in our county of Juneau. I was ordered to appear before the draft board at Mauston, Wisconsin and on January 22nd, 1918 I was placed in class 4, a deferment because I was employed by a railroad, and also because I was married with a family. I was not called for army service after that, but I did my part of the work of the war in the handling of traffic for the war department; troop trains almost daily over the main line through Hustler and extra freight trains hauling war materials. The railroads were the back-bone of the war effort, no other means of transportation being available for the purpose.

Feelings ran high in our community because of the war. Individuals took sides one way or another. There were quite a few of German nationality living in and around the town, but most of them were loyal Americans. There were some who took advantage of the situation to vent their dislike on certain of their neighbors by under-handed methods. One man in particular was the target of unthinking, ill-advised individuals by painting one of his buildings with yellow stripes, denoting disloyalty to the United States government. Such tactics intensified hard feeling.

President Wilson ordered his Secretary of the Treasury, William Gibbs McAdoo to take over all the railroads of the country in the name of the Government under authority of the Congress granted for the purpose. From then on they were operated under the name of the "U.S. Railroad Administration" with W.B. McAdoo the Railroad Administrator. His very first act was to raise the wages of the railroad employees after a survey by a committee. My own salary was boosted from $60.00 per month to $70.00 and later on to $91.65 per month. That was the greatest single event that had ever happened to railroad men up to that time. It was the beginning of a progressive advance towards higher wages and better standards of employment for railroad men. It was not long after that when the 8 hour day became the law of the land for railroad employees under the Adamson Act. Over time pay came a few years later. Time was marching on!

F.E. Nicolas was Division Superintendent of our division'. G.F. Boutlette replaced J.J. Prentice as Chief Train Dispatcher. J.J. Prentice went to Spooner as Assistant Division Superintendent. Practically all railroad officers were chosen from the ranks of the Agent-Telegraph craft. Telegraphers seemed to have an inside track to those higher positions because of the nature of their work, being in the center of operations. He knew what was going on over the entire division by listening to the telegraph wires and what was said over them. The best of them were chosen for dispatchers, the cream of the crop and from there on to the higher positions. I myself was not aiming to anything more than being an Agent-Telegrapher at a local station; I was perfectly content as such. I felt out of place among a group of railroad officials.

Those days there was a telegraph office in a small shack just south of the tunnel between Hustler and Elroy where three telegraphers worked 8 hour shifts. One was John S. Johnson; another Selmer Myron; Kiley; others whose names I cannot recall. They were all young fellows and boarded with farmers nearby except Johnson who owned a farm near there and had a family, a daughter who married Kiley, who later became a train dispatcher at Eau Claire. There were also one or more tunnel walkers whose duties were to walk through the tunnel just before each train was due to inspect it. I recall one of them was a one armed man. The office was called 'Tunnel', office call 'X'. It was abolished a few years later, as were the walkers as being unnecessary. Camp Douglas on the other side of me had a tower at the juncture of the Omaha and Milwaukee Railroads that controlled train movements by interlocking signals operated by hand; three men on duty. The depot was on other side of tracks where C.J.Phelps was agent as well as a freight house. It was a very busy and important station. The Western Union installed a wire power boosting office at 'CD; to amplify, or increase electric power over their numerous wires going through

158

there, which since has been abolished. I think that Tunnel had been used prior to 1914 as a block office for blocking trains manually, as we had at 'WD', Woodville, and elsewhere. My office call at Hustler was 'TR'.

One time the way freight conductor asked me to get some information for him from Elroy 'RG'. The dispatcher was busy; I tried to break in on his wire but he chased me off as he had more important work to do at the time. The conductor was impatient, so I grounded the dispatcher's wire (that seemed to be the only wire we could RG on) and called him for the information and gave it to the conductor, who then left at once. The dispatcher could feel his wire was weaker and he knew at once it was me who had cut his power off south of my office. (Some of it came from batteries at Elroy RG) He was calling me when I cut back in. When I answered, he wanted to know what business I had to ground his wire and cut off the 'juice'. I told him that I did it to find out something from RG for the way freight, and that I got the train moving by so doing. That satisfied him; his only concern was to move trains and I helped him do that in this case.

During the war all agents were ordered to go to St. Paul for an agent's meeting regarding problems incident to the war business, which was enormous. I cannot recall, but I must have closed my office for a couple days, as there were hardly any relief men. After I got on the train, two other agents I knew from Valley Junction and Warrens got on and the three of us stuck together from then on, except for the banquet after the meeting, somehow they placed me in the line far behind the other two I was with. The result was that I ended up sitting next to H.R. Grochau, the freight claim agent, and across from him was a general freight agent from Omaha Nebraska. The two of them talked about claims and law suits that ran into the thousands of dollars. That was big talk to me, a mere local agent. After a while we got acquainted and I went through the banquet without any casualties. They were human, just as I was. Many years later I read of Mr. Grochau's death and that he was a millionaire at the time as a result of some fortunate investments while a young man. He had reached age 90 at his passing. A.M. Fenton was the General Freight Traffic Manager for the company and he conducted the meeting. I recall that F.R. Pechin, General Superintendent gave a short speech as did A.W. Trenholm, the general manager. But most of the talking was done by the agents, and there were hundreds of them. Mr. Fenton as M.C. kept order. Some agents took advantage of the meeting to vent their pet peeves. Fortunately they were very few and were cut as short as possible by Mr. Fenton, who was a first class M.C.

I wanted to try to increase my income some way besides my railroad wages. Jimmie Freeborn who had batched it with me in our rented house, offered to sell us his business, a patent medicine and delicatessen store, as he planned to go to a telegraph school and learn telegraphy. So on Aug. 22nd, 1916 we bought him out for $550.00. Soon after we moved out of the house and into the rear room of the store so as to be there handy to wait on customers. We needed an additional counter in the store to display our wares and I asked my Dad to come and make one for us, which he did. When he completed it, it turned out to be a very fine piece of cabinet work; he was an expert at that kind of carpentry.

Ben, who was less than a year when we moved in, ran all over the place. There was an old gentleman who wore a stub beard and who came in to buy something almost every day, had a lot of fun with the little fellow, as they chased each other around the counters. W.W. Smith, cashier at the bank, also, used to come in every morning and bought a cigar, and he also paid attention to him. On dance nights, which was once a week, we had to remain open until after midnight to serve lunches and coffee. Some of the customers abused their credit privileges and were difficult to collect from. The extra work got to be almost too much for us, and after a couple years of it, we decided to close out the stock. Hattie Maddox Roddy, who operated a drug store at Camp Douglas, bought much of the medicines for her own store. She was the sister of W.R. Maddox, depot agent at Black River Falls. When our stock was down to a small amount, we moved across the street to a building that stood on the site where the present old people's home now is located. The stock we had left was displayed in the front part of it, which had been a store some years previously, and in time sold it all. We moved into the rear of the building and upstairs, and lived there until we moved from Hustler. Later on we sub-let the rear part and lived in the front and upstairs.

We dabbled in real estate during the 1917-1919 period when prices were on the rise. We bought and sold two farms in Polk County at nice profits. We dealt with A.B. Weaner, a real estate dealer in Milltown, Wisconsin. With our profits and savings we bought a small farm near Alma Center in the North Branch community, which turned out to be a bad mistake. Inflation prices then in full force absorbed our savings and profits. If we had been more shrewd investment-wise, we would have bought U.S. Government Liberty Bonds instead, which kept increasing in value in spite of good or hard times. Hind-sight is better than foresight. A small recession set in during 1921, but the real big one finally came in 1929 when prices on everything skidded until the bottom was reached. We finally sold the farm in trade for a house in Merrillan.

Some time after we had disposed of the store stock and fixtures, and while we were living in the store building where the old peoples home now stand, another offspring was due to arrive in our household. This time we would not take chances and engaged Dr. Cron to come when called. By this time he owned an automobile and could come in a hurry. We had Mrs. W.F. Talg as assistant instead of Grandma. This time we were not so excited, having had previous experience in such a matter. So the time finally came for the birth of another human being, a natural process that is as old as humanity itself. It was on a week-day when I was on duty most of the day, but I found time to make several hurried trips home. We called Dr. Cron early in the forenoon, and he made things easy for the mother and the rest of us. A Big Boy was born 11:35 AM January 25th, 19/19, and I was there at the time. The doctor did a good job and everything went fine. He picked him up and shook him and made sure he could breathe and scream. Mrs. Talg was a great help and did everything the Doctor ordered her to do; she was co-operative, very kind and considerate. The Big Boy was fat and heavy. This time we had no difficulty settling on a name, Raymond Arvid Erickson.

When Ray had reached adulthood he came into possession of a letter I had written to Dr. Cron protesting his charge of $18.00 for his services in connection with this birth. Mother and I thought the charge was too high and told him so in the letter, but he would not reduce it and we paid him the full amount finally. Ray had made a joke of the fact that we thought he was not worth $18.00, but of course he was; we merely were trying to keep our expenses down to a reasonable amount.

It was in a room upstairs where he was born, and many years later when we stopped off at Hustler we went into the hotel for a visit and I pointed out to Ray the approximate spot, which was in the hotel lobby, where the great event took place. Mr. Talg, the lumber dealer in town, had bought the old store building and tore it down and erected a hotel on the same site. Ray was attending the university at the time of our stopping off there to see the place. The location where the room had been in the old building was about six feet from the floor up in the lobby, or office of the new one. In later years the Talgs sold the hotel building to the Lutheran Church who converted it into an old peoples home, which it still is.

On the morning of October 28th, 1920, when I opened the depot and went into the office, I saw at once that something was wrong. A window pane in front window was broken and a package of express had been opened. Also the gum machine in the waiting room had been jammed open and the pennies taken. I was not surprised at this because the day before two valuable shipments came by express, one from Madison and the other from Baraboo with C.O.D.s running into several hundred dollars; both shipments of four packages addressed to John Smith, Hustler, Wisconsin General delivery. After I had given my receipts for the values to the train messenger, it was up to me to see to their protection because of their high value. I took the packages into the office at once. I tried to locate the party to whom addressed without results. No one knew John Smith. The postmaster had no knowledge of such a person. When it came time to lock up and go home, I felt that I could not leave those packages in plain sight without protection of some kind. So I took down the ladder that always hung on the depot wall outside, brought it into the freight room and up leading to the attic above the office. I took the four packages up there and placed them between the rafters where it was dark and where no one could possibly see them, or think would be there. When I discovered next morning that the office had been broken into, I hurriedly replaced the ladder to the attic; climbed up and found the packages intact; no one had discovered their hiding place. I felt elated at my success in outwitting the burglars. I wired the express auditor at Eau Claire and he answered to ship the packages back to the shippers, which I did on the afternoon local. In a few days I received a letter from E.E. Westfall, Superintendent American Express Company Milwaukee commending me for my prompt action in protecting the company's interest and for fooling the burglars.

The following day the auditor came and collected all the information he could and copies of my records in the case, which were turned over to their detective force who soon had a good description of the man from the sales clerks at Madison and Baraboo who had waited on them. The packages contained expensive clothing for men. Eventually they were tracked down, arrested and given jail terms. If I had been smarter than I was, we could easily have caught the burglars in the act if I had called the sheriff at Mauston that day and the two of would have lain in wait for them in the depot.

One day I received a letter by U.S. mail that contained $3.00 in bills with a notation 'from the debtor, unsigned. I forwarded the money to our local treasurer at St. Paul who credited it to the 'conscience fund'.

As our first son grew older and bigger, he would come to the depot, which was only a little ways from where we lived, and spend time playing there and in the stock yards, which seemed to fascinate him with all the live stock in pens, especially on stock shipping days. One summer day, when it was warm enough for him to run barefoot, he limped to the open window of the office and screamed for all he was worth. I found that he had stepped on a nail in a loose board, the wound showing in the bottom of his foot. I applied first aid. That was his first lesson to keep away from boards with nails in them.

One morning when I came to work I learned that No. 18, fast mail and express train from Minneapolis to Chicago had run head on into a man standing on the track in front of the depot around midnight. The locomotive hit him and tossed his body to one side, killing him instantly. The train stopped, backed up and the crew found it near the fence of the right-of-way. After notifying the marshal of the village, Melvin Peckham, the train proceeded. He was a young man and later it was learned he had attended the dance in the village hall that night and had been jilted by his girl friend. It appeared that he could not take it as he walked to the depot, waited for the train's head-light, and just as it reached the crossing near the depot, he stepped in front of it when it was impossible for the engineer to stop at such a short distance. It was ruled a suicide by the county coroner. Foolish young man~

Another time the local passenger train from the south in the forenoon brought a passenger who looked different from most men. He was a big man physically and his mouth held a pipe with a long, curved stem and smoke was issuing from it like a smoke stack. He came into the office and chatted with me. He turned out to be W.H.H. Cash. President of Hillsboro and Northeastern Railroad, a short line from Union Center to Hillsboro, Wisconsin. He stated that he was on his way to Mauston, the county seat on business and some one was to meet him and take him to Mauston, probably by horse and buggy, I cannot recall. He was a sociable man and kept talking to me with twinkles in his eyes. He pulled out and showed me a bulky book of passes from many different railroads in his name. He stated, with a grin on his face, "The joke is on all those railroad presidents when we exchange passes; I can travel thousands of miles on theirs, while they can go only 5 miles on mine." Later he repeated his classic remark, to me, "My railroad may not be a long as theirs, but by golly it is just as wide". That remark has been attributed to him as its origin, and it has been told and retold many times; heard it myself several times. In later years when I saw and became acquainted with F.S. Seymour, President of the GB&W RR., he reminded me of W.H.H. Cash, President of the HANE RR. Both men were of the same build, heavy set and wore wide brimmed hats and quite handsome in each their own way. But I never saw Mr. Seymour smoke, whereas Mr. Cash always had that long curved stemmer between his teeth. Temperamentally, they were far apart. Mr. Cash seemed to be genial, good-natured, friendly and of a laughing disposition, while Mr. Seymour was stern, critical, suspicious, and on occasion when he found one of his men had failed in their duties, could be very harsh with him and bawl him out to 'a fare-thee-well'.

165

Another old gentleman, a good patron of the railroad, was also a character in his own personal way, Ole E. Moe of Clifton, an inland town to Hustler. He was the saloon keeper at Clifton had received all his beer at my station. One January day a large shipment of beer in wooden kegs and in cases came for him and it was up to me to protect it from freezing, so I carried all the cases into the waiting room where it was warm, January temperature outside was below freezing, probably below zero that night. I thought surely beer would not freeze in those kegs, so left them in the freight room without heat. But it turned out I was badly mistaken. When Ole came for his beer, he could see at once that the beer in the kegs was frozen and I had to note the freight bill to that effect. I, also, had to make a bad order report to the freight claim agent that it had frozen while in the freight room without heat. He came right back at me with the remark, "What, leave beer in a cold room in January temperature?" But Ole reassured me that he could thaw it out; that I should not worry and that there would be no claim, and there never was in this case. Mr. Moe was a kind-hearted gentleman and would do almost anything not to offend any one. He was always sociable and never complained about anything. Mr. & Mrs. Moe had 5 sons one of whom was Edward Moe in the general store business in Clifton and who did a lot of business with us, both freight and express. They used a team and wagon for hauling their goods and produce. Once a week Ed Moe brought a wagon load of live poultry in crates for shipment to Chicago and Milwaukee, by express. He was a very good business man and well liked.

Pete Strand was the laziest conductor I have ever known. All he did was to stand on the platform with his hands in his pockets and watch the rest of us work. He would not even run a wheeled hand truck to haul the freight into the freight house, nor the checking. I checked the way bills as freight was unloaded. Pete only talked while we worked. I learned later that he had passed on prematurely as a result of a weak heart.

On the other hand, Julius Sontag, the opposite way freight conductor, always did his share of the work by wheeling the freight from way car to freight house over the plank platform that extended from car door to house door. The house floor and car floors were on the same level permitting use of the special plank for that purpose. There were two Sontags, brothers, one a passenger conductor, the other the freight conductor. Both were real gentlemen, courteous and friendly and did their best in the performance of their duties. Some years later as I visited my uncle and aunt's graves in the cemetery at Neillsville, I noted grave markers with the names of both Julius Sontag and W.D. Sontag; they had completed their final runs.

We attended and supported the Baptist church in Hustler. It was a prosperous and popular church at the time, although its membership was not large. Rev. McGorty conducted the services on Sundays, coming over from New Lisbon where he also had a church to serve. Later he was called elsewhere, which left both his churches without a Pastor. During that period, the members put on entertainment features in the church with local talent on Sunday evenings, but kept on with Sunday School in the mornings. One Sunday while visiting in Garden Valley I became acquainted with two young preachers who held meetings wherever they could, and all of us understood them to be Baptists; they did not deny it. I thought it would be a good idea for them to come to Hustler and conduct meetings while we were waiting for another Pastor. They were more than willing to do so. We took them into our house for room and board free. It seemed to be satisfactory to the members to let them preach in their church because they understood them to be Baptists. Their names were Amos Smith from

Dawnsville, Wisconsin and Peter Hanson from Sweden. They were traveling preachers.

Hanson was a good, persuasive speaker and drew capacity crowds. After about two weeks, they showed their true colors when they persuaded half the membership to withdraw and form another sect with him. Towards the last of his meetings, he had nothing good to say about the Baptists and other church organizations, claiming they were all 'man made', etc. The final and net result was that the little Baptist church received its deathblow; it never recovered and was forced to liquidate and to sell the building to the Lutherans, who started to use it for their Sunday School Service. The new sect that was formed, pretty much the same as the Baptists, also in time ceased to exist, so that nothing good was accomplished by the split up. On the contrary, hard feelings and discord resulted, which certainly did not promote the Kingdom of God, as gospel preachers are supposed to do. I am sorry to state that my three brothers and three sisters belonged to this denomination which has a few branches in a few places; but they do not call themselves a denomination, nor a sect; no name whatever. Only Anna May and myself remained Baptists, although we never claimed to be good Baptists. Since then, I have always felt that I was partly to blame for the split-up because I invited them in the first place and kept them in my house. The incident is now closed, except for the record. "Man's inhumanity to men, makes countless millions mourn." Even in the religious world.

--Chapter 9--

We still owned the farm near Alma Center and it was a great temptation to move onto it. We discussed it pro and con and finally decided to try it. That was our first bad mistake. Second mistake was my resigning from the railroad instead of taking a leave of absence. I wrote out my resignation on March 1st, 1921, but the management did not act or would not relieve me until latter part of May. In June 1921 we left Hustler and the job I loved so well. bull-headed stubbornness! So we moved our goods and two little boys from their birth place. We should have considered their welfare rather than our own selfish interests. I loved my family, but selfishness in too many cases takes precedence over love.

I found it very difficult to accustom myself to farm work. My muscles were soft and became sore; my hands and wrists swelled up from the unaccustomed strain on them; my stomach and bowels went out of order and I became ill again. But I stuck to it as long as I could take it, which was not long. Our money ran out getting started on the farm. I was commencing to see our mistake. Another baby was due to arrive. Hilman Neil was born Aug. 12th, 1921. He was frail and puny from the start, due to the extra physical work on the farm Mother had to do during the later months of pregnancy. On Sept. 2nd, 1921 in the afternoon while I was working in the field, the little one expired from convulsions, probably brought on by stomach troubles. Bitterness and grief! Bitter at our folly for what we had done, and grief at losing such a beautiful and well formed baby boy! All this would not have happened if we had remained at Hustler and on the railroad, where I belonged. Another Soul had attempted to live in physical life and benefited there from and failed because of the stupidity of its parents. Many thoughtful people think and believe that the same Soul, or Ego returns again to the same family to be born into physical existence in mother body. I rather think so too.

In July of 1921 we came very near to losing Raymond also. He was under two years of age at the time. He was playing all by himself in the yard, poking into everything, as small boys are wont to do. When I saw him that warm July afternoon, he was sitting on the ground all covered with blood. When I picked him up I could not find a thing wrong with him except that his clothes were bloody and his face and hands caked with dried blood. To find out what was wrong, or where he had been injured, I stripped off his clothes and placed him under the pump and pumped water over him and washed him clean but still I could not find any injuries. Mother brought a quilt which I wrapped around him and carried him inside and laid him on the bed. It was then that I noticed a swelling on the wrist of his right hand. The swelling was right over the pulse and on closer examination, I saw a small hole in the skin where the pulse was located. We concluded that he had been playing with pieces of broken glass and one of them punctured the skin through to the main artery which caused him to almost bleed to death. He was pale and weak when I laid him down on the bed. But he was a strong, healthy and chunky boy and the recuperative powers of nature came to the rescue and stopped the flow of blood through the puncture and saved him. We kept him in bed for a couple of days and fed him well, after which he was a good as new again. Close call! We were being penalized for our stupidity.

After we had buried Hilman Neil in the West Garden Valley cemetery, both Mother and I became disgusted with life on the farm. The checks we were receiving from the North Branch cheese factory were practically nothing as compared with those we received from the railroad. Things were not going as we had hoped, although I thought we could make a go of it in the long run. I was tempted to resume work on the railroad again at the job for which I was best fitted and experienced. So we decided I should apply for employment for that fall and winter and then go back on the farm in the spring but things did not turn out that way.

Railroading really was my life's work, which I could readily see then. An inner voice whispered to me to get off the farm, and quick before anything more serious happened to us! We had paid plenty for our mistakes and did not wish for any more of the same. If I had been on an extended leave of absence as I should have, then I could have gone back to my job at Hustler. I thought the Green Bay & Western would be the most convenient for me, inasmuch as I planned to return to the farm for the next summer. But 'the best laid plans of mice and men, go oft astray', which they certainly had so far for us.

One evening in the latter part of October 1921 I wrote a note to the chief train dispatcher at Green Bay giving him my previous experience and wondered if he needed an agent-telegrapher on his line. I did not know his name at the time, but later learned it was H. C. Erbe. As soon as Mr. Erbe received my note, he called R.J. McDonough at Alma Center on the wire and told him to get in touch with me at once and come to the depot so he could talk to me on the wire. Having no phone, he called our neighbor Otto Kutz, who came over and told me that I should go to Alma Center depot right away as Green Bay wanted to talk to me. I was surprised at such a quick response to my note, at the same time elated, for now I would have a good excuse to leave the farm. Mother, also, was glad, for she could see by now that I was not cut out for farming. We had learned the hard way our bitter lesson.

Next day I 'hitch-hiked' to Alma Center. Mac told me many years later that he could never forget the day I walked into his office. I called 'N' and told H.C.E. who I was. He asked some questions and we talked back and forth like veteran telegraphers. He said he did not want inexperienced 'hams', but experienced men who were good on the wire. He could see I sent good Morse and could read him easily, although he sent fast and furious. It was good to be back on the wire again. 'The sweetest music in this world to me, is the musical click of the telegraph key.' Mr. Erbe never used a 'bug' in all his telegraphing days. His 'fist' was as good as any 'bug'. I did not use one either until many years later I happened to get a vibroplex. Finally Mr. Erbe, (RB as he signed himself) said he wanted a man at a certain station as soon as possible; that I should come to Green Bay to fill out application blanks and get posted on accounting procedure and etc. So he sent me a wire pass to use on the next train the following day.

When I came home Mother was glad for me as well as herself that I was going back to my first 'love', the railroad. The next day, with my suit case of personal effects and my pass, I was on my way; away from the place where we had lost a boy and almost another; away from the farm were I did not belong and where happiness for us could not be had. As I left, I vowed that I would never return, and I never did. But I surely hated to leave my family, who were dearer to me than I had realized before. I promised myself that we would be reunited again in the near future in a better home and a more suitable environment. Henceforth my thoughts and labors would be for them only; for the family for whom I was responsible.

When I arrived Green Bay I went at once to the dispatcher's office on the second floor in the general office building. I found Mr. Erbe middle-aged and a man of few words. He was the chief and did all the dispatching from 8 AM to 4 PM with a side wired man named A.G. Elsner. J.P. Grimes, an old timer was on second from 4 PM to midnight. There was no dispatcher on duty from midnight to 8 AM at the time. After filling out application blanks and getting acquainted with the general auditor J.C. Thurman and getting posted on the duties required of me and receiving instructions form L.P. Wohlfeil the traveling auditor, I took a room at a hotel that evening.

The next day, October 29th, 1921, I and L.P. Wohlfeil and the express auditor from Green Bay boarded passenger train no. 1 for Scandinavia, Wisconsin. When we got off the train, the agent, L.L. Larson presumably was surprised when we walked into the office, but he did not show it and said nothing. Both auditors started in at once checking the cash, books and accounts. He may have expected it, too, as he was in financial difficulties with the companies, and he knew it. He was just a young man and irresponsible. He was checked out and I was checked in that day. One man's loss was another man's gain; thus are the fortunes of life.

I put my whole heart and energies into that job. I wanted badly to make good. I wished to make sure the company officers would not be sorry that they took me on. I certainly appreciated the fact that I was back in the old harness again doing what I had trained myself to do. I went out of my way many times to accommodate our patrons and the company. I studied every phase of my job and did all I could to achieve more efficiency in the conduct of the company's business and operation of trains. I found that such efforts paid off well for myself and our patrons. For the management as well as the dispatcher could see at once that I was more than willing to do my share in the company's interest; none of them ever reprimanded me; they had no occasion to do so.

Scandinavia was a very important station on the Green Bay & Western at that time, being a junction point for two branch lines, one to Waupaca and another to Iola. We hauled everything and had a monopoly on it, passengers, freight carloads and less than car loads, express, U.S. mail, both received and forwarded. We had no competitors. I did all the Western Union wire work for Iola and Scandinavia. I recorded arrival and departure of all branch trains which was sent to the dispatcher. I checked all the L.C.L. freight for both Waupaca and Iola and Scandinavia while men unloaded it and called them off to me.. I handled train orders for almost every train on the main line, there being many trains for which the dispatcher had to figure meeting points. Trains were shorter and more numerous those days due to limited motive power as compared to present day trains. When the branch crews had to cross over the main line tracks to do their switching, it was my duty to give them information about the main line trains and when to expect them. I always had it for them, which they appreciated.

One day the drayman for Scandinavia checked short one sack of sugar for one of our patrons and I had to mark it short on the freight bill and make a short report to Green Bay; I could not dispute him as he gave me the chance to count them myself on his dray wagon, or truck. Next day C.L. Booth agent Iola who was also conductor on the Iola branch train, found our sack, made a regular over way bill for it and brought it back to Scandinavia. The difficulty was that I had checked it off on the original way bill which had been sent in to the auditor's offices and when I made a short report of it, the two did not jibe. I still had the over way bill in my office when one morning F.B. Seymour came on No.1 and strode in with an evil glare on his face. He pulled a file of papers from his pocket, showed them to me and asked me to explain. They were the original way bill for the sugar and my short report for one sack, the way bill not carrying a short notation as

174

required in shortages. As he showed the evidence to me, he glared and was about to accuse me of stealing a sack of sugar when I said to him, "Mr. Seymour, the sack really was short because here is the over way bill for it from Iola; they found it there, brought it back and we delivered it to consignee." When he examined my evidence he muttered something, put his papers back in his pocket and walked out without saying another word to me. I could not help thinking at the time that he felt relieved that I had been able to clear myself so easily.

F.B.S. really had a good heart under his rough exterior, but woe to the man who tried to put anything over on him or his company! He was promoted to the presidency of the railroad in later years; J.A. Jordan was president at the time, while Mr. Seymour was general manager. He was a pioneer railroad man of the old school. He had grown up with the Green Bay and Western which originally had been chartered as the Green Bay and Lake Pepin railroad for whom he worked as a water boy while it was being constructed. He was about 14 at the time. The line was finally completed to Winona Minn. in 1873 and on January 1st, 1874 the first passenger train was operated form Green Bay to Winona with F.B. Seymour as conductor, having been promoted to the job of passenger conductor a year or two previously. He was born in 1856 so that he was only 18 when he made the original initial run.

Beautiful Trempealeau Valley which had slumbered peacefully from time immemorial without benefit of human civilization, was rudely awakened one day by a black monster belching smoke and steam what had been made by men as it was speeding through the middle of the valley on two ribbons of steel. It was an insult to the Gods who had created this fertile valley with its land sloping gently to the hills on both sides of a river that had drained it for unnumbered centuries. Man had moved into it with his railroad, his machines and institutions which always follow the pioneers; men and women who were destined to start the march of progress towards the accomplishment of the command "to have domination over the earth and to make increase of the inhabitants thereof." The Gods were at last turning the valley over to human beings and they decreed that henceforth they would be solely responsible for it.

But it would seem that they would not give up the struggle to relinquish it without a humiliating incident to man and his machines; for the train carrying prominent guests in charge of F. B. Seymour as conductor was speeding merrily along the new rails through the valley until it reached a point one mile west of Independence, Wisconsin when it unceremonially left the rails and landed in the ditch to the dismay of Mr. Seymour and his passengers. As he himself told about it, "I handled the job with such charming success that I landed on top of the right of way fence."

F. B. Seymour was a fine looking man, dark and well built. In later years he became famous with every one along the line for his black sombrero and distinguished mustache. Every one who knew him either feared or loved him. While he was general manager and president of the railroad, his word was law among his employees. Every detail of the operation of the railroad was in his mind; none escaped him. He ruled by hand written notes; he scorned secretaries and type written letters. While he was president I have seen him lay down on the station platform full length in order to inspect and observe the under side of the train passing, something no other president would stoop to do. Even a conductor did not do that, but inspected passing trains standing up. His addiction to details was amazing and he tried to instill like concern in his men for the railroad's interests. Any violation coming to his attention on the part of any employee would be summarily dealt with by F. B. Seymour himself; woe to the man who could not defend himself!

There are in circulation many stories about him. I have in my possession a card that he sent me and others on the date of his 80th birthday with his picture on it and the following notation: "F. B. Seymour 10-3-1856-1936. Do not let the hinges of friendship get rusty." He passed on May 6th, 1939 at age 83. I like to think of him as a human being, just as the rest of us with our undesirable and desirable traits. He had been brought up in a strict pioneer family whose parents instilled in him qualities of frugality, self reliance, independence and devotion to duty. He could be called a 'self-made man' by our standards, not having received much of an education except what he learned in the hard school of experience. He went to work very early in life and eventually reached the top of his vocation, and in the process accumulated a sizeable fortune in money and property. Stern and robust qualities of character are required for such accomplishments. The last chat I had with Mr. Seymour was in his private car spotted on the house track at Whitehall over night. I received a message for him and went to deliver it to him personally. It was just before the new management took over, probably 1933. He was sitting in his upholstered chair in the rear observation section of his car 500. He was not spry any more; it bothered him to walk, so he sat there and let others walk for him. After reading his message, he spoke to me in a pessimistic tone of the condition of affairs in the world, especially those of the railroads. We had been at the time and were passing through difficult times due to the great depression that started in 1929 and the financial panic it entailed. He complained bitterly about the trucks that were commencing to make inroads on the business and traffic belonging to the railroads. He asked, "What will become of them? What is the old world heading for? Will our new president (F.D.R.) be able to do anything about it all, etc., etc.,?" I could do nothing but to remain quiet and let him talk, but I did say a few words to him about the future prospects of our county;

that conditions will change for the better; it always had in the past and will in the future and that the railroads will readjust to the changing conditions and continue to serve and again be prosperous in future time. Mr. Seymour had just about reached the end of his railroad career, for some time later a new and younger president was elected by the board of directors; new and younger managers took over; the oldsters were retired to their 'rocking chairs.'

F. B. Seymour had a brother John J. Seymour, a passenger conductor. I like to relate an incident in connection with him that shows their inner nature, the deep feelings which at times came to light from under the stern exterior. C. R. Van Horn, who had been agent at Whitehall in earlier times, was confined to his home with an affliction that paralyzed his whole body and rendered him helpless. His mother also was sick and unable to move much; both were on their 'last lap' in the struggles of life. People in town were assisting them financially and other ways. When J. J. Seymour found out about the condition they were in, he circulated a petition among railroad men asking for donations. Every one made contributions; even President Seymour and his company made sizable contributions. A long list of names with money was collected that totaled to a considerable amount, all of it from railroad men. When it was completed, John Seymour held his train up at Whitehall one day and asked me to take him in my car to Van Horn's home. I did so while the passengers on the train waited patiently. When we went into the house and John saw the condition they were in, and presented the petition and money to V. R. Van Horn, he actually broke down and cried. After regaining control of himself, he apologized for his display of weakness, extended his sympathetic well wishes and left. On the way back he kept talking about them and their condition and how bad he felt about it. I record this incident as being a fine gesture of love and sympathy for a fellow man in distress, and of the finer more noble nature of two brothers who covered up their deeper feelings with a disguise of a rugged exterior.

I had rented a room upstairs at Nelson's house in Scandinavia and was eating at a restaurant. I was lonesome without my family. I spent some evenings in the depot reading books borrowed from a small library in town. In December I secured a pass for Mom and the boys to come to Scandinavia for the holidays. I will never forget the evening they came on the mixed freight and passenger train. Ray, who was one year and 11 months old at the time, was the first to come into the office with me, when he got down on his hands and knees and spread out pieces of a picture puzzle some one had given him for Christmas and went to work laboriously putting them together, and while doing so, kept talking to me the few words he could say. How proud he was when he had completed and showed it to me! I surely was glad to see them again. We spent Christmas in my room and also at Lutheran Church programs and in the restaurant. Happy days were with us again.

But it was not for long as Mother had to go back to the farm and take care of things after the holidays. The two boys, of course, had to go with her. Early in the spring of 1922 she had an auction and everything was sold except the farm. In the mean time I had rented an apartment upstairs above the restaurant where I ate. After all had been settled on the farm, they came back to Scandinavia with what house-hold goods we had left and we all moved into the apartment. That was April 1922. We were all together again, and no one was happier than myself, unless it was the two boys. Ben was 6 and Ray 2 years old. Ben started school at once, a much better school than the one in North Branch where he attended for a short time.

But we did not remain in the upstairs apartment very long as it was too inconvenient for all of us, especially for Ray who had to run outside all the time. So we rented a part of the large Peterson house near the lake. We had all the rooms on the ground floor; large lawn and ample space outside and inside. We enjoyed this place very much with its beautiful scenery and a nice lake in the rear, and in the distance across the fields the Academy with its buildings nestled in a grove of trees. The Academy was owned and run by the Lutheran denomination, but later disbanded and buildings sold to the school district for a high school. It was about the middle of summer of 1922 that we moved into the large house by the lake.

The winter of 1922-23 was one of very deep snow all over the country. In front of our house it was so deep that Ben could not be seen above the top of the trench he had made in the snow; and it almost buried me. During the heavy snow it became too much of a hard walk through the deep snow by way of the village, so I beat a path in a direct line to the depot through the swamp and woods. The snow went up to my waist. I enjoyed those hard walks through the snow, it was so clean and fresh, the air invigorating.

Later in that same winter of 1923, a sleet storm with more snow and rains came followed by freezing temperatures that froze the rain and snow into a solid mass of ice all the way down to the ground for several feet. This occurred throughout the whole country=side from Green Bay extending in all directions from there and Scandinavia for hundreds of miles. Every railroad and highway in that part of the country froze up solid and traffic came to a dead stop, which lasted for a week or ten days and more. The Iola and Waupaca branch trains did not run for over a week; the two towns were isolated with no freight or mail during that period.

The management tried to open the main line first and it was quite a job. The rails were under a solid sheet of ice of six inches and more, including in between them. A work crew and engine started from Green Bay and worked east. Men with ice tools, picks and axes cut through the ice on the rails at intervals, then the engine tried to break up the ice between the cleared spots. It was slow work but they kept at it night and day until after a few days the work train arrived at Scandinavia.

C. H. Smith, the general manager at the time, was in charge of the crew;. I recall that I had a message for C. H. Smith, and when I went to deliver it to him, he asked me to read it to him so he would not need to stop signaling the engineer to start and stop and start again and again until a portion of the rails were cleared. Whenever he came into the office for information, I had it ready for him, which he seemed to appreciate. I kept myself posted on conditions along the line for all who needed it. Fortunately, our wires were intact and functioning normally.

During all this time I had on my hands four carloads of potatoes in the yards that I was required to keep from freezing, which I did by keeping the fires in charcoal stoves going in each car. They were billed 'Carrier's protective Service', which meant the Company and its agents and crews were obligated to keep the contents from freezing. Fortunately, I had an ample supply of charcoal in sacks on hand in Freight house, which I carried a ways to each car. I had the satisfaction of saving the potatoes from freezing while the four cars were in my yards.

Holger Hanson was conductor of the Waupaca branch train and C.L. Booth of the Iola; who was also agent at Iola. He had a clerk in charge of his office while away with his train. This arrangement was discontinued, after the unions became stronger and more insistent. The potatoes shipping business from Iola and Waupaca was very good those days, all of it moving by rail. Whenever F. B. Seymour came in he always sat at my desk and wrote notes signing them merely as 'F. B. S.' Even as president he kept that up. I recall once his pen dropped into a crack between desk top and the wall, and to get it out, he took out his knife and jabbed the blade into the wooden part

181

of it and drew it out. That required skill and attention to details.

H. M. White was roadmaster and he handled all the details of his job without assistance. He, also, did it by 'notes'. He was a notoriously poor writer and the recipients of his 'notes' had great difficulty reading them. Mr. White was always a polite gentleman; he had a good word for everyone, although he could get tough when occasion required it. But it was not his nature to be rough, but of a pleasant and optimistic disposition. We all liked him. He became a rich man due to his habit of thrift and frugality. When he went out on the line, he always carried his lunch box with him from his home, hardly ever eating at a restaurant. One day he asked me for my opinion as to who would be a good section foreman at Scandinavia to replace a young man who had been killed in railroad service while out on his section. Without hesitation, I recommended John Otterson, who happened to be a neighbor of ours. Mr. White appointed him at once. Advertising jobs with bulletins had not yet come into general use on the GB&W RR.

Some time later, Otterson did something that almost cost him his job. He had left the main line switch leading to the passing track open by mistake and had forgotten to close it before the passenger train came along tearing through it and onto the passing track, instead of up the main line. The engineer fortunately had control of his train and was able to stop before reaching the end of it where the switch was closed. Somehow Mr. White found out about it, probably from the engineer, and came to Scandinavia to investigate. He spoke to me about it; he was reluctant to discharge him, he told me. He said he thought he better give him another chance and that this should be a good lesson to him. I agreed with Mr. White and told him I thought the mistake would make a better workman out of him, and he agreed. Mr. White was a reasonable and good hearted man. He long since has passed on to his reward.

There were two section crews at Scandinavia, one of them in charge of a young man named Jorgenson. One morning as he was riding his motor car with his men, it struck a small obstacle on the rail and derailed it. The young foreman flew through the air and landed on his head and neck, killing him instantly. C. H. Smith, who also handled personal injury claims, had in his earlier years studied to be a doctor of medicine. He came to investigate and also to examine the body. He told me that he had never before seen such white skin on a body, and without a blemish of any kind.

Mr. K. M. Buer, a local resident, had the habit of walking on the Iola track to and from his home. One day Mr. Buer did not get off the track soon enough when the engine, backing up to Iola, overtook him and ran over his foot or smashing the toes on one foot. The engine was headed the wrong way which, under legal procedure, made the company liable. C. H. Smith came to investigate in the role of claim agent; also called on him at the Iola hospital where he was taken and operated on. He even sent the company doctor from Green Bay, Dr. Minnehan, I believe, to see and examine him. I recall he also sent flowers to Mr. Buer while in the hospital. I did not find out, but presumably the case was settled to the advantage of the railroad, as he had always done before.

It was the winter of heavy snow that Sherman was born. We had Dr. Peterson on the job that day, January 29th, 1923. We also had a competent assistant, a woman from town. I was on the job at the office, and in the afternoon I went home as soon as I could get away. It was a beautiful day; the sun was shining over the snow blanketed landscape, its rays reflected by the white snow in dazzling brilliance as it prepared to hide itself in the blaze of glory in the western horizon, while casting long shadows over the snow and through the windows of

the room where another child was to be born.   When I
came the Doctor was busy at his task of assisting Mother
Nature in her age old process of bringing another human
being into the physical world. In a few moments he was
holding a baby boy by the legs, head down, tapping his
back gently as though to welcome him to a new world. The
new arrival answered demanding immediate attention.

When the main task was over with, the Doctor called
my attention to the boy's left foot. It was turned over,
called a 'club-foot', and he explained reassuringly that
it could readily be remedied and not to be concerned too
much about it. He stated that he knew of a specialist in
Milwaukee who specialized in correcting abnormalities
of this kind; that he should be taken there as soon as
the baby would be old enough for the trip. Other than
that, he was husky, well developed and healthy. So in a
few weeks Dr. Peterson went with Mother and Sherman
to Milwaukee by train and called on Dr. Gaenslin who
had a good reputation for that kind of therapy, and also
an orthopedic surgeon in the straightening of bones in
infants and older persons. His treatment in this case
was simple enough, that of applying a boot fitted to the
foot made of plaster of paris and applied while soft and
wet and using pressure on the affected part with his firm
capable hands and held in that position until it dried on
the foot and kept on until the next treatment. The foot
was first enclosed in a soft material to prevent friction
from the hard boot.

Those treatments were kept up for some time, Mom
making several trips to Milwaukee. Later, as the foot
grew straighter and straighter as a result of this method
of treatment, or therapy, Doctor Gaenslin ordered a boot
made of a hard material for him to wear before he started
to walk. It was not long before the foot did not look like
a 'club-foot', but it became necessary, as he started to
walk, for him to wear shoes made by an expert in that
field, a Mr. H. Shinzheimer of Milwaukee, who specialized

184

in shoes for sore and crippled feet. They were made of leather with heavy soles in such a way as to hold the foot rigid and straight,. Two of them were made to match both feet. Mr. Shinezhiemer was a jolly man of German descent, good-natured, who had made custom made shoes all his life, employing several men for the purpose. When Sherman first had to have them by orders of Dr. Gaenslin, I took him to Milwaukee myself on my vacation. Mr. Shinzheimer took measurements of the foot which he handed to his men in their work room and while we waited for a few hours, they were made, charge $10.00. Dr. Gaenslin also charged $10.00 per treatment. I recall that at the Milwaukee road station, while waiting for our train to Green Bay and Scandinavia, I let Sherman walk all over the place in his new shoes. One of the station attendants told me to hang onto the boy; he was running around too much and in danger of getting hurt. As he grew older, his foot became more and more normal as a result of our efforts. This was sometime in the winter of 1924-25. Years later, after we had moved to Whitehall, Dr. Gaenslin came there to put on a demonstration for the benefit of the doctors in the community, including Dr. MacCornack. Sherman was one of the subjects of his demonstration and talk on physical therapy held in the high school building, giving the history of the case from the beginning. We learned that some years later the good doctor had passed away while still in his prime, for which we felt badly as every one thought highly of him and his work. This man had done more good to his fellow-man than all the cruel dictators of history put together.

We were happy and prosperous while living there, healthy and contented except for one thing: an automobile. We needed and wanted a car. So we bought a 'Star' touring car from a dealer in Royalton nearby, cost $500.00. That was April 23rd, 1923. I had never driven a car before and the dealer did not ask if I could or not. He merely delivered it to me at the house and gave me the key and left. That evening I started out with it, thinking I knew all about shifting and driving it. I had no trouble putting it in low and then shift to high and drove down the road around the lake, but when I came to the entrance road to the residence, I wanted to turn around and go back, I was stumped; I did not know how to shift to reverse. A boy standing on the lawn in front saw my predicament and came over to assist if he could. He knew more about automobiles than I did and got in behind the wheel and shifted it to reverse for me and backed out. That was all the training I received in driving a car. No examination and no license, merely plates on front and back that were numbered, issued by the state. I cannot recall what they cost, probably three or five dollars. The car was not enclosed, but wide open for the cold wind and rain, but later we had wooden slides installed that helped keep out the bad weather. We made several trips to Alma Center in it, most always started after six PM. We had the road to ourselves, very few cars. The roads were rough 'wash-boards' and in places deep muddy ruts. There was one place where all cars got stuck in the mud; a man with a team of horses was right there handy to pull them out, charge one dollar. Speed of the engine was limited; tires went flat on the least provocation; a repair kit was a must. No heater, no wind-shield wiper, no speedometer, no mileage indicator. Almost every Saturday night we drove to Waupaca to shop; also to the Baptist Church on some Sundays.

We had been looking around for a house of our own for some time. We thought we would be permanent residents there. Finally we decided to buy a two story house on a side hill with two acres of land and a two story garage building. We moved in during the summer of 1923 some time after we had bought the car. Our nearest neighbors were the Jorgensen's and John Otterson's, good people all. Howard Jorgenson was about Ray's age. Ottersons had a house full of boys and girls. We liked it there; lots

186

of room inside and outside. I fixed up the second story on the garage building to keep chickens, and made good at it. They paid for our groceries. I enjoyed that kind of work. I had my Dad come from Black River Falls to make some improvements, such as a concrete retaining wall along drive-way and lawn. I used one of the rooms upstairs in the house for cabinet work where I made a desk for myself, which I still have. Also, at the Peterson house, I had made a cabinet for clothes, which we also still have. I also made a typewriter desk in the upstairs work room which I later sold to the GB&W RR.

It was the merry month of June, when the birds were singing and all nature was in tune. By the first of April 1923, Mother Nature had awakened from her long winter's slumber and bestirred herself with the task of thawing out the frozen earth, pouring into it warm rays from the sun, bringing with them the necessary stimulus to reawaken seed germs that had been hibernating through the long winter. As a result there came into being a veritable re-birth of growing things, a reproduction of last summer's green leaves and grass; flowers in profusion; a time when vegetable life of all kinds reincarnated into physical existence again. It was at this time in June that another human being was about to reincarnate into physical life again in response to Nature's laws of re-birth. It was at 6:45 PM June 26th, 1024 that a strong, husky, well developed boy was born to us. Dr. Peterson had done a good job. We could not agree on a name for him. Mom wanted his first name to be Myron. I wanted it to be Dallas. So we compromised by naming him Myron Dallas. As he grew up I persisted in calling him Dallas, and it stuck with him. We now had four boys, Ben 8 years 9 months; Raymond 5 1/2 years; Sherman 1 1/2 years and Dallas a baby.

1924 was a presidential election year. Calvin Coolidge was president and he was up for re-election. He had been vice president when President Warren Harding had passed away while on a trip to Alaska. Silent Cal Coolidge ran on his and Harding's record and was easily elected on his own. Times were good. Coolidge had succeeded in balancing the budget and was paying off some of the debt. We as a family unit were prospering. I liked my job with its easy hours and Sundays off. I had 300 laying hens filling up my poultry house, all good producers. We raised potatoes and vegetables for the family. The boys played on the hill and in the woods nearby. We had a good school and fine neighbors. Our place overlooked the village from its high location, with its fine scenery. What more would we want? Sometimes I have regretted that we did not remain there. But regrets are futile; water over the dam never returns except as rain; time does not reverse itself; it moves forward, not backward. Past years and their records have been entered on time's relentless scroll, and are now but memories. The time is now with us to be used as we choose, and the future is ever bright with promise and hope yet to be realized. Anticipation is but a fore-taste of realization. Hope and faith! Can we live without them?

It was under these conditions that I received a letter in May 1925 from Mr. C. H. Smith, the General Manager, offering me the Whitehall Agency. I had not asked for anything better; I was satisfied with my status quo and wished to remain where we were. I think I would have chosen to remain in Scandinavia if it had been left to me only to decide. I was tired of moving. We were now well settled and I was loath to leave for new pastures. It was Mother who insisted we accept the offer. That would bring her nearer her relatives, and of course my Dad, who was growing older. This offer really was a promotion. Mr. Smith liked me, as did Mr. Seymour. I was on very friendly terms with Mr. H. C. Erbe, the dispatcher with whom I worked every day. It would seem to be a shame to turn them down. Mr. Thurman and Mr. Wohlfeil were both agreeable with me from what I gathered. Whitehall was a very important station for the company, although others could handle it as well. They would not tell me the reason for wanting me there so quickly. So it seemed inevitable that I should go. Mom insisted on it, the management did likewise. The cards were stacked against me, and I surrendered. C. M. Penn came to relieve me. He introduced himself as "My name is Penn, not Pencil." On the morning of June 1st, 1925, after loading my typewriter, my typewriter desk and a few other items in the back seat of my Star, I bid farewell to my family, with the hope to see them again soon in Whitehall. It was agreed between myself and the auditors, both freight and express, that I should arrive at Whitehall at the same time as No. 1, on which the auditors would be that day, so that we would all walk into the office at the same time. I started early enough so I would not need to hurry; did some shopping at Neillsville and stopped at couple other places. I was happy for the promotion and the new prospects in the better location as I drove along.

I arrived at Whitehall just a few minutes before No. 1 was due and parked my car near the depot and waited. As the train pulled in, I drove up to the platform so that I and the two auditors got out at the same time and walked into the office together. F. W. Bradison, the agent came in after he was through with the train. He did not seem surprised; I think he was expecting us.

It took the auditors several days to straighten out the accounts and check me in. I merely loafed and looked on in the mean time. They were unable to locate all the items and collect for them. The result was that the shortage ran into approximately nine hundred dollars for the railroad, and about one hundred for the express company and some money for the Western Union. A representative for the bonding company also was there to see what he could salvage and to talk to Bradison about his difficulties. I learned later that he had trouble with his wife for some reason. After some time, she divorced him. I think myself that the job was too much for him;

the management should not have sent him to that station, but to a smaller one.

Thus once again I was called upon to replace a young man who had failed. Thus did I and my family's life commence at Whitehall, the place where we were destined to rear and educate them; where we passed through eventful days of the second world war in which two of our boys enlisted; where another boy and three girls were born to us; the home from which our offspring flew away from their nest and out into the world on their own; where the old folks kept growing older and older in body but never in mind and spirit; when 'silver threads among the gold' replaced the dark hair of youth and the body gradually deteriorated to extinction, as is the lot of mankind in all ages.

--The Song of the River—
by
William Randolph Hearst Sr.

(Selected lines from complete poem)

"So at last when our life has passed
And the river has run its course,
It again goes back o'er the self same track
To the mountain which was its source."

--Chapter 10--

Our family moved to Whitehall in July 1925 into the Alexander house, where Lien's now live. We all liked the city from the start. Ray 6, started in first grade, Ben almost 10 in 3rd or 4th, cannot recall which. All our offspring attended and graduated from the Whitehall High School, one by one. Harold A. Knutson came soon after I did and worked with me as assistant and learned the business. During that period we handled up to 900 pros per month; a pro is the number of a freight bill. That is a lot of inbound traffic, in addition to the numerous forwarded shipments, carload and LCL. We were busy all the time. Express business and Western Union telegrams also kept us on the jump. Two way freights per day, and most days they met at Whitehall; each would have up to 8 way cars from which to unload freight. All the eggs produced in the territory were shipped by rail in iced refrigerators. After way freights had gone, the long platform was filled with freight for the local dray to deliver to merchants. He was Ben Pahnke and he used a team and flat topped wagon. Egg cases came back empty by the hundreds and Harold, being the tallest, would stack them up high. Several cars of live stock were shipped every Thursday. Everything moved by rail.

Pigeon Live Stock and Grain Co., H. I. Everson, manager, handled most of the stock; also hay and grain, as well as receiving cars of feeds. E. C. Getts bought most of the live poultry and shipped to New York City in special poultry cars with Jack Lundstead as caretaker almost every Saturday. Jack always brought me a live chicken every time he billed a car or two. C. R. Van Horn, former agent, who was confined to his house because of illness, bought hay by the carloads from farmers by telephone and shipped by rail, transacting his business by remote control. We handled all the freight business for Pigeon Falls. The drayman was John Skadahl, who used a team and wagon and later a truck when they came out. Ralph Back replaced Pahnke later on and he also used a team and flat topped wagon. The dray line was owned by Mason & Scott, who also were the ice dealers for the town; that was before electric refrigerators came on the market. They also filled the railroad's large ice house the house track for their use in icing refrigerator cars. Ed Scott also bought and sold live stock, while Bill Mason did an occasional contract job, mostly by teams and hired men.

I cite the following as an incident that shows how an agent is responsible for the interests of his company. Soon after I came a shipment of house-hold goods was received and billed on 'order bill of lading', which is negotiable and had to be paid at the bank before delivery, the same as a C.O.D. by express or mail. The agent cannot deliver without surrender of the order bill of lading, which the bank surrenders to the consignee upon payment of the draft. Ben Pahnke had a key to the freight house and would deliver freight sometimes when we were not on duty. On a Sunday he was asked to deliver this particular C.O.D. shipment, which he did, not realizing it was on order bill of lading shipment. Finding out it had been delivered by Pahnke, Monday I called on the consignee, a new arrival in town, and asked him for the bill of lading. He demurred, saying our man had delivered it; he had the goods; what can I do about it? I told him plenty. The drayman was not our man: he delivered without our authority. I said I would give him unto early afternoon to pay the draft at the bank and give us the bill of lading. He did not. I went to M.A. Anderson's law office and explained the situation to him. He made out papers for the sheriff to serve on the man. When the sheriff called on him, he went to the bank and paid and gave me the bill of lading. He had to pay the cost of serving the papers, including the lawyer's fee. Expensive lesson. Afterwards Judge Anderson, who had been a County Judge, called me on the phone and asked if everything was alright, and when I said it was, he said 'case closed'.

E. C. Getts and Ludwig (Barney) Hammerstead received their egg and poultry market quotations by Western Union CND each morning which I delivered personally. That was before radio started to quote them. I believe the charge for this service was $15.00 per month. The market telegram from Chicago was a long one with all figures, and I made an extra carbon copy for Barney. I deducted my commission of 10% on the cash, but was paid nothing for those paid at other end. On holidays such as Thanksgiving and Christmas and New Years, I always went to the office to receive a stack of greeting telegrams for many different people in town which I delivered personally. Whether the patrons appreciated this or not, I had the satisfaction of performing for them an important service, which was sufficient for me.

Many times when Ben and Ray went to and from school, they would stop in the depot and the first thing make a bee line for the typewriter and pound away at it. Sherman and Dallas were kept inside the house by Mother. As Dallas got older, he would make a hole in the porch screen big enough for him to crawl through and get outside when Sherman would follow. They did this when mother wasn't looking, Dallas always taking the lead. In later years, Dallas was the leader of the pack of boys he ran around with. When they were very small, they always asked me when I left for work to bring some 'white and blue candy', meaning chiclets from the gum machine, which I most always did. They were a penny a piece in white and blue packages. I took them for walks quite often.

Once more, this time in the spring of 1926, after old man winter had released his grip on us, and when summer was taking over with her balmy breezes and wars, and when May flowers were in bloom and the dandelions were giving of their nectar to honey bees, another child was ushered into our world, a baby girl on May 24th, 1926 at 6:40 PM. I wanted to call her May for the month she was born in and because she was so welcome as the flowers in May, but Mother would have none of it. Being the first girl in the family, I let Mom name her and she was named Avis Marie. She was a fine looking little girl with the physical characteristics of a beautiful woman to be, and she turned out to be just that. This took place in the Alexander house and Dr. and Mrs. J. C. Tyvand officiated at the great event.

On November 3rd, 1926 Mother and I started on our vacation trip, the first since coming to Whitehall. Previous to that, and since 1914, we had taken a few trips, one in 1920 while still at Hustler, when we traveled to Salt Lake City to visit sister Anna May and her husband Ed. Litchliter. They look us on a sight seeing tour of the city, which of course had to include, as it does with all tourists, the Mormon square where the great Mormon Temple and Tabernacle were located as well as other historic points of interest. We also drove through several of the scenic canyons.

This Nov. 3rd, 1926 trip we left Avis and the boys with Grandma's on the farm and headed by rail for Seattle, Washington. We were gone a month. In addition to visiting some relatives of Mom's at Seattle, Portland and another small town, we made scenic boat trips on Puget Sound and several other places. Dr. Charles S. Price, a famous evangelist, was holding forth in a huge tent in Seattle that Mother wanted to see and hear. We found him to be an orator of the old school, and without benefit of a loud speaker system, he held his audience spell-bound (except myself) with his passionate appeals to the emotions. He possessed an appealing personality, especially to women, and a voice that was clear and resonant, although soft and sympathetic. He used the old fashioned method of the 'sawdust' trail technique and also conducted 'healing' services in public on the large platform in front of his audience, which to me, personally, seemed ludicrous and more of a publicity stunt than an honest effort to help sick people.

His assistants lined up his 'patients' in a single file and as each one reached the 'healer', he anointed them with an oil, probably olive oil, on the forehead at the same time praying for them in his soft, appealing voice. Practically every one of them, and they were mostly women, fell down in a trance and an assistant on each side of them was there and ready to catch them as they fell on their backs on the platform. After giving it some study, I concluded that this phenomena was nothing more than hypnotism. While in their trance condition. most of them kept mumbling something as though trying to speak.; I also learned later, by more study of the subject, that these victims were obsessed while in the trance; that is, influences and entities from outside of them, took possession of their body and vocal chords and tried to speak through the voice. This practice in too many cases also leads to a permanent obsession of mind and body, which eventually causes mental diseases of various kinds. The trance condition is a phenomenon in nature, and should be avoided because one loses control of the body and mind, which of course is very undesirable.

From Seattle we went to Los Angeles to see the sights like any other tourists. One particular point of interest for most tourists, and for us, was Aimee Semple McPherson and her Angelus Temple, which had been in the daily press for some time past. The temple was a huge structure that covers almost a city block. She had founded what was known as the 'four square gospel' church. Hers was a pleasing personality and she was a master of the art of manipulating mass psychology. She could get her audience to respond to almost any mood she chose. Her system was more refined than that of Dr. Price; at least she did not permit her victims to fall down in an undignified position before her audience. I do not know what took place in her 'upper room' where they kept up a prayer vigil night and day. I noted that all her assistants were men; her audience also consisted mostly of men, which was natural as her feminine charms appealed to men. Apparently it was not difficult for a man to fall in love with her.

From Los Angeles we traveled to San Diego and visited my sister Martha and her husband. They moved back to Janesville soon after that. On our way back to Whitehall we stopped off and visited at Yellow Stone Park. Nothing of importance took place in 1927. Going back to 1914 and since, I always managed to take an annual vacation, but short ones, when we would visit relatives and friends nearby. But we did not have the luxury of paid vacations those days; that came quite some time later.

On May 18th, 1928 at 6:20 PM Wayne Douglas was born in the Alexander house. He was taken from us July 20th, 1929 at 4:50 PM. He had contracted pneumonia, a dread disease at the time that could not be controlled as at present. He was a smart, good looking boy with a well developed body. It was a hard blow. Was he taken from us for a purpose? Was it his destiny to be born into physical existence only to be snatched away again? If so, why? So many questions entered one's mind in such cases.

Destiny maketh and unmaketh, mending all:
That it hath wrought is better than had been.
Slowly grows the splendid pattern that it wears

196

Its wistful hands between.

Such is the law that moves to righteousness,
Which none at last can turn aside or stay.
The heart of it is love, the end of it
Is peace and consummation, Obey!

--Tennyson--

In November 1928 Herbert Hoover was elected president of the U.S.A. Times were good that year, but it was in 1929 that the great depression had its start. After all that has been said and done about the greatest depression in history (and there have been millions of words: the fact remains, as viewed in perspective, that it was a good lesson for all of us to learn; that it focused our attention on the necessity for improving our economic system; that the great stock exchanges needed to be reformed so that uncontrolled gambling in stocks by the general public be controlled and prevented; that a system of pensions and unemployment compensation was an absolute necessity and that our government is held responsible through laws in the establishment of measures of social reform that private enterprise cannot accomplish. We learned our lessons well.

In May 1929 we were given notice to vacate the Alexander house. No other house was vacant and available at the time in town, so we moved to the Lowe farm house on the hill just East of Whitehall. We decided at that time to buy or build a house of our own as soon as possible. We were getting tired of being cast 'from pillar to post'. While living there we bought our first radio, a battery set from A. B. Hanson, a dealer. We surely got a kick out of that radio. Ben and I were the most rabid radio fans in the family.

Our Star car was getting old and hard to start, so we traded it in for a used Oldsmobile at a used car sale by the T. B. Olson agency. Lawrence Knutson, who had taken his brother's place in the office some time previously about 1927, also bought a used coupe at the same time at the sale. Harold Knutson, who had learned telegraphy under me, also station work, was sent to Plover as agent-telegrapher. In later years he was promoted from there to be freight agent at Green Bay, a very important position. Both Harold and Lawrence were very good students and made a success in railroading, Lawrence becoming Superintendent and Harold car service manager.

In the spring of 1930 the Wellon family moved upstairs in the Lowe house while we occupied the down-stairs. Our kids and theirs had lots of fun together. They roamed the wide open spaces and swam in nearby Trempealeau River and watched the GB&W trains speed by below the hill, as well as car and bus traffic in front, All of which they enjoyed very much. Ray and Lucille Wellon used to go in swimming together in their birthday suits, about which I used to tease Ray. They thought nothing strange about it, being innocent and not yet self conscious. Ray was about 11. Ben used to catch frogs nearby in the river bottoms and ship frog legs to market for pin money. 'How dear to their hearts are the scenes of their childhood; when fond recollections presents them to view.'

In the summer of 1930 we bought the cottage and lot on which our present house stands from the Clarice Ecker Estate. Charles Ecker was a pioneer agent for the Green Bay & Lake Pepin railroad in Whitehall, probably the second agent. The first depot agent in Whitehall, if I recall correctly, was a man by the name of Camp. Camp also was an artist of sorts. His pen portrait of early Whitehall, or I should say an engraved duplicate of it, was in a large book of history of Trempealeau County in the Whitehall library. I understand Camp made the sketch while sitting on top the hill opposite the town on the north side of Trempealeau River, and taking in a bird's-eye view of the then small and primitive village below him. Charles

Ecker and his wife spent his last years in the small cottage that we bought.

We got busy right away and had the cottage torn down and a large basement dug over which we built our stucco house. Mason and Scott had two of his men with a team and hand scraper dug the basement hole. They also leveled the lawn after the house had been built. Mr. Iverson, father of Dr. S. B. Ivers and his crew did the carpenter work. His son William was one of his men.

Some years later Mr. Iverson passed on from a heart ailment. Evan Finstad did the plastering inside and the stucco work outside, and he did a good job, a good workman. A. W. Wright did the painting and varnishing for the whole house and D. A. Bensend did the wiring and installation of electric fixtures. R. R. Langworthy made the cement blocks and installed them in basement walls and also did the cement job for basement floor. But the stucco was not put on until next spring, as it was getting late for it that year. Ted Koff, who happened to be our next door neighbor, where Stuve's now live, was in the plumbing and heating business. He did the plumbing and installed the coal furnace and fixtures. Correction: Ed Berg did the plumbing work, and Ted Koff only the furnace and pipes. We moved in the fall of 1930 before the stucco had been put on the outside; the walls had been covered with tar paper and steel mesh for the stucco. The whole house was insulated with the then latest insulating material between the rafters. The total cost of all of it, including the lot, came to $4,500.00. We had the cash for all of it. People came to think we were rich, because the great depression was still in full blast. Hank Larson had bought out W. J. Webb the year before, so that our house was the first in town for which he furnished the materials.

The new house was the turning point for the whole family. It came to be our permanent home for the rest of our time on earth, or close to it. If anything can be called permanent here. It was there our offspring grew to manhood and womanhood; where the parents grew old and grey and feeble; the home where we had our happiness; our squabbles and disappointments; our successes and failures and our fruitful realizations; where we worked and played and relaxed; a gathering place for the boys and girls in the community. We tried hard to make it a real home for them. We failed in many respects; we also succeeded in a measure to make it pleasant for them, so that in later years, after they had flown their nest, they were always eager to return to it and renew memories of by-gone days of youth. We may not have been ideal parents, but at least we instilled in them the hard facts and realities of life; that life would not always be kind to them; that it was no picnic, and that they must face up to it and take whatever comes in their stride like good soldiers as they marched along the highways and byways of it.

On June 14th, 1930 I received word that my Dad at Black River Falls had ended his march through life and passed on to the great beyond. It was not unexpected as he was old and had been ill for some time. I had visited him many times before the final close of his life; he said he would be glad to go any time; he was ready for whatever was in store for him. When I arrived at the old home, the undertaker had laid out his long body on pine planks placed on supports in the living room, awaiting internment. As I viewed it, straight and handsome even in death, stretched out to his full length, I was reminded of an old, tall pine tree out down by the ravages of time lying alone in the forest awaiting the final stages of deterioration and its particles returning to their constituent elements to Mother Earth. He had loved trees and the forests, especially the virgin pine that was abundant in the territory in his youthful days, and the wild life the woods contained. He never owned a gun; never killed an animal. He literally obeyed the command,

"Thou shalt not kill." We laid his remains beside his wife in beautiful Shamrock cemetery. He was 79.

My father never participated in any church activities, nor attend any church services during all the time I knew him. But he never said one word against any of them. We could never find out really what his religion was except as he demonstrated it in his daily living, which we think was above the average in good conduct and the Golden Rule of those around him. He was honest, trustworthy and at peace with his fellow-man. Is such a one punished for a non-belief, or a belief that is contrary to the orthodox of his time? Does a belief, a mere belief, or none whatever change the fundamentalism, natural laws to which we are all subject here and hereafter? There are literally thousands of man made beliefs in our world. Surely there must be a system in effect where Devine Justice is done to an individual Ego, or Soul when he arrives on the other side; a system of rewards for good and penalties for evil that are in exact proportion to their extent in accordance with the law of cause and effect.

In June 1931 I bought my first eye glasses for $18.00 from a Mr. Forstrom, a jeweler in Chicago when he was at the Garden Valley Chapel at same time I was. I was 42 and the nature of my work and much reading had contributed to my eyes getting out of focus.

When our new house had been completed inside and out; all painted and varnished and furnished; everything was spick and span and brand new and when the lawn had been manicured and trimmed; when the grass was growing nicely and all nature was in bloom; when the August moon was high in the skies and the honey bee were busy gathering nectar and pollen; when the sun's rays were warm and its energy was shedding on the growing things of earth and vegetation everywhere was green with ripening grains and fruits and vegetables; when the corn was as high as a man and contented cows were growing on the green hill sides and partaking of the abundant foods of Mother Earth, that was the day; It was August 25, 1931 at 3:00 PM when a little girl decided to come out of hibernation and have a look around; to see if conditions were favorable for her to live in this land of milk and honey; and sure enough she found everything Okay and thought she would stay. Who was this little girl, anyhow? We had never seen her before. She was practically a stranger to us. She didn't even have a name. What are we supposed to do with a strange little girl without a name? We adopted her, of course, and named her Leone Arvis Erickson and she became a member of our family and of the greater family of the humanity on earth. Dr. and Mrs. J. C. Tyvand officiated at the great event, for a birth is far greater event than a death for any one. It is the commencement of small cycle, not the ending of it; one of many cycles within a spiral that extends to infinity.

Newcomers were no longer a novelty with us. We were already veterans in the fine art of reproducing the species. We were fortunate in the fact that we were able to care for them properly and give them an education and a fine home in which to live and in which to create a favorable environment.

1932 was a national election year. Poor Mr. Hoover was given rough treatment in the campaign. I don't know how he stood it all. He certainly was not to blame for the great depression, but too many people thought they had to have a 'scape-goat', which was not very complimentary to their intelligence. I could not bring myself to think he was at fault, although I did not vote for him. It was brought about by factors beyond his control, as any one could see who tried to think rationally. There seems to be a certain amount of poetic justice in the fact that Mr. Hoover out-lived Mr. Roosevelt by many years, the man who defeated him at the polls. He was a grand old man with his ability to take defeats and ridicule in his stride as he marched along the pathway of life. Each are the attributes of a Democracy.

In June 1933 our first born was graduated from Whitehall High School. He was 18 and had taken part in many school plays, usually the lead. He was an orator and won the oratorical contest for this district. He represented his school as the winner in oratory at La Crosse. I recall the evening he first presented his lecture in the Whitehall village hall. It was filled to capacity, and his voice carried clearly and distinctly over the audience without benefit of a loud speaker system. As he spoke he make proper gestures in stressing different points. We naturally felt proud. Mom and I both were there and we gave him a Gladstone bag from a mail order house for a graduation present. (Price $4.00)

In the winter of 1933-34 there was considerable interest in the sport of skiing by the small boys of the community. On Allen's hill back of our house a slide and take-off had been built by the kids themselves, with the assistance of their Dads. One fine Sunday a crowd of fans collected to see the kids do their stuff. They had organized this tournament, which was a small scale replica of a regular adult one. The kid skiers on that Sunday put on an exhibition of ski jumping that was long to be remembered in the annals of the sport. A self appointed judge, an adult, judged the jumping, a man who had had experience in the sport. Alvin Windjue, about 11 won first in class A, others in different categories. After the tourney we took up a collection for the kid skiers. Most fans said they had gotten more of a kick out of this than any the adults had put on. Ben had organized the kid skiers into "The Record Breakers Ski Club", a high sounding name for a small outfit. Soon after the first we adults got together and built the kids a larger ski hill and slide where the club put on a regular meet with all the paraphernalia of a regular adult tourney. It included a banquet with all the trimmings in the evening and awarding of prizes to the best kid skiers. What also was on Allen's hill, now a part of the golf grounds? Ray, Dallas and Sherman became skiers and took part. Later Ray became a professional skier and entered in the big meets. Others of the kids later also became professional skiers.

In the summer of 1934 we bought a new Ford 4 door sedan from Auto Sales in Whitehall. Very few cars were being bought and sold those days due to financial effects of the great depression. We paid cash for it, cannot recall exact amount, but it was under one thousand dollars. Some wondered how we came into possession of the money during those difficult time. Actually, we had been saving from my salary, which never stopped; I always received a pay check twice a month throughout the depression.

After F. B. Seymour retired in the fall of 1934, and his death on May 7th, 1939, after 63 years with the one railroad, a new slate of officials from the MK&T Railroad took charge of the GB&W railroad headed by H. E. McGee as president. With this new blood the GB&W started to recuperate from its lethargy and took on a better color in its health; from then on it became a prosperous and healthy railroad again.

The efforts put forth by President Roosevelt and the new measures enacted into law by Congress, were beginning to take effect all over the country and a new confidence came into being as unemployment was being steadily reduced. As F.D.R. said in his inaugural address, "We have nothing to fear but fear itself", a remark that emphasized an eternal truth and will always be remembered and quoted in the years to come. Fear and superstition are two of man's arch enemies, followed by ignorance which breeds cruelty and the other two.

Ben enrolled in the University at Madison in the fall of 1934. He did not return the following year, for which we parents are to blame. In 1935 he did odd jobs around town and also learned telegraphy and station work with me up to August 15th. 1936 when he was called by H.C. Erbe, CTD.,

204

to go to Alma Center and take charge of the station there as relief agent, his first assignment as Agent-Telegrapher. He had previously called on Mr. Erbe in Green Bay and offered his services as relief man. Although he did not care to break in new 'hams', Mr. Erbe did later call on him to go there and relieve the agent. From then on, he has remained with the company, first doing relief work at different stations, and later promoted to Agent at Green Bay and still later to Traffic Representative.

Raymond graduated from Whitehall High School in June 1935. He started working for Iverson-Larson Lumber Co. on May 1st, 1936 on a special permit from the Industrial commission, being only 17 at the time. In the fall of 1937 he enrolled as a student at the University at Madison. In high school his marks were mostly 'A's; likewise at the university.

It was on Feb. 1st, 1936 that the depression came home to me when the management took off the helper job at Whitehall. In addition to other work he had been carrying the US mail from depot to post office and back. That meant that I must do that chore myself. I used my Ford car in doing it and I asked the company for $50.00 per month for the additional expense. C. H. Smith, the General Manager, wrote and said $35.00 will have to be enough for the purpose. For hauling the mail, I constructed, at my own expense, a rack that could be put on the bumper quickly and removed when not in use. Mail was piled high on this rack in front, sometimes nearly obstructing my view.

Warner was postmaster at the time and the post office in the brick building on the corner on Main Street. He was constantly complaining about my handling of the mail. I told him if my service was not satisfactory, to haul it himself. Another time he ordered me to bring the mail sacks inside and place them at a certain spot in the office, instead of throwing them next to the door. This time I really got angry at him and screamed at him, "if you don't stop hollering about my mail carrying, I shall leave all the mail outside on the side-walk for you to come and get it." That stopped him for a while until one day I received a letter from G. C. Byers, the new General Manager, saying the Warner had complained about my services and wanted my version of it. I wrote and told him plenty. He dropped the subject except that some time later the management hired a man to carry the mail. He was Gabe Gilbertson, an old gentleman, who started on Dec. 1st, 1936. Previous to that I asked Warner what his idea was in reporting me to the General Manager. I gave him a bawling out, which he had coming to him, something the others who worked with him did not dare to do. No one liked him.

One day when I had delivered the mail to the post office, Avis was standing near my car at the curb waiting for me when a reckless young driver bumped into her and threw her down on the side-walk where he was trying to park. Tracy Rice across the street saw it all and took her into his car to the hospital. She was pale and shook up severely, but not hurt. I gave the young man a talking to for being so reckless. His mother who was with him, defended him against me. But he received a good lecture on careful driving before they were through with me.

In the fall of 1935, when the frost was on the pumpkin and the fodder in the shock; when the green leaves had changed their colors to the golden hues of autumn; when Mother Nature was singing her lullaby to her brood in preparation for a long winter's nap' the birds were winging their way to the south-land, while some animals were seeking their caves and holes in the ground to hibernate through the long coming winter, an event of great importance occurred on November 6th, 1935 at 12:30 PM high noon when planetary bodies were in favorable positions in their orbits around the sun, an individual was born into this world; a world of beauty, order and system; a female, and we name her Ethel Mae Erickson, who turned out to be the last of this particular tribe. Where did she come from: that is the question.

We knew how the body is created, but not by whom or what. We know there is life in a newly born body, but we are ignorant of what the life really is. Not knowing, some of us are permitted to theorize, to postulate and arrive at reasonable and rational hypotheses that satisfies our questions, at least provisionally until more accurate, scientific information is available. My hypothesis is as good an any one else's:

The life in a body is separate and distinct from the life, or energy that vivifies the atoms in a body. Human life is separate and distinct from animal life, or any other kind of life. Human life is organized into individuals; life in an individual body is composed of, first the Ego, or what religion calls the Soul of man; then mind, potential at birth, but fairly well developed at maturity; then the emotions by which feelings such as love and hate, fear, anger, confidence, etc., are manifested.

Theologians contend that all these are created at same time that a body is. That is not a reasonable conclusion. The more rational one is that they had a previous existence, just as the materials of which the physical body is composed, had a previous existence. In accordance with the universal natural law of physics that nothing is ever destroyed, but merely changes its form of existence to another; life in one form or another has always existed and always will. Originally life, universal life, came from the First Cause, whom religion calls God, who has always existed. In the human kingdom it was broken up into individuals containing this life, very primitive and undeveloped at first, but slowly evolved and developed from one existence to another.

Therefore the life in a baby body, the Ego, the potential mind, the potential emotions and feelings, all had a pre-existence, and also has a future existence. What those existences are, is another subject too long to discuss in a narrative such as this. "This life is a kind of symbolic shadow-show; All that matters is the long adventure of the soul." J. B. Priestly.

--Chapter 11--

When we came to Whitehall, the Baptist was a prosperous, thriving church with quite a large membership and a Rev. Doody as Pastor. We tried to attend their services, and did mostly; also sent our kids to their Sunday School until the time when a break up of the church occurred as a result of an itinerant preacher, when they moved over to the Methodist Sunday School. Rev. C. E. Bowen took over after Doody was transferred to Waupaca. He stated later that his greatest mistake was his leaving the Whitehall Church.

Rev. Bowen went to Cornell one evening to hear this traveling preacher hold forth there in a tent and Bowen was impressed by his methods, so much so that he invited him to come to Whitehall to hold meetings in the Baptist Church. He was a radical type of man with extremes in practically all he did and said, to the extent that he caused such hard feelings in Cornell and was finally compelled by the citizenry to leave there.

Difficulties in the Whitehall church commenced almost at once as a result of his extremes. For one thing, he persisted in kissing the men as they entered the church. I never permitted him to do that to me; neither did Mr. Lewis Rasmussen, a veteran Baptist. He preached and practiced 'speaking in tongues'; falling under the power; baptism of the holy ghost, and so on. The final result that the Church collapsed from friction and disunion and Bowen was dismissed from the denomination. Callahan pulled almost half the membership from the church and started one of his own, which eventually became the Pentecostal, and later the Assemblies of God Church. The Baptist Church remained closed for a period of time. Eventually they reorganized, hired another Pastor and were in business again. We stood with the Baptists and sent our children back there when they reopened.

July 1ˢᵗ, 1936 Ben started the "Lamp Post", a small weekly paper that contained snappy jokes, cartoons and humorous articles and statements. It was mimeographed and circulated among the business men in Whitehall for 23 cents per copy; residents also bought it; a few business firms placed short ads in it; it drew many laughs and favorable comments from readers. It lasted only a few weeks, as he was occupied with other matters.

During 1936 there grew out of the depression many new ideas and schemes and projects about how to prevent another like it in the future. One such a scheme was called 'Technocracy', which was rather complicated and almost too scientific for the average person to understand. It died in birth. Another was Dr. Townsend's $200.00 a month pension plan for the aged that required spending all of it when received. That was supposed to increase consumption and bring about more employment in production of commodities. It was easy to understand for the average person, especially the older persons who supported it by organizing into a body of oldsters. The propaganda that resulted from the plan really did a lot of good, as it stirred Congress to finally do something about pensions along lines of social security benefits.

The railroad men were the pioneers, or at least among the very first to work for a sound system of pensions for retired people on the railroads of the country. A small group organized, published a weekly and bombarded not only Congress, but leaders of railroad unions until they were forced to get busy and conceive and present a solid plan to Congress which eventually passed and became the law of the land. I am glad I had a chance to do my little bit toward that effort. The railroad pension system was the impetus required to push through the social security system later.

There was a Catholic Priest, Rev. Chas. E. Coughlin, in Detroit Michigan who was holding forth on a nation wide radio network every Sunday afternoon with his oratory in well chosen words and a very fine speaking voice. This period was a time of agitation, debates and propaganda throughout the country. On March 13th, 1936 Rev. Coughlin started a weekly periodical called 'Social Justice', a copy of which I have in my possession. His theme centered around the gold standard reforming the money system of the government. As I listened to him I was reminded of my boyhood days and of William Jennings Bryan whose theme was the reforming of the money system. His system was '16 to 1' meaning 16 silver to one of gold. I recall how my elders, especially an old bearded gentleman named Peter A. Potter, argued about Bryan's ideas of improving the financial structure of our economy. It seems that history of human events repeats itself periodically. Coughlin had a golden voice, as did Bryan in his day; each had ideas along the same lines, and each was a good orator. The freedom of speech that both enjoyed, and that we ourselves have always taken for granted in this country, was the means that assisted all of us in the clarification of the issues of the day to a basis of solidarity and good common sense.

Another presidential election year rolled around again in 1936. F. D. Roosevelt had no difficulty at all in getting re-elected. His name by this time was magic to the rank and file. He was given credit for saving capitalism at a time when it was flat on its back; a time when a strong military dictator could very easily have taken over the government and established a dictatorship in this country.

Economic conditions were getting better and better as a result of his leadership within the framework of our constitutional system. I recall that on December 31st, 1936 I had handled 51 Western Union telegrams that day, which I think is an all time record for my office. This was evidence that the people were regaining their confidence in our system and in the business of the country. It also added up to a lot of work for me alone.

In 1937, the GB&W under the new management, put into service the new Mikado type of locomotives on their freight trains which increased tonnage per engine. As an advertising stunt, the management ran a special passenger train over the line Green Bay to Winona with a train of coaches of officers and traffic men pulled by one of the new steam engines. The baggage car was used as a bar to serve soft drinks, beer and candy bars for those who come aboard; all this was a gesture of good will towards the shipping public. Some of the customers got on and off repeatedly for several helpings of beverages and candy. One of the traffic men tried to stop it without success.

June 29th, 1937 Avis was operated on at hospital for a small tumor on the breast, non-malignant, by Dr. MacCornack; charge $35.00. When I visited her she was still under the effects of anesthetics. She recovered quickly.

June 29th, 1937 President Roosevelt signed the railroad pension bill into federal law, which was a very important mile-stone in the march of social security progress. Some time previously Congress had passed and the president signed a bill that was practically the same in its provisions, but the '9 old men' (as president Roosevelt called them) nullified it as unconstitutional; they were far behind the times in social thinking. Eventually the (9 old men), or most of them, retired, permitting younger more social minded men to take their place. It is the younger generations who carry forward and bring about the necessary changes in our civilization.

August 31ˢᵗ, 1937 Sherman was in Milwaukee with the Whitehall city baseball team as a mascot. They had won the district championship and if I recall correctly, they won the first game in Milwaukee when the manager of the team sent a telegram to J. E. Rhode in Whitehall that they had won. I could not find Jack to deliver it to, so I brought it to the barber shop where a group was congregated awaiting news of the results and the barber read it to them. When Mrs. Rhode found out what I had done, she bawled me out for delivering a telegram addressed to Jack to some one else. Such is life.

One day after school Sherman came into the depot and stood in the doorway looking unhappy and forlorn, acting as though he was in pain. He was quite small and young at the time; I could easily carry him. He held one of his arms in one position all the time and said nothing. I saw there was something wrong, but all I could get out of him was 'it hurts' when I touched the arm. I took him to the MacCornack Clinic at once, near by. Dr. Koch could tell right away that his arm was broken. So they put him on the operating table on the lower floor and put him to sleep with anesthetics when both Dr. Koch and Dr. MacCornack worked on his arm through an x-ray screen by which they could see the broken bones and how to put them back into place. But they had taken an x-ray picture before that which showed two bones completely broken off. Later another x-ray was taken which showed them in place. Sherman was given the negatives by Dr. Koch which we kept for him. Dr. Koch did a good job of setting the broken bones and placing the arm in splints. They healed together in time and as good a new. We found later that he had been wrestling with a Smith boy, who was bigger than he was and somehow got his arm under his weight in a twisted manner which broke it. While

Sherman went under the anesthetic, he kept singing and humming to himself.

Speaking of broken bones reminds me of the accident Leone had while out in the country visiting Grandma's; she was playing on a high pile of wood when somehow she tripped and fell on her arm breaking the bone in the upper arm. We started for home at once and took her to the Clinic and Dr. Milenowski set the broken bone, but he did a poor job of it. He was young and inexperienced and it seemed to me, rather careless in his work. Her arm did not go back to normal completely as a result of him bungling, but it healed anyway and did not bother her much if any. She also was placed under anesthetic in the clinic. Dr. Milanowski had only recently been hired by the clinic.

While on the subject of injuries, I must relate the accident that Leone had some years later when she was learning to ride the bicycle. She had some difficulty in riding it properly when one evening she was riding along the road from the creamery towards our house; she and the bike suddenly went off the path and into a clump of brush, her leg striking against a large stick that tore its way into the fleshy part of the leg and broke off, the broken part remaining in the leg. I heard her screams and ran to her. It was getting dark and I took her into the kitchen in order to see and examine the leg. I tried to remove the stick but it was stuck fast. I got out the car in a hurry and took her to the hospital, stopping on the way at Dr. MacCornack's house to tell him, but he was out. Dr. Nerum happened to be in the hospital at the time who took charge; the nurses put her to sleep on the operating table while Dr. Nerum waited in another room; they also gave her an injection. It seemed to me that the doctor should have been there all the time watching and supervising, but he did not show up until all was ready for him. It was very warm that evening. The heat in the hospital and the excitement almost got me. The nurses could see my predicament and tried to help; they let me into another room and put me beside an open window; the fresh air put me back to normal. I watched Dr. Nerum operate; he had difficulty getting out the stick and had to do some cutting; he was spilling blood all over the sheets. Dr. MacCornack came in just then and told Dr. Nerum how to do it; to leave the lower part of the wound open so as to permit it to drain out and the loose sticks and dirt. Correction: they did not put her to sleep but used local anesthetic, so she was able to observe it all and was not at all disturbed. The nurse remarked that I looked more sick than Leone. What a day!

Ben relieved me on October 10th, 1937, his 23rd birthday. I cannot recall where we went, or what we did, but was gone only a week.

September 14th, 1937 my sister Mrs. Claud Harmon (Mamie) passed away from a heart attack. Her husband had gone a year or two previously. This left her two boys and a girl orphans. We tried to assist them, but Floyd the oldest would have none of it. He was an independent and capable and managed the family very well without assistance from any one.

During this period, 1938, Adolph Hitler was defying his neighbors in Europe and elsewhere by threats. He seemed bent on stirring up trouble. Chamberlain of England was trying to pacify him, but without success as it developed later.

April 29th, 1938 Phillip F. La Follette and his brother Robert M. Jr. launched the Progressive Party, a third party movement that got a good start but died out a few years later, as had all third party movements in times past. It seems that the U.S.A. is no place for third parties, as in Europe.

Raymond was doing very well at the university. We received two or three letters from Dean of Men, Mr. Goodnight and also from the Dean of Engineering College reporting the very good progress he was making, for which we felt very proud. When home on vacations he worked for the lumber company.

In 1939 the outlaw Hitler invaded Poland, a crime for which he and his people suffered in penalties years later. It was the start of the Second World War.

July 8th, 1939 Engineer John Ray of the GB&W on No. 2 that morning ran into a C&NW freight train at the Marshland crossing injuring four men on the C&NW and narrowly missed agent Frank Gappa on the depot platform who jumped out of the way just in time. A box car smashed into his depot office and demolished it. He was laid up to a couple days with a heart attack due to shock of the accident. Two or three years later while hunting his heart failed and died at once. His station closed after that when an interlocker was installed at the crossing. Engineer Ray was permanently taken out of service and he also passed away soon after. He had been a faithful employee.

Sherman was helping me out at the depot and learning the business. On July 21st, 1939 he made out his first freight bill, Pro.137 dated that day. September 14th, 1939 Ruth Vinger's picture appeared on a Madison newspaper as Dairy Queen of Wisconsin starting on a trip to California. In the spring of 1940, May 29th, Ray was offered a job as actuary with the Metropolitan Life Insurance Company of New York.

Ben had been assigned the New London second trick telegraph job on bulletin. While there he met Beatrix Roloff and became engaged. They were married in the Methodist Church there on October 19th, 1940 and we attended the happy event. We stayed at Stewart's, a good friend of Ben's, Mom, Sherman, Dallas and myself. On their honeymoon they traveled by train to New York City and on October 21st, we received a telegram from them sent from the top of the Empire State Building.

On November 20th, 1940 Raymond went to Wilmington, Delaware for an interview with the Dupont Company for a job prospect. How it turned out, I do not know. Congress had passed the draft law in 1940 and on October 16th, 1940 16,400,000 young men registered for the draft throughout the United States. October 29th, there took place the first drawing by lot of draft numbers in Washington D.C.. I listened to it over radio in office. The first number drawn was 158. Just after the number was announced, a woman in the audience screamed. It was her son's number. That cry was the first of a long series of cries of sorrow and grief throughout the country. How much sorrow and how many heart-aches it caused is beyond human comprehension. Fortunately our family was spared having to pay the extreme penalty. All this was caused by one man, the worst criminal and most horrible killer in history, Adolph Hitler.

In November 1940 President Roosevelt was re-elected for a third term, the first such in our history. He was severally criticized, but the people wanted him; it was not his fault. In a democracy the voters are the final judges of who shall be president and for how long. Later the two term restriction was imposed by Congress, which I think was wrong. The American people should be allowed to elect a man for as many terms as they wish, especially if he is a good man and does well with every one. Some people seem to think that Roosevelt was a man of destiny, as Lincoln was. He appeared on the world scene at just the right time for certain purposes in history. I like to think that "men are moved and maneuvered as pawns on the world's chess-board by an all-knowing Destiny." In the storms and stresses of life, "God is in his heavens, all's well with the world.: All is well from the standpoint of an over-all consideration; from the stand point of social evolution. It is not difficult to think and believe that a master plan is being worked out, whatever it may be, that required unlimited time in its consummation by the Invisible World Rulers who have our evolution in their charge.

Early in 1941 Raymond was deferred by the local draft board in Whitehall because the Standard Oil Company of California had hired him to do important research work with aviation gasoline that contributed to the war effort. He left for California August 8th, 1941 soon after graduation from the University of Madison. He had previously become engaged to Ruth Vinger. He also had bought a new Plymouth auto. Sherman and Ruth drove in Ray's car to Los Angeles, California and soon after arrival they were married with Sherman as attendant. Happy memories!

Sherman graduated from Whitehall High School in June 1941. He had taken the leading role in the class play 'Poor Dear Edgar". After that he learned telegraphy and station work with the 'old man'. In connection with his learning to send Morse, I recall he had difficulty with his sending hand. Once while sending a Western Union telegram to 'GU' Green Bay relay office, his hand broke out in sweat, became limp and almost useless. The receiving operator became angry and asked what was the matter. I completed sending it and soon after placed him on a 'bug', a vibroplex he had purchased, after which he got along very nicely.

March 11th, 1941 Ben drew Casco agency on the bulletin, his first agent position. He and Beatrix moved there from New London. Lory, their first child, was born there.

During 1941 world events shaped themselves up for world war No. 2. We in this country were doing our utmost to be ready for anything. "Human events cast their shadows before them." Wars are no exceptions to that maxim. In June 1942 Myron Dallas graduated from Whitehall High School. We urged him to go to Ear Claire to learn the tin-smith trade under N.Y.A. a government agency organized for the war effort. We thought it would help him to learn a trade quickly if he should be called upon to serve in the war. After completing this course, he went to Seattle to work in the ship building industry in the fall of 1942 as a tinsmith. April 17th, 1942 Sherman passed the examination in Green Bay as Agent-Telegrapher. Some time later he went to Seymour, Wisconsin to relieve the agent there. He, also, relieved me for my vacation on October 26th, 1942, but Seymour was his first job as Agent-Telegrapher.

It was on Sunday December 7th, 1941 that our war effort really got going. That afternoon I was listening to a Packer foot ball game being broadcast over the radio when H. V. Kaltenborn broke in from New York and stated that Pearl Harbor had been attacked and bombed by Japanese war planes. From then on it was all-out warfare; we were in it at last, for better or worse.

The day after Sherman relieved me on October 26th, 1942, the used tires started to come in, as the government had urged every one to send their used tires to a government agency for the war effort with instructions to bring them to the Express office for shipment. He was swamped with tires and people in the depot and I could readily see that I could not leave him alone to handle all that under these conditions. I remained all that day and the next receipting for tires and preparing them for shipment and filling out government forms for each shipment. Before the day was over, both waiting rooms and the express room were full of tires. Both of us were on the jump constantly. The next day we loaded a four wheeled platform truck of bundles of used tires to move on the afternoon train. As I was lining it up for the train, I turned the front wheels too sharply and the whole load came crashing down, tires and truck on the track, and only a few minutes before the train was due! What a calamity! I called on any one who happened to be near to assist me get it all back on the platform before the train came and smashed into it all. We cleared it just in time. After that fast and furious work, I felt exhausted and almost collapsed from it, but soon recovered after a little rest. After the tires ceased coming in, I sent a bill to the Express company for two days work for me. They refused on the grounds that a commission office has to hire their own help. The commission all went to Sherman and I worked for nothing.

In 1942 in the early spring, Land O' Lakes Creameries commenced to build a large milk, powdered milk and dairy plant in Whitehall. That winter all of us had worked long and hard to get them to choose Whitehall in preference to Independence for the site to build. We finally beat them to it and secured the plant for our city.

During that period business was increasing steadily at my office due to the war. I wrote the management that I simply must have help; that I could not possibly handle it all alone. They finally agreed and established a new position, I simply must have help with hours from 4 PM to midnight. That surely was a relief. From them on, as long as he remained, the two of us handled the business easily and efficiently.

Due to the draft men were becoming scarcer than 'hen's teeth', to work on the railroads. As a result they were compelled to hire women to work on the sections. I asked the road master one day how he liked women laborers. He said he would not have them unless he was compelled to hire them, which he had to do under the circumstances. They could do only the light work, the heaviest was done by men. It certainly was strange those days to see the crew of six or more females in a group trying their best to handle shovels and the other tools. They were kept apart from the men and wore the same kind of work clothes as the men. Surely women are out of their natural element in attempting to do man's work whether at manual labor, running a business or bossing men as executives. It still is a man's world! (We hope.)

Men were in military training all over the country preparing for the inevitable. On September 8th, 1942 I received and delivered the first war casualty telegram from the military to the parents. He was a young man from Whitehall who was killed in an accident while training, Harold N. Stendahl. War had not yet actually started as far as casualties were concerned, but it was very close. December 7th, 1941 was the 'day of infamy' as President Roosevelt named it. The demands of war had been unleashed and were running true to form. Congress declared war on Japan December 8th, 1941 and on Dec. 11th, 1941 Germany and Italy declared war on the United States. Japan never did declare war.

During the next few years so many important events took place that I can touch on only a few them. On March 8th, 1943 Sherman had to give up his job as he had been drafted and had left for Milwaukee with Jack DeBow and Floren Hegge to be examined and all were accepted. They returned later.

On March 16th, 1943, which was my 54th birthday anniversary, the largest crowd of people in any one's memory had gathered at the depot in Whitehall to bid farewell to dozens of young men, Sherman among them, from all over the County who were headed for war. They were waiting for the forenoon train to Merrillan, thence from there to Chicago and various training camps. Both waiting rooms were full, as well as a huge crowd on the platform. Relatives, mothers, dads, sisters and smaller brothers and sweethearts gathered around each their own, spending the last few moments with them. Sobbing women, anxious faces fearful of the future. Would they come back alive? Most of them hid their emotions stoically. It would never do to send the boys away with heavy hearts! They are the ones who were called upon to face possible death. A glad hand and a friendly slap on the back with the words, "Oh, you will be back, don't worry." One girl clung to her sweetheart and cried openly. Mothers tried to hide their feelings, while the fathers took it all in their stride, covering up their emotions with optimistic talk. Some of those boys never did come back. Such as the fortunes and penalties of war!

A few days before that Dallas had enlisted in the Marines, March 10th, 1943; he did not wait for the draft. On March 14th, 1943, a Sunday evening, Sherman took him in our car to Eau Claire together with Roger Therlacker and the two Mattson girls, twins, where the boys entrained for their training centers. The girls sobbed as the train pulled out. Dallas' last words to us were, "I'll be back." He made good on that promise and came back alive on June 12th, 1945. More of that later. After Sherman left on Mart 16th, all our boys had flown the nest; two off to war and other two deferred because of the nature of their work being necessary to the war efforts. Only the three girls were left with us, the old folks; for we were getting old.

For a year or two scrap iron was being accumulated and stored on the vacant ground between the two tracks east of main street until it became so filled up that there were no more room left. This was done toward the war effort and because of the shortage of steel and iron due to the war. Soon they started to load the scrap iron into gondolas and shipped for salvage for making munitions of war. 12 carloads were loaded and shipped. Soon after the GB&W work train hauled in 50 cars of soil and filled in the hollow places where the scrap iron had been stored and the county leveled it smooth with their equipment.

That same summer the GB&W moved the old freight house from its old site along the truck to its present one across main street and converted it into a warehouse for the Whitehall Mill & Power Co. to whom it was leased. The grain elevator which had occupied that site where the warehouse now is located, was moved across main street to the site of the Olson Feed Co., later the Farmer's Union. Later a power shovel was brought in by the GB&W and broke up the old concrete platform and loaded the pieces of concrete onto flat cars for use as cribbing on the line.

This old freight house building, which included an office and a waiting room, was built soon after the railroad was constructed through Whitehall in 1872-1873. The platform was made of wooden planks at the time. In 1909 the old planks were torn up and replaced with concrete. This building served as a passenger and freight depot and office until 1910 or 1912 when the company saw fit to build a passenger station across the main line from it out of brick, a very handsome depot, the best on the line. The old building was used exclusively as a freight house; passenger and freight business was at its peak at that time, for the railroad.

The transportation picture started to change about the time of the depression, or some time before that, when the Roy Hagen truck operated between Eau Claire and La Crosse which gradually commenced to cut into the railroad's loss than carload traffic. How we used to curse that truck! But to no avail. H. D. Briggs started a truck line some time later, as did many others throughout the country. The Greyhound bus company commenced to run their busses from Eau Claire to La Crosse about the time Roy Hagen did, or some time before that. William Mason, later Trempealeau County Highway Commissioner, started a bus service between Merrillan and Winona, which was later taken over by another man, until it ceased to operate for lack of business. Thus did the railroads start to face competition on every hand. That was something new for them; they were not accustomed to competition of any kind except between themselves. The last time I saw F. B. Seymour alive he proceeded to cuss the trucks and busses with vehemence and swear words of which he was capable of using, fluently. That was about all the railroad management could do, to curse them. Instead of cussing, they should have gone into the trucking business themselves, and served their customers more efficiently as the trucks were doing. They could have gotten in on the ground floor of the trucking business and built up 'grand-father's rights' which would have served as a deterrent to other truck lines competing with them. But hind-sight is better than fore-sight. The GB&W eventually did get around to secure authority to run a fleet of trucks paralleling their own line, but by then it was too late; the cream of the business had gone to the established truck lines. Eventually they got out of the L.C. L. traffic completely.

On December 16th, 1943 the GB&W started to build a water tank and stand pipe next to the coal shed and connected the tank with the city water mains and an electric pump that pumped the water into the tank to serve the new big steam engines that had recently been put into service. E. B. Nenncarrow was the engineer in charge, a congenial young man.

January 19th, 1944 early in the morning Mother and I were called by a neighbor out of bed to go and answer a long distance the phone call. We went to the telephone office. It was Dallas at San Francisco. He was all ready to leave on a ship for points unknown. He thought he would have to have a last talk with us, the old folks. At the time it did not bother me much; I had a confident feeling that he would return as he had left. He had said he would. He would only be away for a while. Although it bothered Mother for a short time, she came to take it in her stride.

In the midst of all the warfare throughout the world and the important events incident thereto, Avis graduated from Whitehall High School in June 1944. She was our first daughter to graduate, so it was quite important. There were two more to go. Regardless of turmoil and strife, education went on as usual and life proceeded on its normal course.

Casualty telegrams from the war department are the saddest part of the whole sordid business of warfare. Our instructions from the war department were to use the utmost care and tact in their delivery; not to phone them but deliver personally, unless the party addressed wished to come and get them at the telegraph office; and not to deliver to the Mother unless necessary; always deliver to the man of the house, or a brother.

On September 2nd, 1944 the first casualty telegram I handled was for Mr. R.R. Langworthy advising the parents of the death of their son Archie killed in action on August 20th, 1944. Not being able to get away from my busy schedule and so far to walk, I phoned Mr. Langworthy that I had a telegram for him and he replied, "All right Arvid, I'll be right over to get it." When he came into the office he was as cheerful as ever; he thought it would be just an ordinary business telegram. He was a great hand at telling stories and always had a new one for me whenever he saw me. This time I said to him, "Mr. Langworthy, this is bad news for you." He looked at me severely and said, "What do you mean, bad news?" I said, "Brace yourself for a shock. It is from the War Department." He looked at me a moment, and then at the telegram. He was very slow and deliberate about it. Finally he opened it and read it. He read it over again without saying a word. This was his first reaction: He hit the counter with his fist and exclaimed, "Dam that man Roosevelt." He regained his composure in a few moments and said, "Arvid, do you know my wife had a strange feeling, a sort of an intuitive premonition about Archie the very day this telegram says he was killed?" I replied, "Yes, some women have an intuition in such matters, more so than men." He said, "Anyway, I am glad you called me first. Now it is up to me to tell her, and I don't know how it is going to turn out. I dread it."

Poor man! He walked out slowly; the world had collapsed around him, at least for the time. Archie was an only son. The family's interest was centered around him their only offspring. He had become an artist and an expert photographer and ran a studio in a city in Iowa, when he was drafted for war. Now he was gone from their lives forever, at least as long as they lived on earth. I learned later that Mrs. Langworthy had collapsed completely; a doctor had to be called. Their next door neighbor, Mrs. Arne Rassmussen, came to help them for several days before she recovered from the shock. Five or six years later Mr. Langworthy himself became sick with cancer, and after an ordeal of pain and suffering, he was relieved of his stricken body and from a world of turmoil and strife and warfare. When I called on him at the hospital, he was too far gone for him to be able to see me; just about at the point of death. He had been such a patient and happy soul. He had a genius for architecture. He had designed and constructed many beautiful houses. It was not long after that time that Mrs. Langworthy, also, left earth scenes. We can only hope and believe that the family is together again, wherever they may be.

In October 1944 Sherman was on the high seas for India. He wrote an interesting article for the Whitehall Times which was printed November 9th, 1944, describing the voyage and conditions in India, especially the railroads and their operation, of which he had become familiar in this country before he was drafted. He was in the Air Transport Command of the U. S. Air Force. He was in the communications department, being an expert Morse telegrapher.

In November 1944 President F. D. Roosevelt was re-elected for an unprecedented fourth term, a most unusual happening in this country. Harry S. Truman elected Vice-President.

November 30th, 1944 Stanley E. Hamilton was killed in action. He was a son of Mr. & Mrs. Ernest Hamilton. When I delivered the telegram to them, both Mr. & Mrs. Hamilton took it calmly. There were no display of emotions while I was with them. They took the bad news like the good soldiers they were.

December 2nd, 1944 Grandma Larson passed away peacefully at the ripe old age of 83. Her body had gradually faded away from advanced age. It was time for her to go. She had finished her course; was tired of the race and was happy to leave at least. She left earth scenes in the midst of the world wide conflict, while hundreds of thousands of young men were being sacrificed to the demons of war; she was not alone upon arrival on the other side.

December 22nd, 1944 another young man from Whitehall paid the extreme penalty, Stanley M. Hestiken was killed in action. His folks had passed on and the wire was delivered to his sister Mrs. Norman Garson, who took it calmly. If this portion of my narrative appears to be gloomy with so many deaths, it is because the world was bent of death and destruction during that period, and I must render an accurate account of principle events that took place within my knowledge in my own small circle.

It was not a pleasant task to deliver a casualty telegram to the Edwin Moen's, whose son Ernest M. Moen was killed on board ship near England that was torpedoed by German submarines on Christmas Day December 25th, 1955. "Secretary of the Army has asked me to express his regrets that your son Pvt. Ernest M. Mown was killed in action December 25th, 1944, etc., etc."

Mr. and Mrs. Edwin Moen were at home when I came with the ill-fated message. When she saw me at the door, she seemed to sense what was in the telegram that I had in my hand that she could plainly see, before I could say a word and before it was opened by Mr. Moen. There was terror in her face as he opened it and commenced to read it, and before he finished, she lost control of herself completely. She ran from room to room screaming, crying and wringing her hands. Mr. Moen tried to calm her but could not. When I left she was still out of control emotionally and temperamentally. I could do nothing about it, but had performed my duty, a sad one. The rest was up to them. It was their calamity, their misfortune, although no fault of theirs. It was sad indeed that they should bring up a handsome, tall and husky young man only to be killed in a senseless war that was brought on by the stupidity, greed and jealousy of a handful of selfish men.

On April 12th, 1945 at 4:35PM President Roosevelt died almost instantly from cerebral hemorrhage. He was truly a war casualty. The strain of war duties had sapped his strength and energies to the breaking point. Almost immediately every radio in the country ceased all commercials and devoted all their time to sweet and sacred music appropriate to the occasion for a people in national mourning. We had lost our Commander in Chief in the midst of a war. For three days nothing but classical music, plus news broadcasts and commentaries of the occasion, were heard over our radios.

It was said at the time that in Hitler's camp, there was rejoicing, especially by the war monger himself. He thought surely now he could easily win the war, having lost his chief antagonist. But he was mistaken then, as he had always been from the start to his finish. But there wasn't one moment of let-up in the ceaseless and relentless pressure on the three international outlaws, Hitler, Mussolini and the Japanese militarists. The Japanese war makers soon found that out when the first atomic bomb in history was dropped on Hiroshima on August 6th, 1945 and another on Nagasaki on August 9th, 1945 killing 350,000 people in the first and 260,000 in the second; truly a terrible slaughter of innocent people. Soon after on August 14th, Japan surrendered, closing the war in the Pacific.

Vice President Harry S. Truman took over the presidency, something he had not planned on at all. He was shocked and bewildered at the prospect of being president of the United States. He had not wanted the job, a queer twist of fate. The war effort was intensified on all fronts and at home. All of us were determined to end it as quickly as possible.

In connection with casualty telegrams, I was becoming to be somewhat dreaded as a messenger of bad news those days. I was not told as much, but I could feel it. One case in point: Mr. Charles Keiliholz, who was county sheriff two terms in later years, and his wife had their oldest boy in the service. He came to me one day and told me that, if I should receive a telegram for them, never to deliver it to his wife; that I should hold it for him if necessary, that he would call for it when notified. He wished to protect his wife, as men have always tried to do in times past and at this time. Happily, Chuck's son came back after the war, sound and healthy.

"Despair was never yet so deep,
In sinking as in seeming;
Despair is hope just dropped asleep
For better chance of dreaming."

--Chapter 12--

I received and delivered another casualty telegram for the parents of Omar B. Olson who was killed in action April 28th, 1943. I cannot recall the circumstances in delivering this one to his folks who lived in town. The message for the mother of Ray V. Larson who was killed in action on May 11th, 1945 was delivered to her personally, as the father had passed on some years previously. She did not display any emotions, although it was a hard blow to her; now she was alone in the world as Ray was her only son. Personal tragedy! There were many of them during this period.

The Larson's had been neighbors of ours while Mr. Larson was County Agricultural Agent and our son Ray and their Ray became good friends. They enrolled in the Wisconsin University together and shared a room there while they worked and dreamed together. He had been married shortly before his passing. His bride as well as his mother were grief stricken. With some, sorrow hardens the character, but with those who love and are tender, it ever purifies. Does not the very texture of the flesh of a sufferer, who has in patience and resignation borne his pain, seem luminous and pure, as though through every call there gleamed the light of a hidden fire? How much more so is it with mental suffering?

Are we not irresistibly drawn to reverence one who has suffered much and nobly, and sometimes to love, too?

> "I saw my lady weep, "I saw my Lady weep,
> And sorrow proud to be advanced so
> In those fair eyes where all perfections keep,
> Her face was full of woe;
> But such a woe (believe me)wins more hearts
> Than mirth can do with her enticing parts.
> Sorrow was there made fair,
> Passion wise; tears a delightful thing;
> Silence beyond all speech a wisdom rare.
> She made her sighs to sing,
> And all things with so sweet a sadness move
> As made my heart at once both grieve and love."

Happily there were no personal tragedies in our own family. On June 12th, 1945 (the very month in which he was born) at 10 AM a young man walked into my office while I had my nose buried in books on my desk and said cheerily "hello". When I looked up there was Dallas, well and happy, back from the war. I surely was agreeably surprised. We had not expected him just at that time and so soon. He had returned as he had promised when he went away, "I'll be back." He had arrived at San Francisco June 3rd, 1945 from one of the Pacific Islands.

An event of great importance during those eventful days occurred when Herr Hitler died a violent death on May 1st, 1945. He had finally been run down to earth and cornered. It required a world wide conflagration and millions of casualties to accomplish that feet. His own army officers had tried to do it, but failed. Ironically and as a personal touch, I should relate that Adolph Hitler and myself were born in the same year, 1889. He pursued a career of violence from the time of his youth and on till his violent death, killing many millions of his fellowmen during the process, and now has the distinction, if it can be called that, of being the greatest mass murderer in history. What about myself? I leave that to my heirs, my friends, relatives and neighbors to judge. Hitler's armies surrendered soon after May 7th, 1945. This ended another war in a long procession of them during man's time on earth. Another bitter lesson was learned.

On January 20th, 1945 Adelbert A Bautch was killed in action. His folks lived on a farm a few miles out and I had to hire a car and driver at the Army's expense, as per their instructions, to deliver the telegram. A few days later the Bautch daughter came into the office and told me that she was glad that her mother was not at home when the telegram came, which gave the family opportunity to arrange to advise her in a suitable way.

La Verne Haake's death message also was delivered in the same way, by taxi to his folks on a farm. There were several other telegrams from the War Department containing bad news to parents of boys killed, or missing, or in accidents and so on, the details and names of which I cannot recall at this late date.

On Sunday June 24th, 1945 there was held in the Lutheran Church in Whitehall Memorial Services for Lt. Ray V. Larson; PFC Ernest M. Moen and TSCT Omar B. Olson who had died in the service of their country. That was only one memorial service of the many hundreds of others throughout the country for boys lost in the war.

To return to more pleasant topics: September 9th, 1945 Avis left to attend Bob Jones College at Cleveland, Tennessee September 10th. I left with my trailer on my vacation for a short trip and came back September 17th. Mom never cared to travel with me in my trailer. October 29th, 1945 Ben and his little family moved back to New London to his old job there from Winona. November 27th. Dallas arrived home to stay, having been permanently discharged at a camp in North Carolina. This ended his military career.

After Sherman left his job at depot in Whitehall for military service, I was compelled to put up with incompetent assistants on second trick. Ervin Wolfe was one, incapacitated by a stroke years previously, and was called back to railroad service to help out in the shortage of telegraphers. Later an owner of a small grocery store in Arcadia, who had been a telegrapher in previous years, was hired by the management to work second trick. He was dishonest; took money from the till for his lunches; would not come to work on time; went fishing when he should have been on the job and I had to work in his place, and so on. He made things miserable for me. On December 3rd, 1945 V. R. Zimmerman came to work second trick, having been discharged from army service. Previous to his army service, he had been a student for a short time at Independence depot; was therefore not very competent in the work of a station, nor at telegraphing. But he was a smart young man, willing and able to learn, and he did learn fast; and he was absolutely honest. I had to practically teach him from 'scratch, but it was worth while as he turned out to be a good railroad man and eventually was promoted to agent at Winona, a responsible position.

During the latter part of 1945 my health started to collapse from the strain of over-work 10 - 12 hours per day, Sundays included due to the war and inexperienced assistance; and it continued long after the war had stopped. In addition, my ears had been 'ringing' for a long time with a noise that could not be cured, although I called on Dr. Simons to help me, without avail. My left ear was the worst, the nerves having become damaged some way. I was losing the use of it more and more as time went by.

January 22nd, 1946 at 3:00 PM Ben received a telephone call while at the New London depot from Mr. E.V. Johnson, Superintendent, offering him the position of Freight Agent at Green Bay. He accepted at once; went there and took over permanently after 30 days trial, for which he was delighted; just what he wanted. All of us were glad for him; he was making good in a big way.

March 18th, 1946 we received a telegram from Sherman that he had arrived at San Francisco March 15th, debarked March 16th, and entrained for Camp McCoy, Wisconsin March 17th, and separated and discharged March 22nd, 1946 at 4 PM. He was back in his home town next day. We surely were glad to see him and that both boys pulled through the war without a scratch.

April 1st that year Dallas started to work on the GB&W extra gang. On May 10th, 1946 my office hours were reduced from 9 to 8 hours per day. I was becoming discouraged; every one was making demands on me that I could not meet and received no help from any one. Noises in my ears were increasing rather than diminishing. My stomach and bowels went out of order repeatedly and my nerves were at a breaking point. June 26th that year I bought a hearing aid. This increased the noises, it seemed, thereby bringing about more nervous exhaustion. Many times I felt like throwing everything overboard and getting away from every one, including my family, who were making excessive demands on me that taxed my endurance.

Looking back with hind-sight, that was the time I should have taken a long leave of absence to try to recuperate from the strain and illness. It was my good fortune to have inherited a good, strong heart, without which I probably would have become a war casualty, as Roosevelt was. Instead of applying for a vacation, I decided to get away from the work house I was in as soon as possible and go somewhere where I could rest and recuperate, instead of being hounded almost to death by everyone. When Alma Center station went on the bulletin, I bid it in and moved there with my trailer and lived in it for the next 17 months from July 3rd, 1946 to December 1st, 1947.

For the record, I should state that Whitehall being the County Seat for Trempealeau County, the government established several agencies in the Court House, both during times of the great depression, such as N.E.A.; and others, and also during the war times. There was a Rehabilitation Office and others like it, as well as offices for the draft board of the County. There was also an agency for assisting farmers, and others that were known by their initials, too numerous for me to recall them all. Many of these agencies used the Western Union for communicating swiftly by wire and I had to copy long telegrams of instructions from headquarters to some of them that took up much of my time and energy; and I delivered all of them personally. Almost every morning when I came on duty 'GU' relay office was calling me, and when I answered he sent me a long file of telegrams that I sat and copied on my 'mill' while patrons waited for me to get through.

After the Land O'Lakes plant got going, every morning for a period of time they shipped one and more refrigerator cars of condensed milk and cream, fresh, to various points in the south that had to be made ready and billed for the morning train that was due about an hour after I opened the office; these moved by fast passenger trains via Merrillan, Amherst Jet and New London Jet., for which I had to lock up correct rates, as they were billed prepaid. While I was doing that, 'GU' kept calling 'his arm off' to get me to answer, and when I kept telling him '25' (busy on other wires) he, or she, kept calling me anyhow until sometimes I cut the wire out on the switch board in order not to hear them call me.

During the period of training at army camps scattered all over the country, dependents, wives and relatives of the soldiers all wanted to go to the camps and visit their men, and I had to take much time to figure out routes for them to go via rail; passengers were discouraged to travel by highway due to shortage of rubber, bus or cars.

Trucks, also, were restricted for the same reasons. The only way they could travel was by rail. Later that mode of travel also was discouraged, restricted and sometimes prevented. Some days huge advertisements appeared in newspapers telling the public not to travel in any form, especially by rail, in order to save space and fuel for the war effort. I saved one of those ads. Enlisted men were constantly traveling by bus and train on government 'Requests', which was a standard form to the carrier and authority to furnish them transportation. These had to be handled by the Agent of the carrier, and most of them started their trips from the County Seat of the county they were in at the time. All this took time and effort, and together with the other work, it was exhausting.

Construction of the Land O'Lakes dairy building required several carloads of materials that we handled by rail, which construction commenced in 1942 and completed in time for the last deciding punch in the war effort.

By the time the war commenced, farmers in this territory shipped their eggs by Briggs truck line to Chicago. In order to save space in their trucks Briggs loaded the empty egg cases into railroad box cars and shipped them back by rail. At one time they had as many as 20 and more cars of empties to unload and haul away from our yards. In accordance with demurrage rules, I kept an accurate record of these cars as they were placed for unloading, the time and date for each car. I had to issue written notices called 'Constructive Placement' forms to the consignee for each car and mailed to Farmers Service Company, which was the company George Briggs organized to handle this traffic. It was impossible for them to unload their cars within the free time, 48 hours, and so demurrage charges piled up which Geo. Briggs refused to pay, and turned the bills over to his lawyers. The result was that the Western Weighing and Inspection Bureau, owned by the railroads, sent one of their men to Whitehall to check up on it. He worked a couple days checking my records. I recall he had two books in front of him, checked one with his left hand and the other with his right until every car was checked. He found all my records perfect, and the charge correct and legal. The total amount ran into a couple hundred dollars demurrage, possibly more, I am not sure at this late date. The final result was that his lawyers advised Briggs to pay it in full at once; it was all in order and legal.

While cream and condensed milk was being shipped by fast passenger train service, the refrigerators were billed back to shipper that contained the empty cream cans and the dunnage that was used for packing. Besides Land O'Lakes, the Bowman Dairy Company also shipped these products in the same way, so that we had to be very careful that the right car was delivered to the right consignee. One time there was a mix up; Land O'Lakes cans were in a Bowman car with the result that there was an argument about who should have the car, and there was a shortage of refrigerator cars at the time. Managers of both concerns claimed the car; Roy Rutfeldt was manager of Land O'Lakes; and Bowman was a field representative; neither would give in. So I had to ask the management at Green Bay what to do. They said they would be neutral in the argument and would not advise me anything. When I told both men that, they came to the depot and sat in the waiting room and argued between themselves. Bowman man was insistent, saying they used that car in shipping and were entitled to it' Rutfeldt said the cans are ours; Bowman said you or we can unload the cans and we take the car. That is how they finally settled it; Rutfeldt had to give in, which was gentlemanly of him.

There were also several claims in connection with the cans and dunnage in these cars getting lost somewhere with the result that all this was an extra job for me to handle and make correct CS&D reports. Many times I did not use the correct rate for these shipments, and the tariff clerk in Green Bay sent me one correction after another to make corrections, refunds or balance due collections. That entailed a lot of work.

As evidence of the amount of business we did in Whitehall those days I cite the figures of the December 1945 balance sheet total as being the largest of all of them; an all time record; it was $59,804.75. That included all items, ticket sales; prepaid forwarded baggage; freight received; prepaid forwarded freight; demurrage, etc. etc. That meant a lot of work for one man. Total of the express company balance sheet was $364.36 with $41.00 commission. That was for January 1945. For May 1946 total was $973.75, $57.73 commission. Add to this the Western Union balance sheets for the period, for which I do not have the figures. Plus the gum machine sales.

At Alma Center I really had a good chance to rest for the first time and try to recuperate from nervous exhaustion. I did a lot of sleeping in the office and in my trailer, just what I needed. I was not young any more at the time; I had reached 57.

Sherman took over the Whitehall Agency from me. Later, when the bulletin came out, Rueben L. Magnuson bid it in and Sherman resumed his job on second trick, which had been held for him while he was in the service. That was August 11th, 1946. On September 15th, Dallas enrolled in the University of Wisconsin under the G.I. Bill of Rights Law passed by congress for the benefit of the service men and their education.   November 2nd, 1946 the U.S. mail service on the GB&W was discontinued after 73 years of carrying the mails on the railroad; it was turned over to a truck star route. Things were changing fast.

June 18th, 1947 Sherman was offered a train dispatcher's position in Green Bay by H. Weldon McGee, Superintendent. He accepted and started there September 9th, 1947. August 9th, 1947 Avis started to work as a clerk at the Bly Rendering plant out in the country. We had a family re-union, believe the first one, on August 30th, 1947. September 1st and 2nd. Ray and his family were on their way to California to accept a new position and stopped for the family re-union; all our kids were home at the time. It was a happy time of getting together again after the war.

It was on Ray's trip to California August 8th, 1941 to take a job with Standard Oil Company that we sent the following telegram to him on the train. Raymond A. Erickson, Care Union Pscific Rail Road, Pacific Limited train No. 21 due 1055PM Omaha Nebraska, "Bon Voyage". May the wheels of fortune carry you safely to a land of plenty where dreams materialize into realities." The Family." I forgot to refer to this telegram in previous mention of the trip.

September 16th, 1947 was Avis' last day at the Bly plant. She went to Minneapolis with Josephine Sylla September 22nd, on the Bly truck and went to work for Butler Brothers there. September 6th, 1947 Ray and family started back to California. Thence to Portland and finally to Hawaii where they remained until about January 1946 when they flew back to California and thence drove to New York City to settle down in a new position as chemical engineer. I hope I have this right. (subject to correction)

November 22nd, 1947 Whitehall second trick came up for bulletin after Sherman vacated it to go to Green Bay as dispatcher, in September. I bid on it and drew it, but did not start right away as I wanted my vacation first. I transferred Alma Center station to T.W. Franson and went home to stay on December 1st ,1947. I spent my vacation at home that year and on Dec. 19th, 1947 I started on the 1PM to 9 PM job in Whitehall depot where I had spent so many years of my life, more than at any other office. I surely was glad to be able to stay home again, rather than drive back and forth every week to Alma Center. By going there in the first place I remained on the pay-roll and the checks kept coming, which was very important, and while doing so I had a good chance to rest and recuperate, which also was important. My income would have stopped had I taken an extended leave of absence. In the long range of things, everything turned out fine for myself and my family during those trying years of war, heavy work and ill health. I found that on enforced absence from home for a considerable period of time causes one to appreciate home so much more when one returns again.

Mother was ill disposed also during that period, having to pass through the menopause peculiar to women; we both had to readjust ourselves.

My new assignment enabled me to sleep late in the mornings, something I had never before been privileged to do. I had Mondays and Sundays off without being 'pushed around'. Later I went into the honey bee business as a side line; that gave me opportunities to be out in the fresh air of the country-side; with the bees and the trees and the birds. This set up enabled me to 'Coast into retirement', which was not very far away.

In December, 1947 a radical change in motive power was inaugurated by the GB&W when they started to replace the old steam engines with Diesels, thereby effecting a large saving in operations; eliminating water stations and coal sheds, etc. which resulted in a considerable saving in fuel.

It was on April 27th, 1949 that Sherman brought his girl friend Eva Hawkinson home to see us. We liked her from the start. Sherman always had fallen for the small type of girl' his previous one was small in size. Eva traveled abroad May first that year with her folks, including a trip to Sweden. She returned August first same year. A couple days later, while Eva and Sherman were home here, they drove to the beautiful park at Blair, and it was there that they became engaged to marry; to respond to Nature's call to mate; to imitate the birds, the bees, the flowers and the trees. The park was a replica of the traditional 'Garden of Eden' that contained the trees of knowledge and was the home of the original Adam and Eve. (We should have named Sherman Adam; probably would have had we known he would marry Eve.)

Leone had by this time decided to become a nurse and she started to prepare herself for it before she graduated in June 1949 from Whitehall High School. She was vaccinated May 12th, 1949 and in July of that year started nurse's training at Eau Claire State Teacher's College. A wise step and a worthy profession. She graduated in the Spring of 1952. Another offspring had commenced on a career.

September 1st, 1949 was a mile-stone in the history of railroad labor when the 40 hour week went into effect for non-operating employees. At first I was not in favor of it, being old fashioned enough to think that a man should perform a full day's work for his pay and to remain on the job every day of the week, as I had done all my life. But I got over that idea in the course of time and finally came to like the new arrangement.

February 11th, 1950 most of us attended the marriage of Eva and Sherman in Minneapolis in their Church there. He wished to get out of railroad work and move to California, although he was getting along fine as dispatcher; he decided to seek happiness and fortunes in that state. Of course we were against his resigning from the GB&W, but it was his life to live, not ours and our objections were brushed aside. So after their marriage the newly-weds arrived in Oakland California February 22nd, 1950 where he got to be Traffic Manager for the Dow Chemical Company finally. The move turned out better than we had hoped for. To young people the future always looks bright no matter where they locate.

Another war started in Korea on June 26th, 1950. We thought we had finished with warfare, but it seems that the communists were replacing the Nazis as trouble makers on the world scene. On January 17th, 1952 I copied my last casualty telegram as follows: "Washington DC 1-17-

52 to Mr. and Mrs. Carl J. Finstad, Whitehall, Wisconsin. Secretary of the army has asked me to express his regrets that your son Corporal George H. Finstad was killed in action in Korea September 6th, 1950 He was previously reported missing in action. Confirming letter follows. Wm. E. Bergain, Major General US Army, For Adjutant General of the Army, 422 PM."

On July 15th, 1950 Mother, Leone and Ethel started on a trip to Oakland to visit Sherman and Eve. Came home August 4th.

Dallas graduated from the University of Wisconsin in June 1950 in Commercial Art.

September 29th, 1950 Mom and I made a trip to Ridgewood N.J. to visit Ray and Ruth. Came home October 13th, 1950

On October 25th, 1951 I made a trip to California to visit Sherman and Eva. November 13th, 1950 Avis went to work at Northwestern Schools in Minneapolis as office clerk in the treasury department.

I have given many dates in this narrative that sounds rather dry and matter of fact, but they seemed desirable for the record if nothing else. Many dates were skipped as being unimportant.

There is one date I have forgotten; at least I have not written it down but it was important; that was when the Western Union switched from the old telegraph to the telephone in handling telegrams for the small towns, including Whitehall. It commenced about 1947 and soon after all the Western Union equipment, such as sounders, keys, resonators were removed; but we in our office hung on to ours so that we could work with 'QN' the W. U. office in Winona. Even that had to be discontinued when the GB&W moved their office including the telegraph equipment from the up-town GB&W freight office building at Winona to their freight yards near the Mississippi River railroad bridge which cut off 'QN' W.U. office from that wire. That meant all our W.U traffic had to be telephoned from and to Winona W.U. office. That was not so good; I did not like that at all. That took place just before I retired in 1954 March 16th.

When the telegraph was finally discontinued in the handling of Western Union traffic, that ended an era for me. It was the end of sending and receiving telegrams by telegraph that had been in use since 1840, over a hundred years ago. It ended 44 years of wire work for me for the W.U. I had always enjoyed copying W.U telegrams from the wire on my 'mill' and I tried my best to make each one as complete and accurate as possible and I felt proud of my work.

I recall a day in 1940 on the 100th anniversary of the Morse telegraph we were told to listen to the same message to be sent on our W.U. wire on that date that Samuel F. B. Morse sent the very first time; "What had God wrought." I was right there and copied it at the time when an operator in GU relay office sent it.

Those who are want to sneer at and ridicule the telegraph as out-moded, obsolete, out-of-date and old fashioned should remember that our history in this country is closely tied in with it; we could not have made the progress we have done the last 100 years and were more without it. Every daily newspaper in the country depended on it for their press dispatches, their only means of communications. Every railroad from their very beginning was run by the telegraph in the hands of dispatchers and telegraphers. Every commercial telegram by the Postal and Western Union Companies were transmitted by it. Some historians say that the Civil War could not have been won without the telegraph operator at the front and in every command post and in tents.

I recall how I used to go to the office after my hours to send press dispatches of important events; basket-ball game tournaments by telegraph; receive results of prize fights round by round for local fans; important election

243

returns; send death messages; news of disaster such as floods; and others too numerous to mention. All this was for and in the public interest, and I am proud that I had the opportunity to thus serve the public.

To return to my narrative: Leone graduated from Nurse's training school in Eau Claire in July 1952. She had taken six months hospital training; internship in a Chicago hospital and became a Registered Nurse. In the first year she was chosen by the nurse body as their representative at a Nurse's convention in Atlantic City, New Jersey. She traveled with another student nurse who also was a daughter of a railroad telegrapher, both of them traveling on passes.

In October of 1952 I took a trip to Salt Lake City Utah for a visit with my oldest sister who had lost her husband, Edward Litchliter just previous to that. He died suddenly from a heart ailment while fishing in a mountain canyon stream; age 75. The high altitude was too much for his heart. The year previous to that Mother and I made another trip to Oakland California to again visit Sherman and Eva. During our time we have made at least six trips to the west coast; one to Mexico; one to Canada and New York and Florida and points in between.

December 27th, 1952 Dallas and Ruth Krummenacher were married at Dale Wis. in the Evangelical Reformed Church. They had met at the university where they both studied commercial art. It was a very good match as each supplemented the other in qualities and abilities and were congenial and agreeable to each other. Mother, Leone and Ethel and others of the family attended the great event. 'The old man' had to stay on the job with his 'nose to the grindstone'. Happy days and pleasant memories!

Thursday May 28th, 1953 Ethel Mae graduated from the Whitehall High School. It was a 'red-letter' day in our tribe as she was the last of the brood to do so. Seven graduating nights over a period from 1925 to 1953 makes a lot of history in one family! School days of childhood and youth with their experiences and memories; knowledge accumulated and stored in their minds and lessons learned never to be forgotten! Memories of those good years are pleasant also for the parents as they live them over again in retrospect and recalling events that occurred during that period.

Ethel went on with her education at once when she enrolled in the North Park College in Chicago the same year. Two years later she enrolled at the University at Madison, where three others of our brood and attended and two graduating. Although Sherman could have enrolled under the G.I Bill of Rights, he chose to enter the railroad field and worked with me and finally became a train dispatcher.

August 31st, 1953 Leone went by train from Eau Claire where she was a nurse at Luther Hospital, to Columbia South Carolina to attend Columbia Bible College. There she met her future husband, Lawrence Kaylor. They were married in Sherman's home in Oakland July 16th, 1955 at 400 PM. She was the first of our girls to be married. Mother, myself and Ethel were there for the happy occasion. They were a fine looking couple, both tall. The house was filled with numerous friends and relatives and gave them a great send-off as they drove away on their honeymoon to Northern California.

Nothing further of importance occurred until the time finally came for 'the old man' to be retired from railroad work after 45 years of it. In this connection I am reminded of the time Herb Schriner, a humorist and T.V. personality, was interviewing a retired railroad telegrapher on one of his television programs and asked him: "How come you quit after 45 years of telegraphing?" The old telegrapher answered: "I just couldn't seem to get the hang of it."

It was Saturday March 13th, 1954 that all the boys except Sherman who was too far away, Avis, Lory and Lee barged in on us (they thought to surprise me) to celebrate my retirement on my 65th birthday anniversary. If I recall correctly, Leone and Ethel also were home, but am not sure. They came to pay tribute to an old timer, a veteran whose best years were behind him, whose footprints in the sands of time were but memories.

In the afternoon the boys were at the office to take pictures of me performing my duties for the last time, including locking up the depot door. After I had received and delivered the last train order on my last day on duty, the dispatcher called again and sent me another order, addressed to myself: "Order No. 17 to Operator W. After your long and successful run on schedule, you are ordered to take siding at Whitehall for a long and happy retirement. A.G. E. Complete at 814 PM." The order was duly delivered to myself, and I still have it as a memento.

Mother had prepared a small birthday supper with a cake inscribed with '65' which also was her own 65th birthday February. 3rd, 1954. Mrs. Alice Stuve, a good neighbor, also gave me a small birthday cake for the occasion. The boys presented me with a fine, expensive, light-colored tan sport coat and trousers which suited my tastes and age. The girls gave me an over-night traveling bag and other smaller items. Happy Day! Whether or not I was worth all that attention and well wishes, I certainly appreciated it all with gratitude and humility as tokens of respect and love from people who believed that such tokens are best bestowed while the individual is still among the living. Thank you all from a full heart!

On Monday March 16th, 1954 Mother and I drove to Eau Claire to file applications and necessary papers for our railroad retirement pensions. The papers were complete in every detail so that it required only 15 minutes to file with the Railroad Retirement Board representative. Pension checks started to come a month and a half later and they have continued to come regularly ever since as a result of my having paid my allotted portion into the fund from its very beginning.

July 17th, 1954 I bought a used half ton truck from Ray Hagen Agency and built a cabin on its chassis with two bunks and a gas hot plate with which I took a few trips, carrying my own 'bed and board.' I had planned we both should travel together for a time after our retirement, but Mother could not bring herself to ride and live in it, being fearful of riding and sleeping in it. So I finally traded it in for a used 1955 Dodge two door Coronet with which we did our traveling now and then here and there.

At 9 PM on December 29th, 1954 while I was walking across hall from west room with intention of going into my room, I stepped into the stairway well instead, thinking it was the open door to my room. I fell headlong down the stairs, turning over a couple times (I think) hitting my head and left shoulder against stair steps, breaking shoulder blade and cutting my scalp. In walking up and down those steps, probably a million times, I had always consciously counted those 15 steps, and still do, from force of habit. I am wondering if my sub-conscious counted them at that time as I went down. Be that as it may, I retained my conscious state during the fall and as I came to a dead stop at the bottom I was still fully conscious and, incidentally, in great pain. Dr. R.L. McCormack with the ambulance driver took me to the hospital where I lay for 11 days and nights. I returned home January 9th, 1955. Again incidentally, her son Joel was born to Eve at the very hour and date I had the accident; some coincidence! According to Insurance Company's vital statistics, I should have passed out permanently at that time, as most old people do not survive such harsh treatment at that age. In such case, there would have been no appreciable loss, as Joel came into our world at that time to take my place. Now I view the incident as a form of punishment for something.

March 7th, 1955 I and Mother headed for Florida, as we had planned to do previous to the accident. I found that the southern climate did not agree with me, the sun being too hot for one had been born and reared in a cold climate. Most of our time there was spent in St. Augustine Florida.

The next winter of 1955-1956 we spent in Minneapolis with Avis in her apartment. We found that city more to our liking, especially the climate. There we took in many different attractions for the first time. I and Avis also attended services in each of the many different church denominations in the city, for me mostly to observe and compare them with each other, which was educational as well as inspirational. We returned to Whitehall and the old home in the first part of April 1956, John and Helen Engstrom being so good and neighborly as to offer us a ride with them. Thanks so much.

Soon after our return Avis wrote that she had been invited by the Ostlund sisters, with whom she had roomed, to ride with them to their old home at Tioga, North Dakota. There she met Franklyn Ostlund, whom she married on August 25th, 1956 at First Baptist Church in Williston, North Dakota. We went there by train and attended the great event. They made a fine looking couple he tall dark and handsome, she a beautiful young woman with the attractive curves of a female. He was eager to protect her in the storms and stresses of life, as is the ancient role of man.

Leone and Larry Kaylor flew to Minneapolis the day we traveled home from Williston, and I barely had time to drive to Eau Claire to meet them there. Dallas and family, also Ben and family also came that week-end for a reunion.

During her summer vacation in 1956, Ethel accepted a position in a clinic where Leone worked in Huntington Park, Calif., returning to her studies at the university in Madison September 18th, 1956 to complete her course.

Mother traveled to Tioga and arrived just in time to assist Avis in the birth of her first boy, Steven, who was born June 2nd, 1957 at 1026 PM in a local hospital in Stanley, North Dakota. He was a big BOY, weighing in at over nine pounds. Avis was the first of the girls to provide us with an additional grand-son, for which congratulations.

April 24th, 1957 Ethel's boy friend, Carl Radmer, a handsome young man about her age came to see her; she had been here a few days previous to his visit. He was a student in electrical engineering at Wis. University.

In July 1957 Avis and Franklyn came with their baby boy, a strapping big boy, the image of his Dad. Up to then we had acquired 9 grand-sons, not a girl among them; just enough for a base-ball team.

Since retirement, we had traveled more extensively than ever before. All these trips are too numerous to enumerate in this story.

May 17th, 1958 was the great day for Ethel and Carl. A beautiful ceremony was performed by Chaplain Foss in the Baptist Church at Whitehall in the afternoon with the Church filled with friends and relatives. It was a happy occasion for them and the rest of us; they were such a fine looking young couple, happy and eager for what life had in store for them. She was the last in our family to be married. The best to you and yours!

This biography is being concluded in the first part of the year 1965 and the occurrences that took place from 1958 to 1965 had to do mostly with the families of our seven offspring, which up to that year totaled 21 grand-children. As some of them phrase it, "two for replacements and 1 for the increase." But there was one quite important event in 1964 that cannot be ignored.

It occurred while the City of Whitehall put on their annual 'Beef and Dairy Days', when large crowds of people came for that and also for many different re-unions and celebrations held at the same time. It was August 22-1954 on a Saturday afternoon in the Baptist Church in Whitehall. The occasion was the 50th Golden Wedding anniversary celebration for an old couple who had withstood the ravages of time for 50 years of our time with its stresses and strains; rewards and punishments; successes and failures; accidents; good fortunes and bad; happy moments and sad; an old couple whose balance sheet of life would hopefully show more credits than debits; whose final rendering would enable the Good Law to proclaim 'thou hast fought the good fight, enter thou into the Kingdom of the Gods."

From the stand-point of statistics, we might mention that we had over 200 guests; received that many greeting cards and more; over a dozen presents and almost 200 dollars in cash. A thousand times thanks to one and all.

--Chapter 13--

In the old time telegraph fraternity, 13 means 'I understand', and this chapter being No. 13, it is hoped that what the previous 12 chapters contains can be understood. At the end of this one I shall write 'NM', no more. The old time press writers ended theirs with '30'

There will be no dates in this final chapter; do dry data. Instead I shall try to extract from my store house of memories stories, incidents and events with which I personally came into contact as I traveled the beaten pathway of life, some of them humorous, others tragic and some of them disappointing and frustrating to the individuals involved. A couple of the incidents certainly was not to my credit, but I should tell them anyway, in order to make this chapter more interesting, if nothing else.

I had been visiting my girl friend in Bingham Lake that Sunday, and in the late evening she saw me off on the late train for Rushmore when I was supposed to be on duty at 8 AM Monday morning. I arrived there late and went to bed after midnight upstairs in my room over the restaurant. I slept soundly all the rest of the night until Monday noon when the proprietor of the restaurant wondered why I had not been down for breakfast and noon meal, he came up and wrapped on my door. When I awoke and saw it was noon by my clock I got dressed hurriedly and, without stopping for breakfast, rushed to the depot and found freight and express piled on the platform. When I entered the office, the side wire man and dispatcher were calling 'NU' and burning up the wire, almost, in doing so, I knew I was going to get a bawling out and reluctantly answered the dispatcher. In such cases, the first question, as I have heard on the wire a few times, invariably was "Where have you been?" I cannot remember what I answered him. Next "OS train so and so." I could not because I was not on hand when both the passenger train and way freight had arrived and departed my station. There was nothing he could do about it; am sure he bawled me out, but what he said I cannot recall; he probably cautioned me not to do it again. He understood of course that I was a 'ham', a very young one at that, and I presume he made allowance for that fact and was lenient. Not so the side wire operator who takes the car report from all agents every morning by wire; he had them all but mine. He swore at me, that I can remember. I think I let him rave; I went out to check the yards in order to send him my 'cars' and by the time I got back and sent them to him, he had cooled off. That was all; no letter of reprimand; no more bawling out. That was another lesson learned for me. That was about 55 years ago, from 1965

In the following incident, the shipper was at fault, although he blamed us as Agent for the railroad. I was working as relief agent at Vernon Center Minnesota when it was freezing cold a farmer brought in a case of eggs and left it on the platform for me to bill out by freight. He did not ask for a bill of lading, which is a receipt, as he should have done so that I would have the data by which to bill it. Instead the case was left standing there for several days, long after I had left there, and the eggs froze solid. I think I and the rest mistakenly thought it was an empty case, and did nothing about it. The next I heard of it was while I was at Woodville Wisconsin many months later I received a wire from H. R. Grochau, the freight claim agent requesting information I may have had. What I told him I cannot recall. I understood later that the company claim agent refused to pay the claim. They were not liable.

The young man I worked with in 'A' office as messenger, Geo. GeSauer, was examined by old 'Davy' for a telegraph job out on the line. That was after I left there. He was sent to a station on the Northern Division, I believe. One day while he was working in the depot there the dispatcher called and asked if he could deliver a train order to a certain train that was switching at his station at the time. He said he could, but actually had already given them a clearance, or else his board was clear for them. He copied the order simultaneously with the operator at the other station for the opposing train to meet at an intermediate point, a siding, between his station and the next. After both operators had repeated the order back to the dispatcher, both received the 'complete' with time ok'ed. That released the train at the other station which started to leave for the meeting point. When De Bauer was getting his completed order ready to deliver together with the required release, his train was passing by his station and signal without the order. He became panic stricken when he saw that; ran outside and waved his arms frantically; the whole train and the caboose passed him without any of the crew seeing him or the signal, if it was at stop.

He could do nothing further but to go in and tell the dispatcher. It was his turn to become frantic then; I understood later that he had tried to get in touch with some one near the track who may have had a telephone, but telephones were few and far between out in the country those days, if at all. He could only wait for the inevitable report of a collision and a terrible wreck. They met head-on on a curve where visibility was nil, smashing two steam engines. What the human casualties were, I did not have the opportunity to ascertain at the time. That was the end of the railroad career of the operator as well as the dispatcher. He did not play safe. The operator could have jumped on the caboose as it was passing. If he had his wits about him, and had the conductor stop the train. He was a good player in a band. He probably went into orchestra work after that.

One day many years ago in Whitehall the local train had for us a huge boar (male hog) in a crate by express for one of our patrons. I lined up the four wheeled platform truck to the express car and both I and the express messenger started to unload the heavy crate. While we were doing that, the boar had gotten one of the cross pieces on top on crate loose, and appeared to be getting ready to jump out of the crate. We almost became panic stricken, but managed to hurry up to get it on the truck; I hurried all I could to get the truck into the express room, while the messenger did what he could to keep the big hog inside the crate. I had no more gotten it into the room and closed the door, when he jumped out and was loose in the express room. I got out of there quick and closed the door leading to it. That was a close call. After that it was up to the consignee to get him out of there and he managed to do it, having experience in handling hogs. He was a big vicious animal with huge teeth that looked forbidding.

An annoying incident was when a dog that came in a crate by express got out and away from us and ran all over the place. When we got near the dog to catch him, he darted away fast; he was too smart for us. Finally I had to get some boys to chase him and between them they eventually caught him. I made sure of him after that until it was delivered to consignee.

One day I received a telegram for a personable young lady from one of her boy friends stating he would be there at a certain date on a certain train and wanted to see her upon arrival. When she opened and read it, her expression changed from a smile to a frown. The next morning the young lady bought a ticket to go on the morning train somewhere, seemingly to get away from him. The young man came on the appointed train and time and date, but he could not find his lady fair. He proceeded to her place of employment but could not find her there either. She had 'flown the coop'. The poor guy was out of luck. She took the path of least resistance to avoid him.

A divorcee was living in our city who was willing to date almost any man. A traveling salesman sent her a wire one day that he would meet her on a certain date at a certain place for a certain purpose. I delivered it promptly. In a short time she came into the office and I could see that she was 'hot under the collar'. She wrote out a telegram for the gentleman and handed it to me to send collect. When I read it and counted the words I noted that she had written a most obscene telegram. Before I could call her attention to it and that the telegraph company would not accept and send it in that way, she flounced out and was gone. I did not know what to do with it. But rather than disappoint the man, I changed some of the words and sent it, and it was on its way.

W. J. Webb always sent his telegrams collect, saying "if they won't pay, I'll pay." They always paid. The day I had Ben deliver one to him; when he received it, he told Ben to wait a minute, then opened his safe, took out the cash box and handed him the sum of 1 cent tip.

For a time before their marriage a young man and a young woman conducted their courtship by telegram. He lived in a distant city while she was in the country not far out. I always had to phone them to her and she phoned her answers; she never showed up in person. They believed in doing it the fast way; "Don't write, telegraph" was their slogan. And they achieved good results, for they eventually married and 'lived happily ever after'.

There was a girl telegrapher in GU relay office Green Bay called Julia. She was a sociable girl and always had a good word for those she worked with. Many of us flirted with her on the wire, especially Earl L. Wiedemann, Agent at Blair, who was a bachelor. He hardly ever left his office except to eat and sleep; he spent all his evenings at the depot. Julia used to come to the Western Union telegraph office in Green Bay and talk to Earl hours at a time. Some of the rest of us telegraphers used to listen in and many times would but in and say something to Julia, who would always respond. Earl invited her to come to Blair one evening, which she did. I think she came by train. While visiting him, Earl took her to my office in his car to get acquainted; also to some of the others with whom she had talked on the wire. Apparently what she found was not to her liking, for the wire conversations ended abruptly. Wiedemann married a Blair girl later. Some years afterwards, he died of a chronic ailment on the operating table. Such are the vicissitudes of life.

One winter's day in Whitehall I had a train order for No. 1 and in trying to deliver, or hand it up to the engineer, the engine was passing me as I came out and I had to run to catch up with it to hand the engineer the order. As I did so I started to slip on icy platform and I found myself heading for the wheels of the engine. To prevent that, I threw myself with full force in the other direction, thereby regained my feet. It was a close call for me.

After the express messengers had been taken off on trains of the GB&W, the conductors accepted our remittances and signed for them, express and railroad. I had a remittance of $60.00 currency for conductor Closuit one day; he signed for it and placed in his pocket. The item appeared on my express balance sheet, but the Auditor had no record of receiving it and wrote me about it. I answered that I had a receipt for it from Conductor Closuit. They took it up with him and asked him to 'come across' with the money. He refused. The traveling auditor contacted him, but without avail. Finally the company offered to settle with him for half the amount, which he did. Closout felt bad about it, especially having to 'dig up'. He spoke to me several times and looked all over my office and the waiting rooms, the platform and the snow in front, but we could not locate it. It was my opinion that the envelope had dropped out of his pocket and some one picked it up. $60.00.

While we were unloading freight out of a way car at the platform of the old station one time, one of the men, think the conductor, thought an empty barrel was full and heavy and in trying to move it, he applied all his strength, with the result that he, the barrel and all went sprawling backwards almost the full length of the car. Fortunately no damage was done except ruffled dignity, for which we had the last laugh.

During my time I have handled a great many corpses by express and baggage but only once the cremated remains of a man that came by express for W. J. Web. It was a small wooden box weighing a pound or two that contained the ashes of Mr. Edward Webb, the brother of W. J. Webb, who had been an Agent-Telegrapher all his life for the Great Northern Railway, at Grand Forks North Dakota. Mr. Webb took it to the cemetery and buried it in his family plot where his own body was buried some years later. Edward Webb had spent his whole life time on the Great Northern railway and this was the way it ended, a few ounces of ashes. It seems rather pathetic that the body of a man of which he was so proud during life should reach such a low estate, such an ignoble end. But fortunately Nature has provided a marvelous system for its replacement, each succeeding body some better than the last. Whether a person's body is cremated or permitted to take its course of slow deterioration, is immaterial. In either case, its atoms return to their constituent elements in accord with the fundamental law of conservation.

I have many pleasant memories of friendly contacts with my fellow-man as we traveled life's highway together. Practically all of those I knew and came into contact were good people trying to do a job the best way they know. There were times when many of us became irritated and lost our composures in the rush of work and business. But none of us held any grudges against one another. Most railroad men were generous with their money in cases of misfortunes and illness among their fellows. Some of them were most always, when necessary, circulating petitions requesting assistance and donations for any of them in distress and financial difficulty due to illness.

In cases of rules infractions they protected one another if they could by not reporting them or refraining from testifying against one who may have been in difficulties with the management. That happened to me when I first started and to many others.

As time rolled on, many of my fellow workers have crossed the great divide, having accomplished their mission in life and entered upon life's greatest adventure. For myself, I never could honestly subscribe to any theory or belief that was contrary to the idea of the continuity of human life, of human consciousness; a continued existence of the individual from the present phase to that of the next. The contention of some that this present one is the only existence for the individual to my mind runs counter to a fundamental law of science that nothing is destroyed or wasted, everything merely changes it form of existence. Of necessity, that must include human life and the individual Ego. The law of 'conservation of energy' is applicable to all phases, on all planes of nature. If this present life is the only one, then all our efforts and strivings are futile; they would have no meaning for the individual. Knowledge accumulated, experience gained and all our thinking would be of no avail; the mind, the individuality, the personality and all characteristics, good and bad alike, the spiritual, moral and intellectual attainments will have disappeared into nothingness. Although these are all intangibles, they are fundamental to the evolution of mankind as it marches towards betterment from generation to generation; from life to life through eons of time.

We observe that the universe has meaning in the orderly and timely movements of the planetary bodies of our solar system; of the galaxy to which our system belongs revolving majestically as a huge wheel; the unlimited extent of space and all that is in it. If we see any waste in it all, it is only apparent to us, not real. The sun renews its energy without waste. If there are so called 'dead' worlds in space, they are not really so; they only changed their form of structure, what ever it may be. Human bodies likewise are subject to the same law of change from one form to another. Human life likewise is not destroyed; it merely withdraws from the physical at transition and changes its form, or state of existence.

Universality is the criterion by which we may judge a theory, a belief, a dogma, or a law natural or otherwise. Is it universal? Is it applicable universally throughout? Does the whole of the human race come under it? If a dogmatic belief, religious, scientific, or philosophical, does not stand up under the scrutiny of the human intellect as being universal, then it is not a fundamental law of nature, but a man made one. The code of ethics contained in all religions is a universal one; it applies to the whole of the human race no matter what religion born under. Then what of Christianity and its dogmas? What of all the other major religions of the world and each their own particular dogmas? The correct answer is that all religions exist for the purpose of assisting the different peoples each religion covers, to live better lives; to improve themselves morally and spiritually; to set their fears at rest; to console them and make them as happy as possible under the circumstances of each group of people. That has been a necessity from the beginning of our present civilization. We could not have progressed as far as we have without the many different religions.

But that does not render their dogmas true and infallible; they are only props and straps to hang onto in the storms and stresses of life. They remain that until such time as the human intellect has advanced and evolved to the point where the difference can be noted; when the human reason decrees then to be void unless they can answer to the criterion of universality as we do with the fundamental laws of nature. Until the human intellect reaches that point; unless and until it has evolved towards betterment in thinking ability sufficiently to distinguish and differentiate between the true and the false, then man will hang onto his theological props; until then most men will require his religion to assist him to live peacefully and amicably.

There should be no question in the minds of the thinker, the well developed and scientific thinker, that life itself is universal throughout whether in physical bodies or outside them. Life renews itself in physical forms constantly, all sorts of forms, human, animal, vegetable, mineral, etc. But of course the human life is the highest of all of them, human beings being at the top of creation. The only question is, where does all this life come from?

Therefore I am an individual Entity am indestructible; it never ceases to exist in some form; it changes its form periodically; it is universal; its duration in time is unlimited, just as space is unlimited in extent and in time. All this is true of the life in all human beings on earth. Each to an individual Entity, or Ego, at all times no matter where it exists at any given time, in the higher planes of nature, or on the lower physical plane. Its life on earth is only a small cycle in a spiral that circles to infinity. And during each cycle it improves itself, consciously or otherwise, morally, spiritually, emotionally, and most important, intellectually. Its ultimate destiny is perfection in all respects. "Verily we are gods in the making."

During the 75 years or more that this biography is supposed to cover, so many changes have occurred in our world that it is bewildering to think of them all. If any of us believe that the changes have been too much on the debit side, we should consider those that appear on the credit side of the world's balance sheet, also, in order to arrive at a true and balanced conclusion. Changes towards betterment in all fields have always been effected at a sacrifice; penalties must be endured and paid to achieve them. Changes for the better in practically all fields of human endeavor have occurred except in the field of religion until very recently.

Modern computers can mathematically project results in a given field almost perfectly into the future. Human beings can also with his ability to think project his thoughts into the future and predict what the conditions will be in future times by studying the past and extending the trend in any given field.

In the case of education, the future trend will follow that of ascertaining a child's latent capabilities and bringing them to the surface and developing them, and also to assist the child to expand the imagination and thinking potential.

In the case of religion, the future trend will be to modernize centuries old beliefs and dogmas; or to discard them; or let them die a natural death. Theories that run counter to the natural order will be replaced with those that coincide with the laws of nature as discovered and made known by science.

Under this new and more enlightened system, all Churches will in the course of time become educational institutions for adults; service organizations that cater to the needs of their members, such as marrying and burying; a place to sing and to listen to the grand music of the Church; where a well educated speaker lectures on the problems of life and death; the great scientific subjects of the day; a forum for debate and discussions by interested, intelligent individuals on abstruse matters of science, philosophy, comparative religion and many other subjects.

> "Creation rejoices and sings,
> In tune with a Cosmic Plan.
> Nature eternally brings
> Wonders in stars and man.
> The eagle in the summer sky,
> The worm beneath the sod,
> The sun, the moon and you and I,
> We live and move in God.
>
> --N.M. No more--

--Addendum--

"Early history of Jackson County lumbering and pioneering with lumber barons and towns they established that are now ghost towns", was written by Fred J. Rogers in the 1930's , printed by the Banner Journal of Black River Falls then and reprinted from December 23, 1964 ending February 23, 1965. With permission of the owner of the Banner Journal from Black River Falls, Wisconsin , and added as an addendum are 4 weeks (Weeks 1, 2, 3, and 7) of the series of articles.

This Editor's note appeared in the first printing of these stories: (1936) "We take pleasure in offering a series of articles written by Fred J Rogers on ghost towns of this region. They present information that had been laid away in lavender until dug up by Mr. Rogers. He was stationed at City Point CCC camp as forester at the time. We hope they will give some measure of enjoyment and to refresh memories of the past. Friends will regret that Mr. Rogers has been ill for a time and now lives in New London, December 1936."

Preface to the 1964/65 printing
"It has been 28 years since the Banner Journal published a series of articles on ghost towns of this region and related stories about early lumbering and pioneering

in eastern Jackson County. There have been numerous requests to republish the series of eight stories (weeks) written by Fred J. Rogers who in the 1930's was a forester at City Point and who wrote the series for the Banner Journal. Any one who has traveled the Wazee Trail and who has hunted deer in eastern Jackson County and others interested in local history will find the series interesting." (Preserved by Arvid B. Erickson (3-24-65) due to his interest.)

Week 1

Ghost Towns

Central Wisconsin's Great logging period is nearly forgotten: nothing is left but ghost towns where logging activity was the greatest that commenced soon after the Civil War. The spectre of ghost towns hangs over the tangled mass of slash, charred stumps and desolate lowlands of central Wisconsin, wilderness of Wood, Clark, Jackson, Juneau and Monroe Counties where 40 or 50 years ago (1870's 1880's 1890's) there existed busy, thriving lumbering and logging settlements..

In the so called driftless area where glaciers of eleven thousand years ago did not pass, the topography of this vast area is unusual and rather Western in aspect. Scattered through it are buttes, messas, steep hills, towers and grotesque crags of sandstone that resemble ruined castles.

Prehistoric Lake

Reaching out for interminable distances from the bases of these cantellated bluffs are the dark, almost impenetrable swamps which is the bed of prehistoric Glacial Lake Wisconsin. Once covered with the finest stand of pine trees in the state, this section, one of the last to be cut because of its inaccessibility, still holds the secret of the ghost towns which sank, as if by enchantment, into the bosom of the earth.

The old lumber-jacks

There are a few men living today who once worked and reared families in these villages which long since have ceased to be. A woodsman in his twenties at the time would be 70 and over now. (1836 Most of them never went back after the fineries played out and their memories are hazy about exact dates and locations. However, the old lumber-jacks still living do remember with the aid of carefully preserved photographs the old logging days in Central Wisconsin's Big Swamp. They can recall when the whole area was a beehive of activity: with the woodsmen's axes ringing in the air: saw-mills buzzing and pony railroad trains puffing through the forests. In those days great towering white pine trees nearly six feet through at the base, and containing enough board feet of lumber to construct a small house. It may have taken Nature a hundred years to grow one of these stately pines, but an expert woodsman could fell it with an axe in a few minutes.

And in the cutting there would be much waste, for "waste makes wealth" was the philosophy of the logging operator whose favorite practice was to buy a section and log off the adjoining three or four without the formality of purchase. Man's avarice at its worst was displayed in the rush to massacre Central Wisconsin's timberlands.

According to old timers, large scale logging operations first started in the Big Swamp about 1885, years after timber that was closer to means of transportation had been cut and marketed. In the year (1885) a severe cyclone swept through the center of the area, laying low many forest giants. Saved the trouble of cutting them down, a number of operators rushed in to reap the harvest.

A logging railroad was constructed by the Chicago, Milwaukee and St. Paul from Mather to a point near Saddle

Mound just south of Pray in western Jackson County. At Mather it joined with the main line to Tomah. All along this logging road were spurs to dozens of settlements which sprang up like mushrooms. They in turn had their small, narrow-gauge wooden rail lines back into the cuttings.

Sprayed live steam

Small streams such as Morrison and Robinson creeks and tributaries were dammed up and live steam was sprayed into the ponds thus created during the winter to provide places to dump the logs and float them up or down to the great saw-mills. The supply of logs at that time seemed inexhaustible, and the busy mills were always hungry for more fodder.

No thought was given at the time for a new timber supply. Behind the cuttings there was nothing but devastation: stumps, and worst of all, slash, -tops and branches – an uncontrollable fire hazard, an assurance that natural forestation could never take pace. Not a seed tree was spared: down went all the great pine trees, and with them went the hope that the land would ever again produce anything more, unless planted by man.

Hundreds of able-bodied men from all over the state were attracted to the central pineries where they worked from 12 to 16 hours daily and drew from $12 to $30 per month, while the operators made millions. Some of the men brought wives and families and regular villages with churches, schools, stores, dance halls and saloons were established.

But with the passing of the timber-lands most of the once thriving towns were liquidated, written off the books and forgotten. A few nearby farmers, after the abandonment, came to salvage some lumber, but most of the building (trees) were left standing until completely obliterated by fire.

266

Then, after time's scythe had reaped the timber clean, drainage ditches were advocated about the turn of the century with the promise from high-pressure promoters that this area could be turned into a veritable garden paradise. Thousands of acres were sold to unsuspecting victims. But these settlers in a few years were like ice laying upon the slope in the sun's rays leaking their lives away.

Weeds close clearings

The abandoned buildings of the settlers and lumbering villages decayed to extinction, and under-brush and weeds grew up in the clearings. Year after year of drought followed and with them a new menace to forest growth. Fires leaving a path of barren waste upon which only the despicable aspen could thrive.

Thousands of acres of wild and cultivated cranberry marshes were destroyed. Game was driven out of the country. No one paid taxes, and the land went delinquent and back to the counties that did not want it. The sheer hopelessness of upper abandonment stared out through the eyes of vacant building, logging villages, some of them entirely forgotten, ghost towns, not a vestige of previous habitation remaining. Others are sluggish, sleepy little communities, usually along a railroad where greatness was once measured by the number of thousand feet of lumber cut each day.

Disappear into the air

Unlike Wisconsin Rapids, Pittsville, and countless others whose first permanent buildings were saw-mills, when the pineries were gone these settlements had no future. They just disappeared into thin air, and were forgotten just as quickly. There was no fertile land around them to justify their continuance.

The pine timber in the vicinity of Bear Bluff and Saddle Mound just across from the southwestern Wood county line in Jackson county was the finest ever known. Clustered together in the center of it were Goodyear, Zoda, and McKenna, three of the largest lumbering settlements of the 1880's and 1890's. Not far distant were Rudd, Spurback, Knapp, Withey, (not the Withee in Clark county), Waterbury, Bear Bluff Station, Alva Station, Ada, Rhea, Spaulding and many others.

Farther east toward City Point, itself once almost a metropolis, there were McNutt, Lytle's Mill and others now completely forgotten. Near Babcock there were Daly, Remington, Finley, Mather, Meadow Valley, Beaver Station and others now mere shadows of their former selves. To the south there were Dodge's Mill, Millson and Fallhall Glen.

"King" George territory

In the Dexterville "King" George Hiles territory there were Scranton, Hilestown, New Dam, Vodum, Amelia, Cary Lindsay, Lynn and Romandtke, the end of Hiles logging line in Clark County. Over Hatfield way there were villages at Della Dam, Arnold's, Jonts', Mormon's, Mead's and Avery's Mill at Big Spring, Ross Eddy, Weston's Rapids and O'Neill's Creek. Around Black River Falls there were Halcyon, Irontown or New Denamor, Davi' Ferry, Shepherds, Vaudrell and others.

Perhaps the most famous of the Central Wisconsin Ghost towns and typical of most of them was Goodyear. Many are the wild and fantastic tales told about it, and Charlie Goodyear of Tomah who established the town. Next in the series of Central Wisconsin ghost town will be an account, as accurate and compete as can be recalled by the old timers in this section who worked at Goodyear.

Week 2

268

Hiles big figure in logging days

A history of the Central Wisconsin pineries in the Big Swamp, once so full of thriving lumbering settlements and now nearly all completely extinct, would not be complete without at least a short account of the life of George Hiles. His influence overshadowed all others of that territory several decades ago. He built villages and railroads doomed for abandonment.

It is said the "King George" as he was called after reaching a position of great affluence, rode from his home at Baraboo to the timber lands farther north on a balky white mule whose name was Dexter. He founded a village, where he erected a saw mill and several other industries and named the place Dexterville after his mule.

Amassed a fortune

Hiles settled in the Dexterville country in October 1850, bringing with him H. Searles. Hiles had but $1.50 in his pocket, the indomitable will to succeed and the courage of a pioneer. From that start he amassed a fortune once estimated at fifteen million dollars, and his work became law among the pinery men and logging operators of the past century.

In 1852 Dexterville had but 12 inhabitants, and the progressive Hiles, intent upon developing the resources of the place; applied to the government for a mail route and post office. The petition, however, was not granted until 1857. Nancy Plate became the teacher of the first school.

Hiles's first business venture was the erection of a "Mully", an up and down saw mill which he operated for some time in sawing rough lumber to build a modern mill having a capacity of 75,000 feet of lumber per day. He also operated a general store and a shingle and planning mill. In 1870 the backwoods city, larger than what later became Wisconsin Rapids.

Hub, pail factory

In 1881 the lumber baron built a hub and pail factory which Hiles ran for 10 years and then sold it to E. E. Bowles of De Pere. Bowles bought the factory to avoid competition. Hiles turned the building into a chair factory.

To get his own logs to his mills and to market his lumber products, the logging king built a railroad from Babcock to Vesper in Wood county and another from Dexterville to Ramadka in Clark county, both since abandoned. These he owned and operated for 15 years in logging, business and passenger service. In 1892 he sold his railroad interests to the Chicago, Milwaukee and St. Paul.

With the building of the Green Bay & Minnesota railroad, now the Green Bay & Western, west from Dexterville in 1873, Hiles built another saw mill at Scranton, the present site of the City Point CCC camp. (1936) A point east of there is now called by the same name. A shingle mill was added a little later, and then a church, school, boarding house and a few homes.

L.C. Bullis was one of the first settlers at Scranton, moving there on March 17, 1873. Twin children, Frank and Laura, were born to Mr. and Mrs. Bullis there on February 24, 1874. The population of the community in 1880 was 65, but the village died out as the timber was cut off and the sandy pit land found unsuitable for farming.

There was another Hiles mill and small village at what was called Hiles- town in the southern part of the township of Hiles, Wood county. Lumber was hauled from there to the Green Bay road with tram carts using wooden rails. McNutt was the superintendent.

Another saw mill and village was built at Veedum, farther north in Wood county. Hi Parker was the first settler. A store was started by a Mr. Paulson and a hotel was built in 1899 by Skidmore Land Co. A Lutheran church was constructed of logs and Rev. Bings was the first Pastor, walking from Grand Rapids now Wisconsin

Rapis, each Sunday. Later a Moravian church was built there.

Paul Grims was one of the earliest settlers and he carried his belongings on his back through the wilderness to his new home at Veedum. John Bernard was the first school teacher. Veedum of course, is still on the map, but the community there today is in far contrast to the active village of the old logging days. Hiles also had mills, or points for shipping out lumber and logs along his Dexterville-Romadka line at Amelia, Cary, Lynn, New Dam, Turner Creek and several other points. He had extensive logging operations near Pittsville, although the pine was not so thick in that immediate vicinity.

At new Dam just east of Scranton, a dam was built on the East Fork of the Black river to create waterpower for the Scranton mill. It is interesting to note that the last carrier pigeons seen in that vicinity roosted there. They were once trapped, clubbed to death, netted and shot by the thousands upon thousands around the lumber camps. A Mr. Roice was the saw filer at New Town and Carry. He was said to have invented the first steam hauler. It was like a modern tractor only operated by steam and was used in place of oxen teams to haul loads through the woods. Mr. Rice also, according to legends of the woods, was the originator of the famous "Hodag" story, which he gave to Gene Shepherd who took it up to Rhinelander. The Lyman Lumber Co. of Tomah operated a mill at Cary near Cary Bluff.

Shipping points

Catherine, Amelia, and Cary stations, Progress, Lindsey, Lynn and other settlements, all of them small hamlets today, which were shipping points or saw mill centers in the Hiles empire, all along his private railroad. Then there were New Town 18 miles northwest of Dexterville and Turner Creek down in the town of Hiles.

Babcock, where Hiles also operated, had an interesting beginning. In the latter 1860's a settlement called Remington was started on the west side of the Yellow river opposite the present village site and W. J. Shea conducted a store there. Some time later J. W. Babcock, who operated a saw mill at Nekoosa, learned that the Milwaukee railroad intended to put through a road down to Remington, and he tried without success to buy the village site. He then bought the site where the village named after him now stands. A small saw mill of the "pocket type" was erected there. Trains began running through there in 1873

In 1885 a rescue home for wayward girls was established in a hotel at Babcock. It was run by a Mr. Wagner and later by a Mr. Claire. The home was operated for about six years and then turned back into a hotel. William Hines was killed in the explosion of the shingle mill in Remington in 1892. The year before the big fire in 1892, 50,000 barrels of wild cranberries were shipped from Remington.

A. F. Lynch had a saw mill at Meadow Valley southeast of there, and Oliver Gregory operated another. The village, once the center of the cranberry industry, had a population of 500, but after drainage and the fires, decay set in until there are only a half dozen occupied homes there today.

Massacred Timber

Hiles converted millions of feet of timber into lumber, hubs, staves, laths, shingles, pails, furniture, etc. acquiring over 70,000 acres of land, and the Babcock-Dexterville-Pittsville area flourished while he was in control. He massacred the timber for miles around and became fabulously wealthy. The naked slopes of North and South Bluff, like two bald-headed old men looking across at each other for sympathy, are samples of his wealth.

Then, the lumber king moved to Milwaukee to enjoy his riches, but he died in 1896, and most of the communities he erected soon sank to nothingness, became ghost towns. His remains were brought back to Dexterville, the scene of his humble beginning. There a Vermont marble shaft, costing over $10,000 remains today on the family plot. What future is there for this vast territory denuded by the lumber barons? An attempt to answer that will be made at a later date.

Week 3

Goodyear, a typical Ghost Town – Aug. 16, 1935

Typical of the ghost towns – deserted lumbering settlements – which dot Central Wisconsin today is Goodyear, on Morrison creek about four miles south of Saddle Mound, NW1/4 of NW1/4 of section 15 township of Knapp Jackson County. Once boasting a population of over 500 souls, hardly a trace of former habitation can be found on the site today.

Barely distinguishable remnants of a dam, a 40 acre clearing grown up with tall weeds, an artesian well and a steel shaft or two are there, but the village has entirely disappeared. The last remaining building went up with the fire that swept through the section a few years ago.

Built large saw mill

In 1884 C. A, Goodyear of Tomah built a large saw mill there. It was in the center of what once was the finest stand of white and Norway pine in the state. The mill had a capacity of 100,000 feet of lumber per day and it was only on Sundays that the angry screeching of the saws died out.

Ox teams and horses skidded and hauled the logs to the company's small logging railroad, tram roads with wooden rails. These temporary lines were shifted about as the timber was cut off, led to the Goodyear-Neillsville and Northern railroad, which ran from near Saddle Mound to Mather. It was operated by the Chicago, Milwaukee & St. Paul whose mail line it joined at Mather.

Loaded into standard sized cars, the lumber was sent on to Tomah, head-quarters of the Goodyear Lumber Company where it was sorted and put into piles to dry. It was quite a sight those days, old timers recall, to see the freshly sawed pine boards, pile after pile, acres and acres of them awaiting shipment to help build a growing America.

First Locomotive

The "Polly-wog" wood burning locomotive first used by the Goodyear Co. was a marvel of its kind. Although it was fitted with a spark arrester, it set many fires along the right of way. Constant vigilance on the part of the hand car crew following behind the engine, was needed to put out the fires started in the slash left by the men with axes and saws.

A school, church, boarding house, sleeping quarters and many small homes were erected from rough lumber at Goodyear. The company had a store and commissary. The head official's quarters and community hall were on the Yankee side of Morrison creek near the school. Norwegians and Germans, imported from the old country by Goodyear to keep down the labor costs, lived on the north side of the creek where they built their own bowery.

There was caste in 'them thar woods'. The creek was the dead line and fights were frequent between the crews. Martin Diceront and Frank Albright had a big fight over a girl, it is said. Beer bottles flew, brawny fists struck bewhiskered chins and finally the inevitable "boots" were put to the vanquished. A Dr. John Hallet did the repair work.

Paid twice annually

The company paid off its men twice a year, in July and December, which were occasions for prolonged violent debauches. All the men were given a week off and they went to Tomah to settle up and receive their pay for the previous six months. Then followed the week's celebrations. No work was attempted. A load of beer was brought in. Together with the "rotgut" smuggled with it, liquid refreshments were plentiful and easy to obtain. Those who did not get drunk could blame no one. Jack Barrett nearly lost his job for stealing a keg of beer from one of his bosses.

Charlie Goodyear, the big boss, was an ordinary man, well liked by everybody, according to those who knew him. Many stories concerning his hard-boiled feats softened by acts of kindness are still told about the villages southwest of Wisconsin Rapids where once he was such a powerful figure. Hard pressed for working capital, it is said that he often borrowed money from his workers to help carry on the tremendous operations. He gave turkeys to all his help on Thanksgiving day, however, and could be depended upon to help a deserving man or family in time of stress. On the other hand an eye-witness tells of a strapping young woodsman being killed along the logging road, whereupon Goodyear, who happened to be there, ordered him buried on the spot without ceremony.

Adam Gabe was the camp superintendent at Goodyear and a Mr. Yackel the saw filer, an important post in those days. Pete Scott and Tug Wilson were the engineers, responsible for keeping the shakey old steam boiler in shape, pumping the saws that ate up millions upon million of feet of virgin timber.

Mill burned down

After operating for a number of years, the saw mill burned down from an incendiary origin, for the fire had been drawn from the pump house engine and the automatic sprinkling system tampered with, according to gossip. A new and larger mill was built at once and the work of sawing lumber went on. Besides the rotary saw, a band saw was installed, which greatly increased the capacity of the mill. Later a second and more modern locomotive, the Two-Spot, was added to help out the over-worked Polly-Wog, both operating on the Goodyear, Neillsville & Northern between Pray and Mather. The road was not taken up until 1899.

Fuel wood, of course, was an important problem at the village of Goodyear where temperatures of 40 degrees below zero were sometimes reached during the winter months. Roaring fires were kept in the flimsy iron heaters, red hot most of the time. But the men were not permitted to use the company's time for gathering their wood. Instead, they left a flat car in the woods on one of the small tram lines each Saturday afternoon when they finished work for the week. On Sunday mornings they would go back into the woods and load up the cars with firewood. Then the brakes were released and the force of gravity was just right to bring the loads into camp.

Typical lumbering town

Goodyear in the 1880's and early 1890's was the legendary lumbering town of Paul Bunyan fame. Far back in the farthest recesses of Wisconsin and upper Michigan its counterparts can still be seen today. Full of rough, high spirited young men of all nationalities, closely confined for months, it was only natural that their vitality sometimes found violent outlets.

It was in places such a Goodyear at night after a hard days work in the snow, "grub pile" finished, that the "jacks" spun their tales. Here in the stifling hot sleeping quarters, the aroma of dirty woolen clothing pervading the air, many fantastic tales of the woods had their origin. It was the only amusement.

In addition to the large mills at Goodyear and Tomah, Charlie Goodyear operated another outfit two miles up Morrison creek at Withey. One morning the fireman put on too much pressure and the boiler blew up killing him and injuring several others. Mr. Goodyear also had a planing mill and a large general store at Mather.

Year after year of cutting, however, soon depleted the forests and soon there was little left to cut. Operations come to a stand-still and in 1905 everybody pulled out, and Goodyear became a ghost village. The two locomotives were sent up north to Star Lake region where Goodyear had purchased another tract of virgin pine. Later Goodyear, who passed away in 1920, moved his outfit to Picayune, Mississippi, where a son-in-law, Lamont Rowlands, still lives. One son, Miles Goodyear, lives in San Francisco, California.

Nothing left today

There is practically nothing left today of what used to be Goodyear village. The school house was moved and became the town hall for Knapp, where it is still in service. In the sawing of logs it was necessary to have a constant supply of water to wash dirt and grit off, and the artesian well which remains is what used to be for this purpose. Its clear cold water is still used by the occasional hunters who get into the district.

Another landmark still visible in the "hell-hole", where all of the refuse from the mill was disposed of. A constant fire was kept burning there, a conveyor taking slabs, saw dust, etc., into it. Later a more modern concrete disposal pit or burner was built for this purpose.

And thus the busy thriving village of Goodyear passed out of existence. In the next article there will be a description of two neighboring sawmill settlements, now ghost towns. Zeda and McKenna – of about the same size.

Week 7

Ghost town area being converted to its former beauty

After ruthless cutting of the timber in the vast Wood-Jackson-Monroe pineries of the Big Swamp, the next desecration of Mother Nature's bounty was drainage. All the towering White and Norway pines having been harvested, high-pressure real estate promoters came onto the scene and mile after mile of deep unsightly ditches were easily scooped out of the sandy peat soil.

Unsuspecting purchasers were roped in, one at a time, strange as it may seem. Nearly every acre of land in central Wisconsin was owned by some individual who thought the drained marsh soil could be productive.. Of course they were doomed to disappointment and financial ruin, for the expensive ditches took away from the land the moisture it needed most, and it became unfit even for grazing.

Precluded natural reforestation

Thus central Wisconsin became a tangled mass of slash left by the logging operators; grown up with thick under-brush hiding all vestiges of the ghost towns and made tinder dry at certain seasons of the year by drainage. Constantly recurring fires which swept the country clean every few years precluded any possibility of natural reforestation with merchantable timber.

To combat these destructive fires in the desolate area, the federal government, in conjunction with the Wisconsin conservation department, established state forestry camps near City Point, Arbutus Lake and Finley, the latter having been discontinued some time ago. Called Civilian Conservation Corps camps, each one at certain times had over 200 young men in them doing forestry work. The camps were under the direct supervision of competent foremen, trained in different phases of forestry work and well qualified to carry out the ideals of the Civilian Conservation Corps plan. In the 'CCC' enrollees a vast army of American youth without employment were given work and the appreciation of real conservation.

Into workable shape

Courage, foresight and money were combined to whip into workable shape this area, the one good thing which came out of the economic depression. The inquiring minds of the 'CCC' boys are finding hearty response from these experienced foresters, who are eager to explain the lore of forestry and into whose hands the destiny of conservation will rest in the future.

In the short period of time since the Civilian Conservation Corps camps at City Point, Finley and Arbutus lakes were established, the following major projects have been completed: Thirty five bridges have been constructed. Fifteen concrete dams have been built and rip rapped with 10,000 cubic yards of rock. One hundred miles of truck trails have been built into all sections of this area to be used in getting men to the scene of any fire. Two thousand of five hundred acres of this once denuded land had been planted with 2,736,350 white and Norway pine seedlings. Tree planting, which many misinformed believe to be the major work of the CCC, actually represents about five percent of the work. Fifty years from now this should be a merchantable timber worth millions of dollars. Much of the planting has dual value since it provides protection of water sheds, checks erosion and plays an important part in flood control.

One thousand man days have been spent in fighting fires in the forests, including the great fire of 24,000 acres which nearly wiped out the village of City Point in 1934. Ninety miles of fire breaks have been built. Twenty five acres of landscaping have been done at the camps. Six hundred man days have been made. Forty five miles of trailside clearing and seventy five miles of roadside clearing have been accomplished. Five thousand acres of fire hazard reduction have been done and 2,000 man days of fire pre suppression have been accomplished. Six hundred man days have been put in at the Central State Nursery at Wisconsin Rapids. Over 3,000 acres of mapping have been done. One hundred fifty acres of forest stand improvement have been made and white pine blister eradicated on 8,000 trees.

Work justified

If the camps were to be closed today, the work would be justified, not only from the standpoint of these splendid results of man making, but also from the standpoint of fire-proofing our forests and increasing their productivity. Every possible means is being taken to prevent future devastating fires in this area, a desolate waste for years. Where a lone pine now leans against the moon, with the aid of conservation, new forests will rise up on every side for future generations to enjoy and utilize in a decent way.

The 'ghost towns' of Zeda, McKenna, Goodyear and a hundred others are gone perhaps forever, but the pine forests are coming back. It will take years, another generation, before the lofty pines again swish in the wind, but the ground-work has been laid and nature will do the rest.

Already the benefits of government reforestation and fire prevention are being felt in this section. Last year there wasn't a single fire of any consequence in the entire area. And with the restoration of natural water levels in the low-lands the hordes of wild fowl have returned, affording excellent sport to the hunter.

Lumbering coming back

Looking into the future, it is possible to visualize a different Central Wisconsin in 1960. Lumbering on a lawful, legitimate basis may again become a major industry in this area. But there well be no logging off of "round" sections where no lines have been surveyed; no ruthless slashing of trees; no leaving of slash to create impossible fire hazards, and no drainage or wild-cat real estate promotions.

The state through its forestry crop law and the federal government with its national forests in Wisconsin, will play important parts in lumbering in this state in the future. Many, perhaps most, of the coming forests in this state will be preserved inviolate for the enjoyment of vacationists and as flood and erosion control projects. Some trees no doubt will be legitimately harvested. But there will be no devastation such as that which took place in the century just past.

In the process of land utilization in a new country, it is gradually becoming recognized that certain areas of the land is adapted to certain things only, and attempts to violate this concept results in inevitable failure.

The central Wisconsin peat lands produce millions of dollars in cranberries and sphagnum moss and also provides excellent sport for the hunter, but above all it can grow fine pine trees.

About the Author

Arvid B. Erickson was born in 1889 to immigrants from Sweden. Though the family had minimal worldly goods the children lived with examples of love, thrift, learning and improving. As a young boy Arvid wanted to be a telegrapher, a goal he achieved providing for him the opportunity to contribute to mankind and to support his own family. (see Arvid B. Erickson's preface to his book) His longest held assignment was as Depot Agent - Telegrapher in Whitehall, WI (see picture above). Every one of his children graduated from Whitehall High School each moving on to his/her destiny. He and his wife, Sarah, were strong examples of loving, independence, kindness, generous spirit, and sense of responsibility.

Daughter's Note: I invite you to the Facebook page - "Life Before Eighty" - to comment as you wish. :-) Leone Erickson Kaylor